Gardening with Young Children

Gardening
with Young Children

SARA STARBUCK, MARLA OLTHOF, AND KAREN MIDDEN

Redleaf Press®
www.redleafpress.org
800-423-8309

Published by Redleaf Press
10 Yorkton Court
St. Paul, MN 55117
www.redleafpress.org

First edition published 2002. Second edition 2014.
Cover design by Erin Kirk New
Cover photograph by Marla Olthof
Interior design by Erin Kirk New
Illustrations by Karen Midden
Typeset in Berkeley Oldstyle Medium
Printed in the United States of America
21   20   19   18   17   16   15   14   1   2   3   4   5   6   7   8

Library of Congress Cataloging-in-Publication Data
Starbuck, Sara, 1955-
 [Hollyhocks and honeybees]
 Gardening with young children / Sara Starbuck, Marla Olthof, Karen
Midden.—Second edition.
       pages cm
   Summary: "Packed with colorful photographs and updated to address
many childhood issues and gardening trends that have erupted in recent
years, it reflects the growing concerns for children's nature deficit and the
obesity epidemic, and it provides a wider variety of gardening projects, like
vertical, green roof, and container gardens for limited-space or urban areas.
It also contains gardening activities for children of all ages—including experiences for infants and toddlers, because even the youngest children can
and should be involved in gardening"—Provided by publisher.
   Includes bibliographical references.
   ISBN 978-1-60554-157-0 (paperback : acid-free paper)
   1. School gardens. 2. Children's gardens. 3. Gardening—Experiments.
4. Gardening—Study and teaching—Activity programs.   I. Olthof, Marla,
1970- II. Midden, Karen, 1952- III. Title.
  SB55.S78 2014
  635.083—dc23
                                        2014002770

Printed on acid-free paper

To my mother, Kathy Starbuck, who gave me snakes, saved painted turtles, and never met a wasp she couldn't catch. Your delight in the wonders of nature was an invitation to a young child and continues to inspire me. Thank you for this gift. —*Sara*

To my daughters, Haleigh, Taylor, and Avery, who love to learn as much as I love to teach. To all my past students and parents from the Child Development Lab at Southern Illinois University Carbondale—now that I have kids of my own, I realize that you taught me more than I ever taught you. —*Marla*

To my students, past and present, who have chosen a career in connecting people with plants through landscape horticulture and forestry. We are all big kids in gardens. —*Karen*

Contents

Preface

When we published our first edition of this book in 2002, we never would have imagined where we would be today and the changes we have seen in the years since we started gardening with young children. When we wrote our first edition, *Hollyhocks and Honeybees: Garden Projects for Young Children*, our work was based on our experience building and living with our gardens at the Child Development Laboratories at Southern Illinois University Carbondale. Our work began with our roles there. Sara was the director of the program, Marla was the master preschool teacher, and Karen was a landscape architect and an associate professor in landscape horticulture, as well as the parent of two preschoolers.

We began our journey gardening together when one of Karen's graduate students, Jessica Chambers, proposed building a series of children's gardens as her master's thesis project. Jessica developed a wonderful design for the gardens, and before we knew it, families, staff, university faculty, and community members had joined in to make our garden come to life. Over the course of the next five years, the garden became a key part of our curriculum from spring through fall.

We initially wrote *Hollyhocks and Honeybees* to share what we had learned from that experience both because we had a lot to share and because it had been difficult for us to find quality materials on gardening with young children. We feel like we succeeded at that task. As we look back at our first edition, it reflects the work we did and the wonderful times we had at the Child Development Laboratories.

But we have moved on. Sara is now an associate professor in Human Environmental Studies at Southeast Missouri State University. She has continued to follow her interest in connecting children to nature through her involvement in many activities, including participation in the World Forum Foundation's Working Forum on Nature Education and membership in the

Nature Action Collaborative for Children. She presents regionally, nationally, and internationally on topics related to nature education. Marla is now a stay-at-home mom, planting flower and vegetable gardens at home with her husband and three daughters in northwest Indiana. Currently she is working to coordinate a raised-bed garden project at their elementary school. Karen's daughters are both in college, and she is a professor still teaching landscape horticulture at Southern Illinois University. Her interests in sustainable landscape practices, urban agriculture, and children have led her to explore gardening projects on the ground, on walls, and on rooftops. She continues to emphasize the value of stewardship of the earth and the positive human response in supporting that concept as we plan and live our lives.

As we have moved on, so has the rest of the world. As we looked ahead toward this new edition, we wanted it to reflect the many changes we have seen over the past decade, including concerns that children are becoming alienated from nature, that they do not play outside enough, and that childhood obesity is becoming an epidemic. We also wanted to reflect a wider range of gardens. In our first edition, we told our own story. In this edition, we share stories from other people with different gardening challenges. We share ideas for people who live in limited space or in urban areas. And we showcase some of the great projects we have found around the country. We also provide more information for those working with infants and toddlers, because often these youngest children are left inside. They also need to be involved in gardening.

Most of all, we want to inspire teachers and family members to involve their children in gardening. Pick up a shovel or go buy a pot and some potting soil. Grab a packet of seeds and start planting. There is wealth to be found in the soil.

Acknowledgments

The first edition of this book was based on our personal gardening experiences with children. This revised version has been enhanced immensely by including the experiences of multiple diverse programs through the selfless assistance of many people. We never could have written this edition without their cooperation. Our gratitude to these friends, colleagues, and family members is immense. Listed here are only a few of those involved:

Tammy Davis, instructor in Human Environmental Studies at Southeast Missouri State University and forever an infant-toddler teacher, provided direction in our work related to infants and toddlers. Tammy's assistance was instrumental in the development of chapter 6, providing inspiration, suggesting topics of discussion, and writing her own story for us to share. Tammy also assisted with photography and notes during our visits to infant and toddler classrooms and shared her own extensive photo library with us.

Marissa Argus, K-1 teacher at the Indianapolis Public Schools/Butler University Lab School, allowed us to photograph her massive garden workday and graciously provided access to her class blog and documentation panels. We also want to thank Principal Ron Smith for his cooperation and Andrew Lucas for tirelessly tracking down parental permission forms right up to our deadline.

Cassandra Mattoon, preschool teacher at the Thomas Metcalf Laboratory School at Illinois State University, hosted a photo shoot in her garden, allowed us to photograph a field trip, shared her expertise on the use of electronic tablets in the garden, and much, much more.

Barbara Meraz, site director of the Sikeston University Child Development Center at Southeast Missouri State University, assisted us both in her current role and her prior role as twos teacher at the University School for Young Children. Barb photographed and recorded her work with the two-year-olds, wrote stories about her experiences, assisted us in photo shoots at the Sikeston Center, and worked to assure we had permission forms for all the children.

Tamra Bottomlee, director of the Purdue University Calumet–Charlotte R. Riley Child Care Center, and lead teacher Kate DeRolf cooperated in multiple photo shoots, shared their own photographs, and introduced us to the Grow NWI (Northwest Indiana) organization, which connected us to additional schools with gardening programs.

Barb Gustin and Arcilia Ramirez, of School City of Hammond Head Start tracked down photo and artwork permissions from past students so that we could share gardening explorations of the following teachers: Jennifer Wachowski, Janet DeZarn, JoAnn Guevara, and Carol Haynes.

Amy Weimann Collins and Colleen Bandy, of the Elgin Child and Family Resource Center, gave us access to photograph cooking activities and provided Spanish-speaking translators as we sought permission from parents.

Principal Peg Harangody and Dyana Butcher at St. Michael's School showed us the incredible power of container gardening. We also want to thank third-grade teacher Maryann Tonkovich, who shared her iPad photos and student drawings.

Michelle Bowen and the teaching staff at the Hilltop Neighborhood House allowed us to take gorgeous photographs of their students in the garden, including the one on the cover of this book.

Crown Point Christian School Principal Carol Moxey, and teachers Elaine Nosich and Betsy Zimmer, allowed us to document learning as well as implement/photograph classroom activities.

Becky Moore, site director, and the teachers of the University School for Young Children at Southeast Missouri State University assisted us with projects and photographs. Special thanks to Megan St. John, Kim Rueseler, Alicia Pavelka, and Amanda Morris for allowing us to work in their classrooms.

The teachers and staff at Sikeston University Child Development Center of Southeast Missouri State University graciously allowed us onto their Nature Explore Outdoor Classroom and into their classrooms.

Christine Kiewra, education specialist at Nature Explore/Dimensions Educational Research Foundation, graciously spent time talking with us about her experiences using a greenhouse and then went out of her way to take a photograph we could use to accompany her story.

Kristi Draluck shared her stories and impressive images of Wooly Pocket vertical gardening with her kindergarten class in Sonoma, California for us to include. We're only sorry that we were unable to post the video in our book of the baby birds whose nest was discovered in one of the pockets and that we couldn't make it to their salad buffet after the harvest.

Beth Krieger, the Director of Communications at The Calhoun School, West End Avenue in New York arranged for us to visit numerous classrooms and join an evening picnic on their green roof. We would like to thank the many teachers, students and parents, as well as Beth, for sharing their gardening curriculum and picnic food with us.

Nikki Cornelision, Sheila King, and other parent/teachers from the Dayemi Parent-Child Collective School in Carbondale, Illinois welcomed us to their planning sessions to renovate their outdoor classroom. We appreciate their students' input and the Southern Illinois University students' involvement as we planned, took pictures, drew ideas, and shared great discussions.

Andy Pense, the Farm to School Coordinator in West Virginia, enthusiastically told us garden success stories based on his work. He is very active in bringing gardens to kids and kids to gardens.

Add Roosevelt took time at the end of a busy day to allow us to photograph her and her children at her child care home.

Marty Gottlieb shared his images and knowledge of Smart Pot container gardening.

Monica Lehnen, Melissa Himstedt, Hollie Eenigenburg, and Crystal Klomp assisted with photo shoots.

Steve Buhman, our good friend and SIUC photographer, took time on a Saturday to take author photos.

We would also like to thank the group of parents and their children who allowed us to take pictures as we planted annuals on the green roof at Southern Illinois University.

And, of course, we once again thank Jessica Chambers who continues to inspire us with her creative gardens and garden activities. If you are ever near the Illinois State University campus in Bloomington, Illinois, definitely visit the Horticulture Center where Jessica is the Horticulture Coordinator.

Each of us owes recognition to our families. Charles, Sara's husband, could have a new garden built before we finished discussing his contributions (and he would be cooking us a meal at the same time). Her daughter, McCartney, during precious visits split time with demands of the book. Chris, Karen's husband, and her daughters, Lonzie and Nyssa, always willingly joined her in garden visits or projects. Todd, Marla's husband, and her daughters, Haleigh, Taylor, and Avery, were very patient with her as she tackled her first professional project in several years and took multiple out of town trips for photo shoots, including one on Taylor's ninth birthday.

All of our families understood when we needed time to meet, write, sort photos, and immerse ourselves in our passion for engaging children in gardening. We love and thank them.

Introduction to the Second Edition

If you are reading this book, we assume you are interested in gardening with children. We wrote this book as a resource for anyone who works with young children from infancy through third grade. We want it to appeal to a wide audience, not just teachers and caregivers in traditional school settings and child care programs, but family child care providers, Head Start programs, homeschoolers, and parents interested in introducing their children to gardening. We hope infant and toddler caregivers and teachers will introduce even the youngest children to gardening. We also want to give primary teachers examples of how they can actively engage their children in meaningful curriculum through gardening. We have included examples of both rural and urban gardens, and we have provided ideas for those who have little space and few resources, as well as those who have more. We have reached out to programs and teachers throughout the United States, who have helped us by sharing their stories. We hope that you will find what you are looking for here.

You may choose to read *Gardening with Young Children* from start to finish, but that is not the only way to read it. You may find that one or two chapters contain the information that is most pertinent to your needs, and you can begin with those chapters. Each chapter can be read individually. You could also begin by flipping through the book, looking at pictures for inspiration or ideas. However you decide to read the book, know that all the subject matter weaves together to create the whole.

Chapter 1 explains why gardening is important for young children. This chapter will give you the rationale for developing a garden program. Read it if you need to rally support for creating a program. Also, read it to deepen your understanding of how children benefit from gardening. We stress the importance of contact with nature for children's physical, social, and emotional development and how changes in our society and the physical landscape have impacted childhood over the past few decades.

In chapter 1, you will come to understand the scientifically proven benefits of letting children get dirty. We discuss the international movement to connect children with nature. We also explore the deficit many children have in their understanding of the source of their food and how food moves from seed to table. The role of the teacher is examined as we seek to assure teachers of their competence and capability in gardening with young children. The section "What the Teacher Needs to Know" actually applies to anyone who works with young children, whether that person is a teacher, parent, grandparent, nanny, curriculum coordinator, caregiver, or "educarer." We also share information for administrators about some of the obstacles they may face as they begin building support for a garden program.

The subject of chapter 2 is engaging children in gardening. We want children to be intensely involved, not just observers. This happens when garden projects and plans develop from the children's own interests. It results in the most meaningful learning. In chapter 2, we discuss how to prepare the children for gardening through exposure to materials and experiences in the classroom, how to help children discover what their interests are, and how to build a garden curriculum based on those interests. Chapter 2 covers specific techniques teachers can use, such as "think aloud," talking tubs, and talking and thinking floorbooks. We also discuss in depth how to maintain intellectual integrity in the curriculum, that is, how to assure that what you are teaching the children is worth learning, that the material being presented is true to the discipline, and that the children can relate the content to their lives in a real way.

In chapter 2, we explain how understanding concepts can help us both in our planning and in our teaching. We discuss the creation of concept webs, which can help you come up with questions you want to answer during the life of your project, building a road map for your curriculum. In this chapter, you will also learn how you can build an integrated curriculum incorporating various content areas and how the project approach fits into the garden curriculum. We share how to interact with children in the garden, facilitate peer interactions, and foster learning by asking good questions and using the scientific process. Chapter 2 guides you through engaging children in fieldwork and giving specific suggestions for preparation and follow-up. We also share ideas for using technology for both research and documentation. Finally, we include an extensive section on how to integrate what is going on outside in the garden with your indoor classroom.

Chapter 3 walks you through the process of planning your garden. We begin by helping you explore your goals. We provide an inventory to help you select your garden site. We share ideas for involving children, teachers, volunteers, and others in decisions about the type of garden to construct and the garden design. Chapter 3 covers the advantages and disadvantages of different types of gardens, including container gardens, raised beds, in-ground gardens, gardens grown vertically on a wall or fence, and rooftop gardens. We also offer sample garden plans with themes to help you get started. Throughout chapter 3, we include lots of tips for including children in the garden planning process.

In chapter 4, we explain how to build your garden. We begin by sharing suggestions for obtaining resources, materials, and funding, as well as true stories from programs that have been successful in procuring outside resources. We discuss how to involve the children in building the garden and why it is important. Chapter 4 provides specific details about building each type of garden presented in the book—selecting construction materials based on your garden plan, acquiring labor and materials, and then building your garden.

Chapter 4 also covers plant selection and many related considerations, such as whether to plant from seed or transplants. Selection is discussed in relation to garden conditions, curriculum goals, and available resources. Native plants and plants to avoid are also discussed. Suggestions for using a greenhouse and preventing vandalism are included in this chapter.

Chapter 5 is about working with children in the garden. Here we share information about how to work with children to plant and maintain the garden. We address maintenance issues such as mulching and pest control. We explore the garden ecosystem, which involves organisms in the soil, insects and other small creatures, and animals, such as birds and squirrels. We discuss which of these are beneficial and which can be harmful, including suggestions for both.

Harvesting is the reward for all of the hard work you do in the garden. In chapter 5, we share suggestions for picking, tasting, and cooking activities. We also include ideas for using nonfood products and how to harvest and save seeds. We conclude with a discussion of how to document and share the work with others through displays and a culminating event.

In chapter 6, we focus on gardening with infants and toddlers. We have singled out this age group because of their specific needs and because we believe it is the group most likely to be neglected when it comes to gardening. We discuss the importance of relationships during the infant-toddler years, both in terms of human relationships and relationships with nature. We include specific suggestions for introducing infants and toddlers to the outdoors, plants, and garden animals, as well as stories from teachers who have been successful in doing so. Tips for choosing plants for this age level are included. We also discuss how you can educate family members about the importance of taking infants and toddlers outside.

We wrote chapter 7, "Universal Garden Learning Experiences," with the goal of suggesting experiences that are not dependent on a specific plant or environment but can be done in any garden. Here you will find a wealth of activities, including tried-and-true recipes. Each activity description includes the concepts to be learned, materials needed, step-by-step instructions, extension ideas for diversity, and, if necessary, safety considerations.

The purpose of chapter 7 is to give you specific ideas for learning experiences both indoors and outdoors. These activities were designed so that they are not plant specific. In fact, many of them don't even require a garden. You may want to go straight to this chapter and explore some of the activities before you begin building your own garden. These activities may help build interest among your class about gardening. We also hope that these experiences will spur your thinking as a class and inspire you to come up with new ideas of your own. This is only a beginning. Your garden will take you on a journey that is yours alone.

We hope that you find this book a valuable reference. Don't be afraid to take it outside and get it dirty. Happy reading and happy gardening!

Chapter 1

Why Garden?

It is said that every snowflake is different—no two ever the same. This could be true of everything in nature. Every leaf is different, every pinecone, every flower. You don't believe this? Go outside, and take a child with you. Try to find two leaves that are identical. There is more to be learned outside than there ever was in a classroom, and children long to be outdoors. Children are drawn to nature. They pick the tiny flowers growing in the grass, unearth the pill bug from underneath the rock, and capture the tiny toad hiding near the sand box. Children notice what has become old to adults. To children, the natural world is still a source of awe.

Children Need Nature

Unfortunately, children are spending less time outdoors than ever before, not only in the United States but all over the world. Changes in the past few decades have impacted how children play in ways we never could have imagined fifty years ago. Many of us grew up outdoors, whether we were playing in small towns, on city streets, or on farms. We ran, explored, made up games, chased lightning bugs, and dug in ditches. Ask any group of adults over age forty about their childhood memories, and you will hear fond stories of time spent outdoors. Sadly, this has changed.

Richard Louv, in his book *Last Child in the Woods,* called attention to the significant changes that have occurred over the past decades in children's experiences with nature. Louv coined the term *nature-deficit disorder* to refer to "the human costs of alienation from nature, among them: diminished use of the senses, attention difficulties, and higher rates of physical and emotional illnesses" (2005, 34). A number of factors have influenced children's withdrawal from nature, but a few stand out: increased interaction with technology, the disappearance of natural areas, and adults' fears about letting children roam free or interact with nature.

The changes in technology over the past twenty years have been transformative. As authors, we couldn't bear the thought of having to bang out this book on a typewriter. We remember our precomputer days and the painful process of retyping pages with errors and worrying about what would happen if we lost our only copy. And as teachers, we know that many new technological tools are amazing. They allow a child to immediately search for and identify the insect that is eating the cucumbers. They give her the opportunity to photograph it, type out her story, and then save or print it with the accompanying photograph. When we were teaching, we were unable to provide enough reference books to equal a small portion of what is on the Internet. And if we took photos, film strictly limited how many photos we could take and how we could process and print them. We appreciate what technology has given us, but we also know that this transformation has come at a cost.

From their earliest years, children are caught up in computers, games, and tablets. In the waiting room of the doctor's office, a mother hands her infant her smartphone, entertaining the child with an app while they wait for the doctor. In an earlier time, the mother might have spent the time talking with the child to keep her occupied. Parents and caregivers are using phones and tablets to provide entertainment, and toy manufacturers are pushing this trend, creating screen toys for young children and products that encourage the use of screens in ever-younger children. (The toy voted Worst Toy of 2012 by the Campaign for a Commercial-Free Childhood [CCFC] was the Laugh & Learn Apptivity Monkey by Fisher-Price. It is a stuffed monkey with an iPhone in its belly marketed for children as young as six months. In 2013 the winning toy was an iPotty by CTA Digital, a potty chair with a stand for attaching an iPad so the child can use the screen while toileting. Shortly after awarding the 2013 prize to the iPad potty chair, CCFC disclosed that Fisher-Price had released a new infant bouncy seat with an attachment for an iPad.) Research done in 2003 found that children under age six spent about two hours a day with screen media, including TVs, computers, DVD players, and video games (Rideout, Vandewater, and Wartella 2003). It is likely these numbers would be higher now, as so many more opportunities are available. As their world has narrowed to the size of a screen, children have come to lack curiosity about the outdoors. They watch TV shows about exotic creatures far away but may be ignorant about the wildlife living in their own backyards (Louv 2005).

If children do want to go outdoors to explore, they face other barriers. Many of us can look around our communities and point to areas, once open and wild, now covered by housing developments, shopping centers, or office parks. As development has taken over, there are fewer open natural areas where children can play. Their world has been landscaped and cemented over, leaving fewer green spaces to explore.

In the past, children tended to play outside and to be a given fairly wide range in which to explore without adult interference. Children had ample opportunity to explore natural areas, build forts, explore creeks, and examine small creatures they came across. However, this radius has been shrinking over the past decades as parents keep closer watch on their children than ever before. Parents are afraid, citing crime, stranger danger, and even nature itself as threats to their children's safety.

At the same time, people are concerned about the future of the planet as development cuts into natural areas and the habitats for many species disappear. Woodlands, wetlands, and rain forests are shrinking, and pollution is an

ever-growing concern. Concerned adults want to raise children who are sensitive to these issues and who care about the earth. Wanting to be proactive, teachers wonder how they can best foster in children a love of nature and a disposition to be stewards of the environment.

One instinct is to teach young children about what is happening to the earth and to engage them in activities to help save the planet. David Sobel cautions against this approach. When children are asked to solve monumental adult problems beyond their comprehension, they are not only likely to be unengaged but may also develop anxiety and what Sobel refers to as *ecophobia*, a "fear of ecological problems and the natural world" (1996, 5). Sobel indicates that exposure to curriculum focused on solving environmental problems may actually result in disempowering children and leaving them with feelings of hopelessness. Instead, teachers should find ways to foster *ecophilia*, a love of the natural world, in children. Sobel says that at each stage of development, "children desire immersion, solitude, and interaction in a close, knowable world" (1996, 12). Look for ways to give children uninterrupted time where they can become deeply involved and engaged in the natural world, whether it is exploring outdoors or working in the garden. Giving children the gift of time to explore, observe, notice, and contemplate is essential to building a bond with nature.

Many children today know a lot more about animals in faraway ecosystems than they do about the animals in their own backyard. They watch TV and movies and learn about exotic animals. However, it is hard to form a true

connection to animals you meet through a screen. As Louv points out, "Such information is not a substitute for direct contact with nature" (2005, 23). When children work in a garden, they observe closely the bees and butterflies that gather nectar from the flowers. They hold the ladybug they find resting on a leaf and examine with a magnifying glass the spider that has spun a web between the vines. On their hands and knees, they count the ants and study them as they carry food back and forth to their anthills. Children discover that snails like to hide under the stones where it is damp and that the bunnies are coming into the garden to eat the lettuce. Nature is real. They touch it, draw it, photograph it, and study it over a period of time. The story is their own story and not the story someone else has photographed, edited, and told to them. And because it is their own, it is woven into the fabric of their lives and becomes part of who they are.

Adults who care deeply about the environment cite two factors that have contributed to their love of nature: time spent playing in nature as a child and an adult who fostered love and respect for nature (Sobel 1996). An adult who introduces a child to gardening—who takes the time to slow down and be with the child as she digs in the soil, who sits inside the sunflower house, who shares joy in the dance of the honeybee—that adult can be the person who helps the child discover the joy and wonder of nature.

Physical, Social, and Emotional Development

The health of America's children is at risk. For the first time in history, children face a future where they may face life spans shorter than those of their parents. According to the Centers for Disease Control and Prevention, in 2007 parents reported that 9.5 percent of children between four and seventeen years of age have been diagnosed with ADHD, an increase of 21.8 percent from 2003 (2010). Obesity has grown at an alarming rate, and children are less physically active. Richard Louv (2011) argues in his book *The Nature Principle* that nature has transformative powers and that vitamin N (for nature) is an essential element in enhancing physical and mental health.

Research validates the important connection of nature to children's healthy physical and emotional development. Nancy M. Wells and Gary W. Evans (2003) found that children who spend time in natural environments are more physically active and experience psychological benefits, including reduced stress. Andrea Faber Taylor and Frances E. Kuo (2011) found that children playing in greener environments had reduced symptoms of ADHD. Studies have shown that heart rate and blood pressure are lowered just by being in a garden (Cleveland Botanical Garden 2014). Even living plants in classrooms have been shown to have a positive effect on children's behavior, emotions, and health. Being near nature creates what Louv calls the mind/body/nature connection that is necessary for our mental and physical health. Living things make people feel good.

Young children are sensory learners, and gardening calls to all their senses. The visual impact of flowers, vegetables, and living creatures pulls them into the garden, where they immediately reach out to touch the growing plants. They notice the fragrance of flowers and herbs, hear the grasses rustle in the wind and the hum of the bumblebee as she settles on a coneflower. They pick mint, perhaps tasting the herb for the first time in its natural state. Later they harvest vegetables and herbs to use in cooking activities. Maybe they try a new food for the first time because they grew it themselves.

Gardening is movement, and children need to move. They can't help it. Ask a group of three-year-olds to sit still and then observe how much harder this is for them than running and climbing. We have always known that movement helps bodies grow, and now researchers have confirmed that movement is also necessary for brain development. A garden gives children a place and a purpose to practice both fine- and gross-motor skills. Children dig holes to plant seeds or seedlings. They pick up tiny seeds and place them in a hole or broadcast them carefully over a wide space. They collect mulch in wheelbarrows and spread it on the garden, then hold the hose as they sprinkle water over the growing plants. Weeding requires careful selection and removal of unwanted plants. Picking flowers takes skill and practice—pull too hard and the roots come up, cut too high up and there is no stem to put in the vase. Some flowers can be broken off; others need to be cut with scissors. When the children harvest vegetables, they must use just the right amount of pressure in removing the desired part of the plant to avoid damaging the remaining part.

Social growth occurs when children work together in the garden. They learn to listen to each other and share what they know. Because their experiences differ, they learn from each other. They develop social skills as they encounter situations that involve taking turns, compromising, and sharing. Patience and the ability to tolerate delays evolve as children learn that their turn does come when they work cooperatively with others. Children and adults all have to work cooperatively in the garden. Gardening is a group project, and negotiation is sometimes necessary when determining what to grow, who will do what task, how to carry out a needed job, or what to do with the harvest. Everyone has to work together to solve problems when they occur, building a sense of teamwork.

Children develop confidence as they work in the garden. They conquer fears as they encounter new creatures in their explorations, examine them, hold them in their hands, and return them to their homes. Even children who don't like to get dirty are drawn to a session of planting flowers. They dig with trowels, and though they may don gloves or grab the stem of the plant to avoid touching the soil, they participate. The garden is responsive to children

with disabilities or to those who are just learning the common language of their school. A good teacher can find ways to include everyone.

Gardens are beautiful. In recent years, many teachers have begun to recognize that institutional-style buildings and classrooms lack the aesthetic qualities that are necessary to foster a deep appreciation of life in children. The Reggio Emilia approach, which emphasizes the relationship between the children and their environment, calling the environment the third teacher, has been instrumental in this new awareness. Adding a garden softens the outdoor classroom area and adds a focal point that changes the quality of the playground experience. By bringing flowers or foliage cuttings from the garden inside, children and teachers can do the same for the indoor classroom. Some plants can be grown indoors as well.

Anyone who enjoys gardening knows the sense of calm that comes from handling soil, tucking seedlings tenderly away, watching the plants and animals that inhabit the garden. The garden demands that people wait. Plants grow at their own pace. The garden gives children opportunities to slow down and take time to explore in detail. Children who observe closely will notice small changes from day to day, large changes from week to week. They learn the need for patience and careful observation. They begin to nurture.

With gardening, teachers can create private spaces for children. Much has been written about the need for children who are in group programs for much of the day to have some privacy. In fact, while teachers occasionally take breaks, children are usually not allowed to leave the classroom. They are often expected to remain with a large group of people for nine hours a day, or even longer. As adults, we know the importance of building in time to be alone, to think, to observe from a distance. Garden spaces can give children an opportunity for privacy or alone time. Teachers can build a special structure, such as a trellis house, with this end in mind, or design the garden so that small,

protective spaces are available. Whether the space is under a low-hanging tree, behind a bush, between rows of plantings, or within a carefully constructed sunflower house, children will appreciate the joining of solitude with the comfort of natural elements.

For some children, the peaceful quiet a garden offers and the interaction with the garden ecosystem may be particularly impactful, even therapeutic. Horticulture therapy is used in a variety of situations, from children's hospitals to treating adults with chronic health and mental health issues. While teachers are not skilled therapists, they can take advantage of the restorative value that gardening offers. Nurturing plants is an empowering process. One of the key features in horticulture therapy is this element of control (Millet 2009). As children interact with the plants, they provide the elements that the plants need to grow. When the child plants a seed, he begins the life cycle of a plant. As he nurtures the plant, it responds and grows. To a child who may have little control in his life, this is a powerful experience.

The sensory elements of the garden are also restorative. Many hospitals are now installing healing gardens, and doctors note that patients who can see the gardens heal faster and with fewer drugs than patients who cannot. Children who have stressful lives or who suffer from trauma may find peace in the garden that is not available in other areas of their lives. Teachers can foster this sense of serenity by creating spaces to be alone, where a child can think or read or draw.

Dirt Is Good

As early childhood educators, we clean things. We wash hands, sanitize surfaces, disinfect dishes, and do all we can to keep our children away from those nasty germs. This makes perfect sense, especially when we have large groups of children who are together for long stretches of the day. Any one of these children may have a contagious disease. At the same time, bacteria are getting

stronger and more resistant to antibiotics, and more of our children are developing diseases, such as allergies and asthma. What is happening?

Teachers who have worked with young children for over the past two decades or more are witnesses to the skyrocketing levels of allergies in developed countries. Once peanut butter ruled supreme in the classroom. Children happily rolled peanut butter balls for snack and munched on peanut butter sandwiches for lunch. The gooey substance is now banned for fear that allergic children will develop anaphylactic shock at the mere touch of peanut butter residue. Most teachers in the United States now deal with allergies regularly. The Asthma and Allergy Foundation of America (2014) states that one in five Americans suffers from asthma and allergies. One theory for the escalation of allergies is the hygiene hypothesis, which states that "excessive cleanliness interrupts the normal development of the immune system, and this change leads to an increase in allergies. In short, our 'developed' lifestyles have eliminated the natural variation in the types and quantity of germs our immune systems need for it to develop into a less allergic, better regulated state of being" (UCLA Food and Drug Allergy Care Center 2014). The hygiene hypothesis has been reinforced by recent studies that show that children who have dogs as pets during their early life (Bergroth et al. 2012) or who are raised on farms (Lewis et al. 2012) have stronger immune systems. As explained by Mary Ruebush in *Why Dirt Is Good*,

> From infancy onward, every germ you fight off increases your ability to fight that germ off again later on even more effectively. Every germ you fight off also strengthens the communications among your immune system cells and lets you mount an offense against an invader that much more quickly. When your immune system doesn't encounter a lot of dirt, it doesn't get challenged. Instead

of responding quickly and accurately to germs, it reacts slowly, leaving you open to more frequent and severe illness. And when kids don't get exposed to enough dirt, their immune systems start making the sort of serious mistakes that can lead to autoimmune illnesses, allergies, and asthma. When your immune system is exposed to plenty of dirt on a regular basis starting when you're very young, it gets the regular workouts it needs to build up defenses and stay ready for action. (2009, 101)

Given this evidence, it makes sense that all children, from infancy on, should play outside, touch plants, and dig in the soil. We should not be afraid if they get their hands and the rest of their bodies dirty. It doesn't hurt us to eat a little dirt. It may just make us healthier in the long run.

Children Need Time Outdoors

Over the past decades, there has been an effort to make playgrounds safer and easier to maintain. Unfortunately, as a result, many outdoor play spaces became sterile, and some completely devoid of nature. Grass and trees have often been removed to clear space for large pieces of climbing equipment and the resilient ground cover that must surround the equipment. Sometimes playgrounds are completely comprised of resilient ground cover and man-made surfacing rather than natural materials. In these spaces, children have little opportunity to connect with nature.

Nevertheless, the movement toward more natural play environments for young children is strong and growing. Recognition that these fabricated industrial environments are not serving children's needs, along with concern that natural spaces are disappearing, is producing a movement to connect children with nature. One example has been the development of the Nature Action Collaborative for Children (NACC), which has sponsored the Working Forum on Nature Education, beginning in 2006. NACC is an interdisciplinary group comprised of sixteen hundred members from six continents, including early childhood educators, environmental educators, health specialists, landscape architects, and environmental activists.

Working groups of NACC have various goals, one being to create natural play spaces for children in preschool settings, schools, and communities. Nature Explore, a collaboration of the Arbor Day Foundation and Dimensions Educational Research Foundation, has been a leader in this movement and a sponsor of the Working Forum on Nature Education. Nature Explore defines a set of principles to use in designing an outdoor classroom, provides certification to programs that follow these principles, supports staff development, and encourages family involvement. There are currently over one hundred certified Nature Explore classrooms in the United States.

A natural playscape may contain many different natural materials—logs, sand, mulch, rocks, wood in many forms, pods, shells, and seeds for children to explore. However, plants are the key to making a natural play space come alive. In fact, Nature Explore certification requires the installation of either a garden area or a walkway through plantings. Plants not only bring life to the environment, but they become an incubator for other living things. Subterranean creatures, such as worms and grubs, move in. Insects arrive to check out the plants or each other. Butterflies and bees feed on the nectar in the flowers. Birds and small mammals find places to nest and food to eat. In a short time, a new ecosystem evolves. In chapters 3 and 4 of this book, we offer suggestions on the best way to assess your environment and resources to plan and install a sustainable garden in an outdoor nature playscape.

Learning from Seed to Table

One of the most notable results of children spending less time outdoors is the continuing rise in obesity rates, even among preschool-age children. According to the Centers for Disease Control and Prevention, one in seven low-income, preschool-age children is obese. In fact, since 1980 obesity among children and adolescents has nearly tripled. About 17 percent of all children ages two to nineteen are obese (Centers for Disease Control and Prevention 2014). Why is there is an obesity epidemic in the United States?

Lack of exercise is clearly part of the equation. Children need to spend more time moving. In addition, the overconsumption of fast food and highly processed food has become a serious problem in the United States. Children today often lack a clear understanding of where food comes from. Meat appears in plastic-wrapped containers in supermarkets. Fruits and vegetables come from cans or appear on plates—sliced, mashed, or fried. Some children live in *food deserts*, areas of the country where fresh fruits and vegetables are unavailable. These children may have no exposure to unprocessed food because their families are unable to buy fresh produce.

Jamie Oliver's (2010) TED Talk gives us stunning insight. Oliver shows a video of himself interacting with a kindergarten class in Huntington, West Virginia. He holds up a bunch of ripe, red tomatoes. "Who knows what this is?" he asks. A child answers, "Potatoes." Oliver offers a head of cauliflower to a blond-headed boy. "Do you know what that is?" The boy shakes his head. Oliver asks a second child, "Do you know what that is?" The child's answer: "Broccoli?" Oliver shows the children an eggplant. "Who knows what that is?" A child responds, "Uh, pear?" Finally, Oliver holds up the staple of many children's diets, an Idaho potato. Surely, they will know what this is. "What do you think this is?" he asks. The response was, "I don't know."

How can it be that children don't recognize the source of their french fries and mashed potatoes? Have they never seen them made from scratch? Have they never seen fresh vegetables? Are we really becoming so far removed from the source of our food that our children don't even recognize basic vegetables? As Oliver states, "If the kids don't know what stuff is, then they will never eat it."

Gardening gives children the opportunity to see food develop from seed through all the changes and processes until it arrives at the table. Children plant squash seeds on a small hill of soil, then water them, waiting to see the small seedlings emerge. Soon those seedlings are growing a sprawling vine of large, green leaves. The children observe as big, yellow blossoms develop on

the vines. If they look carefully, soon they see small squash forming where some of the flowers are attached to the vine. As the green squash get bigger, the children notice stripes on the zucchini. If they touch the leaves or vines, they notice they are a little bit prickly. They wait and watch. Time must pass. The children begin to understand time in a new way. Food is not automatic; it is slow to develop. Finally, they can pick the zucchini. They explore methods to cook and eat it. They prepare the squash different ways—steamed, baked zucchini sticks and zucchini bread. They may compare zucchini picked at different sizes and learn that the smaller zucchini is tender, while the squash that gets too large is tough.

Research has indicated that children who grow their own vegetables, engage in cooking activities, and are repeatedly exposed to the same vegetables over a period of time show an increase in preference for those vegetables (Kalich, Bauer, and McPartlin 2009). Gardening connects children to food in a way nothing else can. They made the food happen. They know whether it came from the root or the stem of a plant. They know about the flower that bloomed before the vegetable grew. They washed off the insects that tried to eat the leaves of the plant or built a fence to keep the rabbits away. They know the food intimately. They are more likely to try this food than they are something that just popped up on their plate. With repeated exposure to foods they have grown themselves, children are more willing to eat them and more likely to prefer their taste.

The Role of the Teacher

Teachers initially may be hesitant to take on a classroom garden, particularly if they haven't had any personal experience with gardening. They may question whether they know enough about growing plants to teach children. All of us have had the experience of obtaining a plant only to have it inexplicably die. Teachers tell us all the time, "I can't grow anything. I have a black thumb." We want to reassure you that your past experience doesn't matter and that you don't have to be successful in everything you try to grow with children. Some things work; some don't turn out so well. It is about the journey, and everyone can go on a journey.

What the Teacher Needs to Know

The best thing about gardening with children is that anyone can do it. Even if you have never planted a seed, you have what it takes as long as you have a positive attitude and the will to learn. When we started our first garden, only Karen had a real horticultural background. Sara's gardening experience was limited to small projects with preschool children and to growing roses at home. And although Marla had grown up working in gardens on the farm with her parents and grandparents, she didn't garden at all when our initial

project began. Fortunately, teachers of young children don't need to have a lot of gardening knowledge at the beginning. What you need is an authentic interest that drives your explorations as you learn with the children. You should be able to admit when you don't know something as you guide children in search of answers. With such modeling, children will be able to ask questions freely.

We can make two promises. First, no matter what your level of expertise, you will learn something new from gardening with children. Second, you will learn much more from your failures than you will from your successes, as long as you're willing to try again when things don't work out as you had hoped. As a teacher, you must be a role model of interest and curiosity. Your enthusiasm is essential if you want the children to be enthusiastic. And you must express a sense of wonder if the children are to be free to express the same. This shouldn't be hard. Even avid gardeners still feel that sense of awe when a shrub first begins to bud after winter dormancy or when a half-inch seed produces a ten-foot sunflower.

In his book *Sharing Nature with Children*, Joseph Cornell (1998, 13) suggests, "Teach less, and share more." This is the best possible advice for a teacher of young children. You can do this by telling stories about your experiences with nature. Talk about your feelings rather than your knowledge. Express the amazement you feel. Take cues from the children. Find the delight that exists within you and share it. Express your disappointment when things don't turn out well. Follow that up with the determination to try again. Provide abundant resource materials, and use them constantly. When you find a new insect, get out an insect reference book or go online to look it up. Even if your classroom is high-tech, provide reference books. When you do, you'll find children spend long stretches of time exploring them. Plus, children can read reference books alone or with a friend, in the garden or the classroom, without worrying that the books will get broken. Once, after looking up cicadas and Japanese beetles with a teacher, two of our children spent another thirty minutes looking through the book *Bugs* by Frank Lowenstein and Sheryl Lechner.

You are the key to a successful garden study. You don't need to know all the answers, but you must be curious, interested, and willing to help search for answers. The garden should not be seen as a list of plant names to be memorized or characteristics to be studied. Avoid trying to fill the children with information and following up with questions to test their knowledge. It's less important for children to learn facts about the garden than it is for them to develop concepts. The children will learn naturally when they are intensely involved. They will become intensely involved when you are able to model enthusiasm and respond to their cues.

Be willing to let children explore incorrect answers. Part of the scientific experience is testing hypotheses and dismissing them. Don't be in a hurry to dismiss the child's conclusion. Hands-on experience with gardening is crucial to the young child's understanding of scientific concepts, and the best approach is to view it as research. Some plants will not grow well, while others will flourish. Some will become bug infested or be devoured by rabbits and squirrels. This is all part of the process of investigation. Our role as teacher is to guide children so that these seemingly unsuccessful experiments become meaningful learning opportunities.

Dying or half-eaten plants often leave children with many questions, such as "What happened to the lettuce?" or "How can we get rid of these slugs?" As adults, we often have answers handy and offer them quickly to children. But we provide a better learning experience for children when we let them lead by asking them to create some sort of hypothesis: "You know, that is a very good question. What do you think happened to our lettuce? Have you seen any visitors in this part of the garden lately? What do you think might have happened?" Allowing children to make predictions adds to their learning. Once children have given it some thought, you can discuss ways to verify their predictions: "Would you like to set aside some time tomorrow to sit quietly and observe the vegetable garden to see if you are right?" or "Maybe you could interview the other teachers and children to see if they have seen any creatures in this part of the garden." Once the children have more experience conducting these types of projects, you can simply ask, "How do you think we could find out more about what has been going on with the lettuce?" The child's response will provide information about his developmental level and problem-solving abilities.

Be willing to take things slowly. Observe the children. Cherish the time it takes to get down to the children's level, nose to nose with a dandelion, if necessary. Stop to see what has caught the children's attention. Focus their attention on new sights and sounds. Your role is a crucial one because children are very sensitive to what is important to adults. If the natural world is important to you, it will become important to the children. Keep in mind that a sense of joy should permeate the gardening experience. If gardening becomes a set of chores, the children will back off, and your project will fail. If your garden is very large, the children will not be able to do all the work. We realized early on that parents and staff would need to find time for weeding because our garden was so large. The children did enjoy weeding, and they did pull weeds, but they were never forced to do so. It was treated as an enjoyable activity. Don't worry if not every child participates in the work or shows a great deal of interest in gardening. The children will benefit from simply being near the garden, watching tiny seedlings develop into beautiful plants, playing under dancing flowers while butterflies float on the breeze and bumblebees zip past their ears.

This book tells you everything you need to get started. While we won't give you all the answers, we will share basic information with you and share activities you can try. You will discover much on your own as you take the children on a journey into the world of gardening.

What the Administrator Needs to Know

Earlier in this chapter, we discussed the fact that children are spending less time outdoors than ever before. Through our work in higher education, we have discovered that the young adults who are moving into teaching positions may have also grown up without spending much time outside or have distanced themselves from nature since their younger years.

Sara's Story

I teach a class at Southeast Missouri State University that includes, for many of my students, their first formal experience with preschool-age children. Each week they work three hours in the classroom at our lab school, and they attend a two-hour lecture class with me. Observing these students has given me insight into the way they see nature and the outdoors.

In one class session, the students are asked to compare learning experiences that hold intellectual integrity with experiences that do not. I have the students conduct some of the experiments with earthworms that are included in this book (pages 201–205). As the years have passed, I have noticed that fewer and fewer students will even touch a worm, much less pick one up. Consistently, the students discuss how "gross" and "disgusting" the worms are. In recent semesters, if I can get two students out of thirty to touch a worm, it is a good night.

I had pretty much adapted to the fact that most of my students were never going to like worms, when a few years back I was showing a slideshow on environments. My intent was to help the students understand how environments influence how we feel and how we behave. I showed a series of photos and asked them how they would feel and how they would behave in the places in the photos—a formal restaurant, a picnic spot by a lake, a traffic jam. Their responses were predictable. Then I showed a slide of a photo from our garden at Southern Illinois University. A teacher was sitting on a blanket inside a sunflower house, reading a book to some children. The photo made me feel warm and happy. I expected it to make the students feel good too. "How does this make you feel?" I asked. "Yuck," was the response, not just from one student but a chorus. I was shocked. "Why 'Yuck'?" I asked. "Bugs, messy, dirty," they replied.

Since then, I have shown this same slide to many students, and I get similar reactions. In fact, research I have been doing with colleagues since this incident seems to be indicating that our preservice teachers have a discomfort with nature. This discomfort seems to be most profound when messes or creatures are involved, for example, in situations where the individual is close to plants and, presumably, "bugs," such as sitting in the sunflower house. Students also showed anxiety about walking close to tall flowers, holding a bird's nest, and allowing children to mix water with dirt or sand.

If you are an administrator and your goal is to introduce a school garden, it is important that you be aware that your teachers may not be comfortable working with children and nature. They may have some degree of *biophobia*, or a fear of nature. In our experience, it is difficult to change someone's comfort level. We have had success, however, educating students about how to work with children outdoors.

Talk with your staff, and encourage them to share their feelings. When teachers with no background or hands-on experience are presented with a garden, they tend to be afraid to become involved for fear they will make mistakes. And they do make mistakes. We know of many instances where someone pulled up the plants someone else had carefully planted, thinking they were weeds. A school garden works best if everyone knows about the garden and feels comfortable enough to guide the children in pulling up weeds when they crop up or checking the leaves of the plants for insects. We also stress to teachers that while it is okay for them to feel uncomfortable around insects and other creatures, it is not okay to pass their fear on to children. For instance, a teacher should not say, "Worms are disgusting," or "That bug is icky." And teachers should never kill a creature and should always teach a child not to do so. A teacher who is fearful could say, "I feel uncomfortable around worms, but I am trying to learn to feel more comfortable." By being honest about feeling uncomfortable, the teacher acknowledges what is true and may be obvious to the child. By saying he is trying to learn to feel more comfortable, the teacher shows the child that even adults have room for growth.

Most of the schools we know that have a school garden have at least one staff member or parent who is passionate about nature and gardening. This person often becomes the natural leader, and cheerleader, of the garden project. Their enthusiasm and expertise will naturally inspire and energize the group. For Saint Michael School in Schererville, Indiana, this cheerleader was Dyana Butcher. As the school secretary, this Master Gardener could see the potential learning opportunities and positive benefits of having a school garden in an asphalt-filled courtyard behind the school. She determined to make her dream of a school garden a reality. This is her story:

Right before our open house in January, I asked the principal if I could make a sign and post it in the gym where all the parents gathered for the book fair. It was a brown tree with apples on the branches. At the top, the lettering said, "Help Our Garden Grow." Each apple had the name of something we needed for our garden, including three bags of potting soil, a hose, a planter box, garden tools, and a "friendship plant," which meant a division of one of their own perennials. Parents picked apples and asked when the supplies were needed. The word was out. We moved the sign to the front hallway by the office. A gentleman came in one day and saw the sign and said if we paid him for the wood, he would make the planter boxes. We also had containers donated—a child's yellow dump truck, an owl planter, and a ladybug planter. In March, K–3 students, with the help of fourth and fifth graders, planted their seeds in starter containers. These were cared for in their classrooms. Planters arrived, and we placed them outside. When visitors came, we showed them the garden space, and we started to get interest from places of business where parents visited or worked. In May the students planted their seed plants and flowers that were donated by two area farmers. On the school picnic day, the students came outside and painted their own designs on the wooden planters. Flowers were planted, in containers of all kinds, as well as

tomatoes, herbs, and some perennials. We also included the wish of our principal, Peg Harangody—a small potted tree, which would have lights for Christmas. Parents and students came through the summer to water the garden. The student council purchased a bench for the garden. A local business paid for an electrical connection. An older gentleman installed a water hose connection closer to the garden. Teachers now use the garden for science lessons and reading time. The students are so proud of their garden.

Dyana's dream of a school garden provided the energy to get the project off the ground. If you happen to have, or be, this passionate person, you are off to a great start. In chapter 3, we share how you can build a team of people who are invested in your garden project. Of course, in an ideal world, all of the teaching staff would work together to plan and learn about the garden. There are several ways you can involve the entire staff. To create interest, you can arrange for your staff to visit a nearby school that has a strong gardening program. If this is not possible due to time or expense, you can do an image search on the Internet and create a slide show of successful school gardens. You can have staff meetings where a Master Gardener guides the staff in activities in the garden. You can give each staff member an area of the garden to help the children design, plant, and care for. You can have workshops on gardening that involve the staff in garden activities to give them more knowledge about how to garden. Also, make sure that you actually have the teaching staff in the garden during the training. We made the mistake once of inviting a Master Gardener, who spoke to our staff in a classroom. Although he shared excellent information, the training was not effective. Because they didn't actually go into the garden, the teachers didn't develop the intimacy with the garden and the confidence they needed to do the work we wanted them to do with the children. Just like young children, adults benefit from hands-on learning experience. Plan to give them plenty of opportunities to work alongside avid gardeners and nature lovers, because over time, this confidence can be contagious. Whatever you do, make sure you are working together and that you are providing teaching staff with the information they need to be successful gardeners.

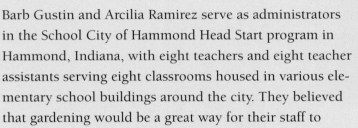

Barb Gustin and Arcilia Ramirez serve as administrators in the School City of Hammond Head Start program in Hammond, Indiana, with eight teachers and eight teacher assistants serving eight classrooms housed in various elementary school buildings around the city. They believed that gardening would be a great way for their staff to meet the federal Head Start program performance standards involving health, nutrition, cognitive development, social skills, parent involvement, and outdoor play experiences. In early spring, Marla and Sara provided a hands-on training workshop about gardening using the project approach. Some teachers seemed hesitant to engage in gardening for various reasons, such as challenging space issues or lack of personal knowledge. To motivate their staff, Barb and Arcilia decided to host a "friendly competition." They asked each team of teachers to create a garden with the children and document the process however they desired. As the school year ended and summer approached, the staff were asked to submit presentations of their garden project documentation to a panel of judges made up of a Geminus Head Start administrator and a School City of Hammond school board member who was a Master Gardener. The presentations were judged based on photo documentation of the project, presentation format, best use of space (related to space limitations at a site), creativity, educational value, parent involvement, and amount of time invested. The teachers created posters, trifold displays, and large books or journals that included photos and children's work products to document the process. This allowed the staff to feel a sense of accomplishment in their garden project and share their ideas and successes with other teachers.

Chapter 2

Engaging Children in Gardening

Successful curriculum engages children mentally, physically, and emotionally. To do this, a gardening project must have an on-site garden at its core. Children must feel ownership through the acts of planning, planting, tending, observing, and exploring. Any gardening curriculum that does not involve children in these types of activities will be short-lived at best. As the proverb says, "I hear and I forget. I see and I remember. I do and I understand." If you want children to learn about gardening, then they must do it daily for some length of time. They need repeated experiences to solidify and refine the concepts they learn, such as what a plant needs to grow. Children need time to become attached to the garden, to treasure it, to study it, to play in it, and to understand the intricacies of its living parts. In this chapter, we describe how to

- foster personal investment and common knowledge,
- engage children in the process of developing an emergent curriculum,
- assure that children are intellectually engaged in meaningful learning,
- integrate the garden curriculum across the content areas,
- use the project approach,
- participate in the garden with children,
- engage children in the scientific process,
- plan fieldwork,
- document children's learning, and
- extend the garden curriculum indoors.

Fostering Children's Interest in Gardening

When beginning the garden curriculum, teachers must first foster children's interest and personal investment in the idea of gardening. Your goal here is to create a common background of experience for the class to enrich their discussions and interactions before they begin actually gardening. In the spring, children are often fascinated by the changes they see in the outdoor world

around them. You can capitalize on this natural curiosity by adding books about gardening to your class library. Introduce gardening poems, songs, and storybooks at circle time to initiate discussions of gardening. Hang posters of gardens or flowers around the room, or take a nature walk to look for signs of spring as motivation for children to verbally share their past experiences with plants and gardening. If you are beginning in the fall, you can look for plants going to seed and collect seed pods to examine. Provide familiar gardening props for dramatic play to help children access memories of garden-related activities and inspire more discussion. Over a period of several days, you will discover which children have prior experience working in gardens or flower beds. Encourage children to share personal stories at group meeting times. Foster conversations among children throughout the day about previous experiences with planting, growing, and harvesting. All of these activities will allow children to recall basic knowledge and vocabulary related to gardening.

Using Emergent Curriculum as an Approach to Gardening

Many early childhood programs plan activities for children around a theme the teacher has chosen ahead of time. Often the theme is the focus of all the activities—music, art, reading, and group times, as well as room displays. The problem with planning this way is that sometimes the activities do not relate meaningfully to the children's lives or their interests, and because the children do not connect deeply to the work, they do not engage in real learning.

Instead of planning your garden curriculum ahead of time, we recommend that you follow the children's lead and let the curriculum emerge through developmental theme planning. In *Reflecting Children's Lives*, Margie Carter and Deb Curtis recommend the following:

- Observe the children. As you discover the themes or deeper meaning of their play, add materials to sustain their efforts and further their pursuits.
- Explore the children's questions. Think about their lives and relationships, and work to understand what interests the children about this particular investigation.
- Provide materials for investigation. Plan experiences that provoke curiosity. When misunderstandings occur, help children reexamine their conclusions. (Avoid correcting children when they are wrong. Instead, help them investigate further. They will eventually discover their own errors.)
- Place emphasis on "doing to know." Encourage the children to investigate materials, explore ideas, and interact with people as they connect with concepts and language.

- Plan based on children's strengths and interests rather than their deficits.
- Learn to integrate early learning standards with what children are interested in and what they want to know.

As you observe the children, let them guide you in selecting the next concepts to be explored. In *Bringing Reggio Emilia Home*, Louise Boyd Cadwell (1997) compares this responsive teaching style to the exchange of a ball on a court or playing field. Sometimes teachers have the ball, as they set up the environment, lead discussions with stimulating questions, and provide exposure to new tools or techniques. At other times, the ball is passed to the children, who steer the curriculum in a certain direction by providing input and sharing decision making.

One way to pass the ball to children when planning the garden is to record questions children ask about the garden or things that are happening in the garden. Keep these questions in a central place, perhaps where the class meets for group times, so that you can come back to the questions. During group discussions, write down the children's questions word for word, just as they phrase them. Elizabeth Jones and John Nimmo (1994), authors of *Emergent Curriculum*, suggest thinking of the teacher's role as that of scribe, rather than editor, to show respect for children's growing language abilities. You can write the children's names after their specific questions, if you wish, in order to follow up during later discussions. For instance, you could later prompt, "Jeremy, remember last week when you wanted to know about what plants eat? Well, today in the book area, we have a book that may help you answer that question. Would you like to read it with me at work time?"

We have also found that we sometimes need to model question formation for a group that has difficulty getting started. We do this by adapting a reading instruction strategy called "think-aloud." When children have difficulty forming their own questions and the discussion is stalled, you can say something like, "Well, I have always wondered if there are any plants that will grow in the shade. Has anyone else ever wondered about that? Do you think we should write that down as something we'd like to learn as we garden?" If children respond positively, write the question on the chart and then ask the children, "What else do you want to know? Who else has a question?" This modeling should provide a sense of framework to the task and get the group going.

Claire Warden (2006) advocates the use of "talking tubs" to stimulate children's thinking. A talking tub is a box that contains three-dimensional materials selected to stimulate observation and conversation. The box is decorated to enhance the experience. Warden uses question marks on her boxes to reinforce the idea of thinking about the items, but you can be imaginative in your decoration as long as you keep in mind that you want to convey the message that this box contains objects that are worth thinking about. The items are

carefully selected based on the goals of the teacher. For instance, a garden tub could contain gardening gloves, a trowel, seed packets, a flower bulb, the root of a plant, a dried flower with a seed pod, a watering can, mulch, a rain gauge, or other items related to a garden. Keep in mind that with a garden talking tub, you can represent both the beginning of life (seeds) and the end of life (the dried-up flower with seed pod). When presenting the box, show one item at a time, and invite reactions from the children. Assure them that there are no right or wrong answers. As the children respond with their thoughts about the items, you can jot down notes about their responses. Warden stresses that the aim of the talking tub is to stimulate discussion, so all connections that children make should be encouraged. When you look at your notes of the children's thoughts, you will see what Warden calls "possible lines of development" (PLODs) emerge. These PLODs are areas of interest to the children, which you can follow to see how the curriculum emerges.

Warden has also introduced the use of "talking and thinking floorbooks." The floorbook is large and can be either made or purchased. Warden gives directions for making floorbooks in her book *Talking and Thinking Floorbooks*. Because the books are large, children can gather around them on the floor. The books are used for planning and recording experiences. For example, the teacher could help the children make a web of what they are thinking about the garden at the beginning of the book, or the teacher could write, word for word, the children's answers to the question, "What do you want to do in the garden?" As the children work in the floorbook, the teacher gathers PLODs and writes them in the floorbook near the work that inspires them. Children contribute to the floorbook on an ongoing basis in a number of ways so that it becomes a kind of journal of their experience. They write about their experiences, draw pictures, and include photographs and artwork. Warden suggests providing precut "writing bubble" thought shapes on which children can record their ideas, and envelopes into which children can place important items. The floorbook is available to children at all times to review and to share their thoughts, plans, actions, and observations. Children can record what challenges they have had, what solutions they have tried, what worked and what didn't. The floorbook becomes a place to revisit what the group has done, creating deeper learning as the children study what they have done and what has happened in the garden over a period of time. Higher-order thinking is stimulated as children make connections and as they explore, observe, and adapt to new ways of thinking and doing.

Assuring Intellectual Engagement

If we are to do our best for children, we must plan for their cognitive development by ensuring intellectual integrity. It is easy for us to fall back on curriculum that is "cute" or "fun" without regard to what the children are actually learning. Lilian Katz and Sylvia Chard stress the need to focus on intellectual goals when planning curriculum. They believe that "children's minds should be engaged in ways that deepen their understanding of their own experiences and environment," and add that "the younger the children, the more important it is that most of the activities provided for them engage their intellects" (1989, 4).

It is easy, in designing experiences for the young learner, to dilute the message or even to provide information that is inaccurate or confusing to the child. In *Reaching Potentials: Appropriate Curriculum and Assessment for Young Children*, Sue Bredekamp relates a story about an experience from early in her teaching career. She had planned what she thought was a "cute" activity: cutting the tops off potatoes, replacing them with cotton balls, and planting grass seed on top to simulate hair. Although she enthusiastically checked on the progress of the "potato-head faces" each morning, she noticed that the children were not interested in the project. After reevaluating the activity, she concluded, "Grass doesn't grow on cotton balls, grass doesn't grow on potatoes, and potatoes don't grow hair! It seems fortunate that the children did *not* engage with this project, because if they had, it is hard to imagine what learning would have resulted and what relationship that learning would have had to reality" (Bredekamp and Rosegrant 1992, 39).

Any veteran teacher can tell such stories. This is why it is so important that whenever words such as "cute" come to mind, we should ask ourselves what the child will actually learn from the activity. If we cannot find value in the activity beyond this adjective, if we cannot determine what concepts the child will be learning from the activity, or if the learning is not true to the academic discipline the activity springs from, then it is likely that the activity does not have intellectual integrity.

In addition to learning, we also want children to enjoy their work in the classroom. But in the same way we want to avoid "cute" as a criterion for curriculum, we also want to avoid planning activities just because they are fun for the children. For example, picking all the flowers from the garden and throwing them in the air may be fun for the children but will likely fail to teach them anything meaningful. Katz and Chard (1989, 5) state, "While enjoyment is a desirable goal for entertainment, it is not an appropriate aim of education. A major aim of education is to improve the learners' understanding of the world around them and to strengthen their dispositions to go on learning. When educational practices succeed in doing so, learners find their experiences enjoyable. But enjoyment is a side effect or by-product of being engaged in worthwhile activity, effort, and learning."

Through a garden project, children are guided in scientific discoveries, not encouraged to believe in magical thinking. For instance, it would be easy to let children believe that the beanstalk grew because the beans were magic, but it would not be true to the discipline of science.

In addition, we must consider the developmental level of the involved children, the relationship of the curriculum to the world that they know, and their ability to participate actively in their learning. To be appropriate for young children, curriculum must be presented in a manner that respects their intelligence while adapting to their ability levels and their knowledge about and relationship to the world around them. To evaluate an activity for intellectual integrity and appropriateness, ask yourself the following questions:

- What is the concept behind this activity? (If you have difficulty naming a concept, the activity is possibly frivolous and may not be worthy of the children's time and attention.)
- Is the activity of interest to the child?
- Is the information that this activity presents accurate and credible?
- Is the information that will be presented worth knowing?
- Can the information be presented to these children in a manner that is meaningful to them?
- If the content is related to a discipline, such as math or science, is it true to the knowledge base of the discipline?
- If the content involves literature, poetry, art, or music, is the work of recognized quality?
- Can the children relate this activity to what is real in their lives and the world they know?
- Will children be actively involved in the learning process?

Focusing on Concepts

It is a teacher's job to determine what to teach. While focusing on facts is easy, and adults often respond positively when children are able to recite a series of facts, the simple memorization and regurgitation of information do not attest to real learning. Indeed, many preschoolers can recite the alphabet or numbers from one to twenty without having any understanding of what they represent. Facts change and become outdated with time. Think about information you memorized as a child that no longer holds true. Science marches on, disproving what was once considered certainty. In addition, some facts are simply not worth knowing. Most adults can conjure up some memorized material from early in their primary schooling that has been of little use since. The value of filling up children's heads with information and asking them to repeat it back is questionable at best. At a minimum, facts must connect to the child's world in a meaningful way to be useful.

On the other hand, concepts revolve around meaning. Concepts are ideas or basic understandings within a discipline that result after analyzing data from a number of experiences. Concepts build from where the child is and become more refined with time and experience. As children's brains develop, so do their concepts of the world, moving from the concrete (plant, flower, insect, roots) to the abstract (growth, beauty, care, cooperation), from the general (plant) to the specific (marigold, impatiens, rose, strawflower). The creation of the associations necessary for children to refine their thoughts over

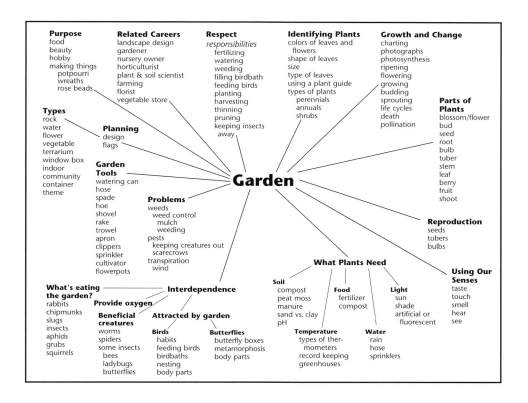

time results in more intellectual development than simple memorization of facts ever could.

To insure that children gain understanding while investigating gardening, you should have a clear idea of what concepts are involved. To clarify this in our own minds, one of the first tasks we undertook in beginning our garden project was the development of a concept web. You can examine our concept web to get an idea of the many opportunities for study in a garden curriculum. It is also a good idea to make your own web. This initial web is really to help you, as a teacher, think about and prepare for ways the curriculum could develop.

Our initial web is very broad and covers many different aspects of the garden. As you engage in studies with your children, they will be narrower in focus. Topics such as bugs, flowers, creatures that visit the garden, seeds, vegetables, and so forth can be explored. In fact, the best projects often focus narrowly and intensely on one specific topic. Once you have discovered that the children are interested in a certain topic, making a web with the children is a good way to find out what they already know about the subject. According to Judy Harris Helm and Lilian Katz (2011, 25), "Webs are graphic representations of the relationships between the children's comments or questions." When children work on a web together, they talk to each other, contributing to the common knowledge base and helping each other become more familiar with the vocabulary of the topic. Remember, the web serves as a map, keeping you aware of the possible destinations and what awaits you if you decide to go there. You won't necessarily cover every topic on your web. Allow the children's interests to be your guide.

After completing the web, think about how the concepts could be stated in simple terms by the children. Some examples of concepts follow:

* Plants are living things.
* Plants need water to live.
* Some insects eat plants.
* Weeds are plants that we don't want in our garden.

Older children or children who have had more experience with gardening will begin to refine the concepts they are learning and come up with more detailed information:

* Some plants become dormant in the winter and come out of dormancy in the spring.
* Different kinds of plants need different amounts of water to live.
* Some insects eat the insects that eat plants.
* Weeds take the nutrients that other plants need to grow.

Once you are able to state clearly the concepts the child is learning, it becomes easier to evaluate the quality of the experiences you are providing for the children. In fact, careful observation of the children should lead your curriculum. By thoughtfully watching the children as they play, work in the garden, and interact with materials, you will be able to determine what direction you should go in your curriculum planning. By following the children's interests, you can use your web as a road map. By responding to the children, you will keep them eager and involved.

The children's learning will be built upon year by year, experience by experience. Some concepts, such as planting, weeding, and watering, are universal, while the related careers and purposes for gardening that you study will vary by region, culture, and age of the group. We recommend that rather than feeling pressured to investigate every concept, you follow the interests of individuals or small groups as they develop.

Integrating Learning

Young children are integrated beings. Their physical development affects their cognitive development, which affects the development of language, which affects social development. From working with young children, you know that you can't divide a child up, dealing first with one part and then another. Instead, you focus on the child's overall development by integrating activities to address the whole child. By focusing on a topic, such as gardening, and carefully designing experiences that address many curricular areas, you help children build conceptual development and deeper understanding (Bredekamp and Rosegrant 1992).

Consider a typical experience in which children may participate during a garden project: making individual pizzas from English muffins with green peppers and tomatoes from the garden. As they follow the recipe, the children are exposed to literacy. They talk and, with the teacher's help, are exposed to new vocabulary words. Children practice social skills as they take turns and negotiate tasks. The children use fine-motor skills in cutting the vegetables and preparing the pizzas. They participate in math as they classify, count, and divide the vegetables into pieces. They divide the English muffins in half and are exposed to fractions. They count the number of pizzas they are making and experience one-to-one correspondence as they place ingredients on each English muffin half. The children have observed scientific processes as they watched the changes in the tomatoes and peppers growing in the garden. Now they will see the insides of the vegetables and notice the seeds (basic biology). They will watch the changes that occur in the pizzas as they are heated (changes in state—physics). Later they will record their experience in their journal (more literacy). One could go on and on. Rich classroom experiences bring many disciplines together.

A garden project is full of opportunities to integrate the curriculum. Every aspect of the curriculum can be woven into a project on gardening, and a wise teacher plans ahead to include each discipline within the activities planned for the child. Be cautious, however, not to focus solely on gardening. Many teachers remember experiences in college when they were expected to plan units revolving around a specific theme. Sometimes the expectation was that every planned activity would be based on this theme. So teachers struggled to come up with art activities related to insects, or fine-motor activities that involved pets. Some teachers still do this. This kind of planning often results, however, in contrived activities that have little meaning to the children and lack intellectual integrity. To avoid this trap, plan several strong experiences related to gardening. Then plan other activities that are simply good activities involving basic materials and equipment, not necessarily connected to the garden, such as science experiments, parachute games, block play, puzzles, woodworking, dramatic play, and music and rhythm. Remember, every song doesn't have to be about the garden, and every art project doesn't have to involve a flower or a butterfly. Children need to continue to explore all their interests and express themselves in a wide variety of ways. If you feel like you are straining too hard to come up with a certain kind of garden-related activity, you probably need to pull back. If you have to stretch to make a connection, the children probably won't get it.

Integrating Gardening across the Curriculum

As you proceed with your garden curriculum, you'll want to be sure that you are integrating all the disciplines into the gardening experience. This book is designed to enable you to create a rich curriculum for children by responding to their interests and following their lead. Periodically take the time to review your project to ensure that your in-depth study of the garden provides a breadth of experiences.

Science

Science is the most obvious area of learning associated with gardening, and the garden is rich in science learning. It would be almost impossible to list all the science concepts that can be included in a garden curriculum. Of course, children will observe plant growth and life cycles. When gardening, they also learn about the entire garden ecosystem. Once they have planted, the children and teachers must contend with weeds, insufficient rainfall, and pests. They also observe other animals that are attracted to the garden, such as large bumblebees, butterflies, and birds. They learn about creatures such as worms, which are useful in a garden. Other creatures have little impact on the growth of the plants but are interesting to study. For example, some children will spend hours examining pill bugs they've dug up from under a rock or log.

Although gardening is a method of controlling the environment, control is limited, and children are exposed to unexpected elements of the natural environment. Children gain an appreciation for the environment when they are exposed to nature. This awareness at an early age is necessary if children are to grow into adults who care about the environment, who see how we are connected to the earth in the most primal ways. Ask any adult who cares intensely about acting responsibly toward the environment and she will be able to tell stories of how she bonded with nature at a young age. When we garden with children, we allow them to become responsible for a small part of their world and give them the opportunity to connect with the earth and its creatures. Through gardening, children begin to see their place in the ecological web that is our world.

Literacy

The most obvious learning from a garden may be in the area of science, but the garden also offers tremendous opportunities for language development. Even adults will learn new vocabulary words as they explore gardening with children. Children love repeating complicated Latin names and identifying such colorfully named plants as dragon's blood sedum, New Guinea impatiens, mammoth Russian sunflower, and birdhouse gourd. They will also need to communicate as they plan and complete tasks, make observations, and record their findings. Literacy skills develop as children read books, do research, label plants, follow recipes, and make representations of what they see.

Math

Children use math skills often when they work in the garden. They count seeds as they plant, using one-to-one correspondence if they are placing seeds in individual containers. They observe growth and may measure certain plants, for instance, comparing the size of the giant sunflower to other objects in their environment or even to themselves. They classify as they observe and record data, often graphing their findings and drawing conclusions. When the time comes to prepare food from the garden, children count and classify, compare size, and measure as they follow recipes.

The Arts

The garden readily lends itself to exploration through the arts. Children construct images from the garden through drawing, painting, and modeling. The teacher can introduce songs and fingerplays about gardening. Children respond readily to creative movement and dramatic experiences that revolve around the garden. For example, they grow like trees, fly like birds, sway in the wind like tall flowers.

Social Studies

With the study of gardening, children also begin learning about their social world. They look beyond their own garden to other gardens in the community. They may visit related businesses, such as greenhouses, nurseries, florists, and produce markets. They begin to understand the economic web of a community, and they make connections with community members.

Perhaps the most important contribution of gardening to the curriculum is that it offers an opportunity to encourage dispositions in children that create sensitive, caring, lifelong learners. Curiosity, initiative, and responsibility are rewarded in the garden. Because children are eager to explore, they are rewarded with discoveries. Because they choose to work, the work is enjoyable, and they continue to choose it. Because their continued efforts pay off, they learn the value of accountability. Children become resourceful as they explore ways to accomplish tasks or solve problems. They learn that persistence pays off as they try new solutions and eventually experience success. As they learn more about the creatures in the garden, they develop sensitivity and respect for others.

Using the Project Approach with Gardening

When we were working together at the Child Development Laboratories, we used the project approach in designing our curriculum. This teaching style is a form of emergent curriculum and, like that of the Reggio Emilia schools in Italy, enables teachers to immerse children in a topic of interest over an extended period of time while integrating various disciplines, such as science, language arts, social studies, math, and the fine arts. During a project, children actively engage in learning and in sharing their new knowledge with others. This approach creates a community of learners in which every member's contribution is valued. Those contributions may come in the form of questions, observations, background experience, or representation of thoughts and ideas. Katz defines the project approach:

> A project is an in-depth investigation of a topic worth learning more about. The investigation is usually undertaken by a small group of children within a class, sometimes by a whole class, and occasionally by an individual child. The key feature of a project is that it is a research effort deliberately focused on finding answers to questions about a topic posed either by the children, the teacher, or the teacher working with the children. The goal of a project is to learn more about the topic rather than to seek right answers to questions posed by the teacher. (1994, 2)

A project differs from a theme or a unit in that it is child driven. The teacher begins with what the children already know, focuses on the interests of the children through conversation and observation, and helps children identify and find answers to their questions through their own investigations.

Gardens lend themselves well to the project approach because of their complexity and the variety of different ways in which children can become involved. Through gardening, children have the opportunity to discover the immediate and useful connections between science, math, literacy, and social studies. The learning gained through this type of project will continue to be meaningful and relevant in their everyday lives. In addition, among the variety of tasks involved in creating and maintaining a garden is something to capture the interest of every child in the group.

If you are interested in using the project approach in your classroom, we recommend two books. *The Project Approach: Making Curriculum Come Alive* by Sylvia Chard gives a quick overview of the project approach. *Young Investigators: The Project Approach in the Early Years* by Judy Harris Helm and Lilian Katz is more detailed and includes a project planning journal that you can use as you work your way through the process.

Being in the Garden with Children

We caution teachers to preserve a sense of wonder as children investigate the garden. Adults easily go into "teacher" mode; in other words, they begin to

quiz children about their knowledge and to point out scientific facts about the plants and creatures in the garden. These are not good educational techniques, and they fail to build in children the dispositions that will make them lifelong learners and stewards of the environment. We believe that adults should join children in exploring and investigating the ever-changing garden ecosystem and become colearners as they work with children in the garden. Teachers will find that this awakens their own sense of wonder and leads to more meaningful experiences for the children. When this happens, children become inquisitive and observant. They learn to ask questions and seek answers.

Often adults should simply be silent. The garden is a place for noticing, appreciating, and reflecting. Teachers will serve children well if they take the time to observe them carefully before intervening. When a child is caught up in a moment—observing a butterfly or intently watching ants working—a teacher's interruption can spoil the moment and the learning. Children, like adults, need time to think and process. Adult input during these times can be intrusive rather than helpful.

When adults do talk, they should have honest conversations with children. This is most likely to happen if you spend real time with children. If you are working together in time, rather than pushing a preplanned agenda or thinking ahead about what you want to teach or say to the children, you will be open to learning and sharing in new ways. You can also strengthen and retain children's natural dispositions to seek knowledge and understanding by talking about your own discoveries with the children. One good way to do this is to start sentences with the stem "I notice." For example, you can say, "I notice that this leaf has some holes in it," or "I notice that something is growing here where the orange flower used to be." Children will pick up on this cue, and they will begin to observe more closely and share what they notice as they explore.

Facilitating Peer Interactions in the Garden

Adults should encourage peer-to-peer interactions. Katz (1984) describes four principles for facilitating communicative competence in young children. Children must interact, and they must have content about which to interact in order to develop competence in communication skills. In addition, the content must be meaningful to the participants and related to their own interests. Katz points out that the greatest communicative competence, as well as interpersonal competence, is developed when turn taking in conversation occurs, with one child's response dependent on what the other child said previously. When teachers can facilitate these types of interactions, they are providing opportunities for children to develop strong communication skills.

Gardening is rich in these opportunities. The garden provides vast content for young children and endless opportunities for children to interact. The

content is rich and familiar to the children, relating to their interests through the food they eat, the creatures they discover, the scents and sights of the plants that grow, the changes that occur daily, and the closeness they develop to the earth as they tend and water the soil. Teachers can facilitate reciprocal conversations by encouraging the children to talk to each other as they work in and explore the garden. Prompts such as "Tell Alex what you discovered under the leaf" can be the beginning of a conversation. This can be especially helpful if you know a particular child is interested in some aspect of the garden. For instance, if Amber is fascinated by snails and Jeffery finds a snail, suggesting that Jeffery tell Amber about the snail may begin a conversation between the two children.

You can also facilitate communication by pairing children to work together in the garden, encouraging them to jointly record their work or discoveries in a journal or for display. Another method is to document changes in the garden by having one child interview another while being recorded either with an audio or video device. The wide availability of video recorders makes it easy to record such an interview and transfer it to a computer for playback.

Asking Questions

Questions have the ability to provoke thought, to challenge perceptions, to invite reflection, to spur action. Questions are important if children are to reach beyond the obvious in their explorations and make new discoveries. A disposition to question is essential to a lifelong learner and one attribute common among people who rise to greatness. Teachers need to model questioning in order to build this disposition in children. They also need to ask questions to encourage children to think and evaluate, to look beyond the obvious, and to stretch their minds.

One way that teachers can model a questioning disposition is to use the sentence stem "I wonder" while investigating with children. When you say, "I wonder," you demonstrate the art of questioning as an approach to learning. "I wonder" statements also can act as open-ended questions, allowing children the freedom to suggest possible answers or solutions. Some examples are, "I wonder how those holes got in the leaves," and "I wonder what that is that is growing where the flower used to be."

Teachers need to be mindful when asking questions. Some questions have the capacity to stop children in their tracks, to impede learning, to discourage. Think of a social situation where you are uncomfortable and trying to involve someone in conversation. If you ask a simple yes-or-no question, it will probably receive a quick answer. The same may be true if you ask a question with only one correct answer. Unless you are dealing with someone who enjoys talking or you hit upon a subject the other person is interested in, you may find that such questions actually stop conversation. Watch a talented interviewer on television. She carefully constructs questions that will cause the person being interviewed to share, reflect, and expand on thoughts. Likewise, good teachers give ample thought before posing questions to children.

First, consider whether a question is convergent or divergent. Convergent questions, sometimes referred to as "closed" questions, have a single, correct answer. Some adults feel most comfortable asking closed questions and will ask a number of them in quick succession: "What color is that flower?" "Is it big or little?" "How many petals does it have?" Children often feel uncomfortable being quizzed for the "right" answer, and they gain little through this process. Think about why you are asking closed questions. In most cases, you already know the answer, and you know what you want the child's response to be. Sometimes teachers think that they should ask questions to find out what children know, but teachers can make most of these discoveries through casual conversation or more meaningful interactions. Katz (2009, 4) calls these "interrogatory" questions and states that when a teacher does need to ask such a question, for instance, to find out if the child knows her home phone number and address, "It is a good idea to start by saying something like, 'I want to know if you know your address. Can you tell it to me?' When phrased in this way, the question is genuine, and its purpose is clear to the child. So perhaps we could call this kind of phrasing a 'checking question' rather than an interrogatory question."

Sometimes a convergent question can help start a conversation, for example, by helping children recall prior events: "What was the first thing

that happened to the seed after we put it in the soil?" You should not stop after asking such a convergent question but continue to encourage the child to extract meaning from the experience and seek out new experiences that expand on learning. If the child is to be challenged to learn and to think creatively, the teacher must follow convergent questions with divergent questions.

Divergent questions, often called open-ended questions, can have many answers. They encourage children to consider what has happened, explore further, examine relationships, and discover answers for themselves: "Why do you think there are holes in the leaf?" or "How could we stop the aphids from eating our plants?"

In *Science with Young Children*, Bess Gene Holt examines and evaluates eight types of questions teachers ask. Holt concludes, "Questions are best and most successfully used to start discussion if the teacher does not already know the answer, if there is no generally correct answer, or if the question asks for the opinions and experiences of each person as her own authority" (1989, 75). She suggests that if teachers want to test children to find out if they know something, they be honest and tell the child this before proceeding with the question, and that if they have information they want to share with the child, they simply tell them. By following these guidelines, teachers develop honest relationships with children that will serve them well as they become partners in investigating and learning.

Types of Questions Teachers Ask

Types of Questions	Who Knows the Answer	Advantages	Disadvantages
One correct answer	Almost everyone	Few advantages	Risks insulting the children. ("Does the teacher think I'm stupid?")
One correct answer	Teacher knows, is virtually certain children do not	Few advantages	Not very sensible. Why would someone who knows the answer ask those who do not? Discourages reverence for questioning attitude.
One correct answer	Children know, teacher does not	Legitimate request for information; recognizes that children have information teacher needs	May be used as a means of enforcing limits. ("Who left their coat on the floor?)
One correct answer	Teacher knows, some children know and some do not	Good for beginning discussion or responding to child's response with another question	May lead to teacher dominating conversation rather than encouraging children to talk to one another
Any question	No one present knows, but the teacher thinks he does	No advantage	May expose children to inaccurate or misleading information
No correct answer	No one knows, and people know this	Communicates respect for unknowns	Can lead to misinformation if teacher is unwilling to admit she doesn't know
Probably has a correct answer	No one present	Can lead in a search for correct answers through research or experimentation	None
Many correct answers	Each person has own answer	Great for starting discussions	None

Joan Packer Isenberg and Mary Renck Jalongo (2001, 332) recommend including thinking words in questions. For instance, instead of asking, "What do you think will happen when . . . ?" the teacher would ask, "What do you *predict* will happen when . . . ?" Instead of asking, "How do you know that is true?" ask, "What *evidence* do you have to support . . . ?" This technique gives children a beginning understanding of the scientific process and shows that you take their investigations seriously.

Katz suggests that questions posed by children be offered to the whole group by writing the question down and giving all the children an opportunity to provide answers. She also advises that teachers follow up reasonable answers with the question, "What makes you think so?" Katz explains, "In this way, the teacher supports the disposition to examine the basis for one's views and opinions" (2009, 5).

Jean Harlan and Mary Rivkin (2012, 34–35) describe seven types of divergent questions. The following chart shows examples of how these can be adapted to gardening.

Seven Types of Divergent Questions

Purpose of Question	Examples
Instigating discovery	What kind of environment do earthworms prefer? How do the leaves of different flowers look different? Why are there holes in the leaves of our beans? Why is the tomato lying on the ground with a bite out of it?
Eliciting predictions	What do you predict will happen if we don't water this plant? What do you predict will happen if we plant the sunflower in the shade?
Probing for understanding	Why do you think this marigold is taller than that marigold? Why do you think that plant died?
Promoting reasoning	Why do you think the worms crawled under the damp paper towel? What evidence do you have to support that? What conclusions can you draw from that?
Serving as a catalyst	What could we do to keep the birds from eating the berries? What could we do to keep the soil from drying out so quickly?
Encouraging creative thinking and reflection	What would happen if the stores quit selling vegetables? What would happen if plants never stopped growing?
Reflecting on feelings	What was it like sitting alone inside the sunflower house? How did you feel when you found the big pumpkin in the garden? What was the best part of watching the ants working in the garden?

Engaging Children in the Scientific Process

The garden is its own world, an ecosystem where plants and animal life coexist, reproducing and interacting together. The rich life that exists in the garden makes it ideal for scientific study. The National Science Education Standards (NSES) stress the importance of teaching scientific inquiry, the process scientists follow in asking questions and investigating phenomena (National Research Council 1996). The NSES list five abilities necessary for scientific inquiry. As you work with children, be intentional in your interactions in order to foster these skills. Also, remember to connect science to other subject areas. You will find that during scientific inquiry, connections often occur naturally in the areas of literacy, math, social studies, technology, and the arts. Other times you will need to adapt the experience to assure that additional connections are made. Following are the five abilities for scientific inquiry (National Research Council 1996, 122) as well as suggestions for assisting children in each.

1   Ask a question about objects, organisms, and events in the environment.
   * Model observation skills by showing curiosity about the garden and focusing on details. For example, point out the tiny insects on a leaf or a new shoot growing on a plant. Use all your senses as you observe, looking closely, smelling, touching, listening, and tasting when appropriate.
   * Describe what you see using a rich vocabulary. Use the complete name of the plant. For example, let the children know that the beans are scarlet runner beans or that the sunflowers are mammoth Russian sunflowers. Use scientific terms like *predict, observe,* and *estimate.*
   * Observe the children carefully and listen for questions that they are asking and make note of them. For instance, if a child is counting ants, you can say, "You are wondering how many ants are coming out of that anthill." You can expand on this by helping the child write down the question and document his findings.
   * When children ask questions, encourage them to share the questions with the group. You can do this by posting the question in a specified place in the garden, in a garden journal or floorbook that all the children write in, or on the board during a large-group activity. Children learn that questions are powerful when they see that they are important enough for others to consider.
   * Have a question posted each day in the garden in a specified spot, such as on an erasable question board. In the beginning, the teacher can generate these questions. Children should be encouraged to think about the question as they visit the garden. An example is, "Notice that one of the tomatoes is on the ground near the marigolds. How do

you think it got there?" After children have seen the teacher's models, they can begin to investigate the garden and come up with their own questions for the question board.

2 Plan and conduct a simple investigation.

- The simplest investigations are based on regular, planned observation. Encourage children to observe to discover what is happening in the garden. If a tomato shows up away from the tomato vine and part of the tomato is missing, the children can watch the garden regularly to see what could be disturbing the tomatoes. If some of the plants seem taller than others, the children can check regularly to see how often those plants are in the sun. Children can put out a rain gauge to determine how much water their plants are getting.

- Provide ample time for children to explore. Children need time to become deeply involved in their investigations and to make discoveries. When teachers rush children from one activity or routine to another, they disallow children the opportunity to engage in the intense engagement that is necessary for higher-order learning skills to develop.

- Provide children with real experiences with real things. Often adults want to give children a sanitized experience. Instead of letting them explore real worms, the teacher puts plastic worms in the sensory table. The teacher gives children a simple drawing or a cartoon picture of a flower to look at or use for an art project instead of bringing in real flowers. Children explore plastic fruits and vegetables in the dramatic play area instead of touching, cutting, and tasting the real item—a much different experience. When children explore the real thing with all their senses, they can manipulate the object to learn about

its properties, observe how it reacts to change, compare and classify objects, and connect these observations to what they already know.

- Encourage children to predict the outcome of the investigation. Prediction is an important skill in scientific inquiry that involves gathering all the available knowledge, thinking about it, and drawing a conclusion about what is likely to happen. When you work with children, use the word *predict* instead of the word *guess*.

3   Employ simple equipment and tools to gather data and extend the senses.

- Provide children with simple tools that will expand their learning beyond what their senses can tell them. Keep some of these tools outdoors in a shed or storage area where they will be readily available.

- Provide tools to magnify, such as simple magnifying glasses. If you can, provide a microscope. This will give children an opportunity to see some of the smallest creatures that inhabit the garden and fine details of plants and animal life.

- Provide small, safe digging tools for everyday use. Trowels and cultivator forks allow children to dig and discover plant and animal life living under the surface of the garden. It is wise to provide some space in the garden for the purpose of free exploration since children can learn a lot from digging and exploring.

- Include tools for measurement. Children will benefit from rulers, yardsticks, tape measures, string, beam balances and weight scales, rain gauges, and thermometers. These tools will allow them to measure distances, keep track of the growth of plants, measure and compare the size and weight of produce, and keep track of weather conditions.

- Whenever possible, have a camera or a tablet available for children to use. Digital cameras have become inexpensive, and children do not need an expensive camera to record their work. Children feel empowered when they are able to record their own observations. If

you have access to a tablet, children will also be able to do research from the garden and can do on-the-spot journaling including photos, observations, and new knowledge.

4　Use data to construct a reasonable explanation.

- As children collect data, we want them to think about the data and use the data to construct an explanation. For this process, scientists use evidence they have found through their observations and the scientific knowledge base. Keep in mind the following:
- Help the child focus on the evidence. If Arthur says, "I think the tomatoes are falling off the tomato plant because the wind blew them off," you could ask, "Have you noticed that it has been very windy lately?" This focuses the child on the evidence.
- As children practice using data to formulate explanations, help them judge the strength of the data. Ways to do this include checking with other children and/or adults to find out about their experiences and observations. For instance, Jeremy thinks the squirrels are pulling the tomatoes off the plant and eating them. He could do a survey of the other children and teachers to see if anyone has seen the squirrels near the tomato plants. This is also a good time to use resources such as reference books or the Internet to check the child's explanation against scientific knowledge. A quick web search of "Do squirrels eat tomatoes?" will answer the question.
- Avoid outright denying a child's explanation even if you know it is wrong. You could say, "Oh, Arthur, the wind didn't blow those tomatoes off the plant. It wasn't even windy last night. Don't you see they have been eaten?" This may correct Arthur's thinking, but you would also stifle his curiosity. Letting a child go for a while with an incorrect assumption is better than dampening his willingness to think through situations and consider different possible explanations. Instead, encourage further investigation.

5　Communicate investigations and explanations.

- Children and teachers will talk as they work, explore, and discover in the garden. An important part of scientific inquiry is sharing what is learned with others. This sometimes occurs through simple conversation at the time it is happening. However, much is happening in the garden that children will want to communicate to others.

Scientists publish their work, and children can publish their findings through a variety of methods. This can be as simple as posting a question and answer on the wall, or it may involve a long-term study as children photograph, draw, and describe the stages of growth of a plant over its life cycle on a mural or in a journal. Throughout this chapter we discuss a number of ways

The Garden Project: Terrariums

As part of our garden project, we have been studying habitats. We discovered that different types of life prefer different environments to suit their specific needs. We created mini habitats called Terrariums with Indiana native species. When we were about done planting, Journey suggested something wonderful, *"Why don't we put some of our worms in our terrarium? They would love it!"*

Two months later, the terrariums are healthy and thriving. We believe this is in much part to the worms' continual contribution to the health of the soil.

children can share their learning, including journaling, thinking and talking floorbooks, graphing, and documentation boards.

Fieldwork

Taking a trip to a special location for the purpose of research enhances any study as children seek answers to questions for which they feel ownership. We refer to these trips as fieldwork, rather than field trips, because the role of the child resembles that of a scientist more than that of a "tourist" on a traditional field trip. The best way to select a site for fieldwork is to get to know your community. Check local listings or online for businesses or locations where you can explore concepts or find answers. Ask parents and coworkers about personal contacts they have related to your topic. Possible fieldwork sites related to gardening include the following:

- the garden tool and supply section of a local discount store
- a local nursery
- local parks with community gardens
- a flower shop
- the home of an avid gardener

One of our favorite fieldwork trips related to gardening was arranged by a preschool parent and took place at a local greenhouse. The children first planted seeds in flats at school. The parent then transported the seeds to the greenhouse for early care and sprouting. A few weeks later, we arranged for the children to visit their seedlings and learn more about the greenhouse. The children observed, touched, sniffed, and sketched the plants. They also learned firsthand about the overhead sprinklers! Eventually, the seedlings were brought back to school and planted in our garden. This led to meaningful hands-on gardening and continued personal investment on the part of the children. During our project, smaller walking trips were also taken to various nearby flower beds and landscaped areas on the university campus, including a Japanese garden.

Before the Trip

Meaningful learning doesn't just happen on a fieldwork trip. You need to set the stage for maximum learning opportunities. Poor planning on your part could actually lead to situations where children are prevented from noticing and recording the detailed information they will need later in the project. In this section, we describe how to set the stage by

- visiting the site in advance,
- keeping adult-child ratios low,
- preparing fieldwork backpacks, and
- creating research teams within your class.

VISITING THE SITE IN ADVANCE

You can increase learning opportunities by spending a short time visiting the site prior to the actual trip. This will also allow you and the site expert to feel confident and prepared. Remember to consider safety factors in the environment and communicate your research goals to the expert. You will probably need to be very specific with the site expert about the attention span of the age group you are serving. Expecting three-year-olds to listen to a twenty-minute lecture on fertilizer would be as inappropriate as only allowing five minutes for kindergarten students to draw the inner workings of a greenhouse. Yet those who do not serve young children on a daily basis may not have this knowledge and will need your professional opinion on such matters.

KEEPING ADULT-CHILD RATIOS LOW

Another fieldwork strategy involves limiting the number of children who attend at one time or increasing the number of adults, so that children can get a great deal of support while observing, asking questions, and recording data. Always invite family members to volunteer on fieldwork trips to provide the extra eyes, ears, and hands needed to keep everyone safe and focused. You could also consider hiring extra staff, such as substitutes, on these days to increase the number of adults on the trip. Or ask your supervisor or principal to attend the trip and support the class in doing research. When we were working together, we split our class in two, taking half in the morning and taking the other half in the afternoon. With preschoolers, this technique works beautifully to ensure that children who nap consistently do not miss fieldwork opportunities. This technique also gives parent volunteers an option to take off half of the day rather than miss an entire day of work. Your actual adult-child ratio on these trips will depend on your state laws and on safety factors specific to each fieldwork site.

PREPARING FIELDWORK BACKPACKS

For every trip, you should prepare several items to take along. We created a "fieldwork backpack" that was taken on every trip and restocked upon return to school. We used a traditional school backpack. The pack included a clipboard for each of four teams. To each clipboard we attached several sheets of blank white paper and a ziplock bag with colored markers or pencils. When selecting writing utensils, remember that children need to document what they see using a variety of colors. Therefore, a full set of fine-tipped markers or sharpened colored pencils is recommended for each team. When clipboards are well stocked in this manner, one set of documentation tools can be handed out quickly to each research team upon arrival at the fieldwork site. In addition, we included emergency items such as medical/contact information sheets for all children, a first aid kit, latex gloves, and antibacterial wipes. The pack is also a nice way to transport a camera or tablet.

CREATING RESEARCH TEAMS

When planning fieldwork, you can assign children to specific research teams that balance their developing skills. For example, each team needs one child who can draw, one who has emergent writing skills, and one who is confident enough to ask questions of the site expert. You could arrange for the youngest children, or children with the shortest attention spans, to have their own team. This way special activities can be planned for them while the other groups continue their research. Once, on a trip to a local nursery and garden store, we arranged a scavenger hunt for the three-year-olds while the older children sketched and printed the names of their favorite plants. The teacher visited the site ahead of time and made a list of objects for the three-year-olds to find, such as a red flower, a frog statue, and a wind sock. This activity helped time pass quickly for both children and adults, while allowing detailed research and data collection to continue.

Within your defined research teams, children will meet regularly prior to the trip to talk about what they may see, divide responsibilities, and brainstorm specific research questions on which to focus. One trick we find useful for preschoolers is to write or type each child's research questions on a computer address label, along with her name. On the day of the trip, stick these to the children's shirts or jackets so volunteers know the children's names and can remind them of their questions. This technique helps each team to focus on collecting specific data. Another idea is to type each team's list of questions and distribute these to the parents and volunteers who attend. You may even want to forward these lists to the site expert a day or two before the trip so she can be sure to highlight these issues during the visit.

During the Trip

During the fieldwork trip, challenge children to listen to the site expert and look closely at the environment while thinking about their specific research questions. Be sure to allow plenty of time for each group to ask questions, record answers, or draw sketches on their clipboards. Encourage parents to take dictation from children, adding it to drawings and labeling their sketches. Take plenty of photos, especially of the plants, equipment, and structures that the children attempt to draw. This will allow children to add details to drawings in the days ahead. Encourage family members and staff to take photos or videos during the trip. If only one video source is available, circulate among each research team, and videotape at least a portion of the events or objects most clearly related to their research questions.

If site experts use terminology that is beyond the understanding of your group, ask them to say it another way or explain it in more detail. If necessary, you can adapt the words of the site expert to a level your group can comprehend and record. Remember to help children compare what they hear or see on the trip to their previous knowledge. For example, you could say, "If these plants like to grow in shade, then they might like to grow at our school in the shade behind the shed or under the big oak tree." As you return to school, remind everyone to turn in or save all field notes (sketches, written data, samples) collected during the trip for follow-up study.

After the Trip

The day after the trip, meet with each research team to assist them in reviewing their field notes, watching video clips, drawing conclusions, and formulating new questions. At this time, you can also help the group decide on a way to represent and share with others what they learned on the field trip. There are many formats for representing what children have learned to others. Photos can be used in a homemade book or bulletin board. Answers to questions can be typed, printed, and distributed as handouts. When children refer to photos and video taken on the trip, their sketches can be refined, labeled

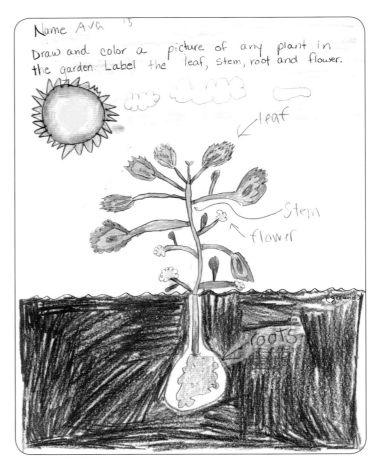

in detail, and mounted on cardboard for display. Sketches can also be scanned and viewed on a computer screen or projected through the use of an LCD projector or Smart Board for discussion with the entire class.

Another option is to use digital photos to create a computerized slide show to accompany an oral presentation. Since some children will freeze in front of the group and forget what they were going to say, it is best to tape their narration by meeting with the team privately in advance. We had great success with this strategy. Each photo was numbered, then shown to the children, and a question was posed about the photo, such as, "What do you remember about this photo?" or "What do you see in this photo?" Then we recorded the children's responses one at a time about each photo. Again, sometimes you will need to remind children of what they saw on the trip just prior to making this tape by reviewing with them your notes or their sketches. Class time for making these types of presentations should be arranged and scheduled so that parents, administrators, or other classes can be invited to attend.

In the process of helping children to represent their learning, some teachers find that children are missing key pieces of information. This sometimes sparks a return trip to the fieldwork site the following week. The entire group can visit the site if it is within walking distance of the school or if transportation is readily available. If this is not feasible, the teacher or a parent can return to the site to take additional video or photographs to use in rounding out children's observations, sketches, and research findings or for answering new questions that have developed.

Graphing with Children

Graphs can provide an effective way to collect and record data. They can also serve as useful tools in solving problems and making decisions related to gardening. A garden project offers many opportunities to involve children with graphing in meaningful ways. Because children at this age are concrete learners, the best way to help them understand graphing is to begin with real graphs. These graphs use actual objects, such as people or vegetables, to form the graph. The use of real graphs forms the foundation for other, more abstract graphing activities.

Opportunities to create real graphs can be planned. For example, a real graph using people could answer the question, "Which garden job would you like to do this week—watering or mulching?" To answer this question, you would post two pictures on the wall or floor, one of someone watering and one of someone mulching. Then the children would select the task they want to do by standing in one of the two lines. You can make this experience even less abstract by using real objects rather than pictures to identify the lines. For example you can say, "If you watered the garden this week, please line up behind this watering can." We call this sort of graphing "people graphing."

Once children are in their lines, you should help them count aloud the number of children in each line. Then you can ask a series of questions, such as

- How many children want to water the garden?
- How many want to mulch?
- Which line has the most children—watering or mulching?
- Which line has the fewest children?
- How many more (or fewer) children watered than mulched?

Initially, you will want to limit children to two choices, but once children have experience using people graphs, you can let them choose between three options, such as watering, mulching, or weeding.

After much practice with real graphs, the children should be shown how to record this information in the form of a picture graph. For the above example, you would give each child a small photocopied or computer-printed picture of someone either watering or mulching, depending on which line he is in. These pictures would then be taped to a graph that was prepared in advance. You would then ask the same series of questions as above.

Real graphs can also be completed using three-dimensional objects, such as fruits and vegetables. For example, you could say, "Today we picked cherry tomatoes and sugar snap peas. Are there more tomatoes or more sugar snap peas?" The children would then create a line of cherry tomatoes next to a line of sugar snap peas. With this type of activity, it is sometimes helpful to have a blank laminated graph with evenly spaced squares to make comparison easier. Then one sugar snap pea or one tomato would be placed in each square.

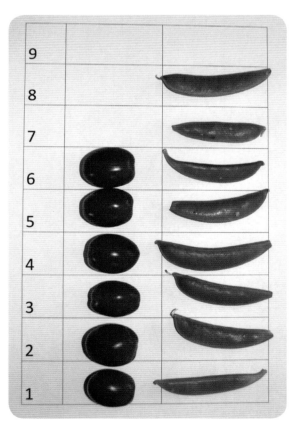

Ideas that are repeated many times in various ways have the most impact on children's learning. Real graphs should be used repeatedly, until children begin to spontaneously ask to create a graph to solve a problem. Some planned and spontaneous graphs we have created answer the following questions:

- Should we bake or mash the potatoes we harvested today?
- What do you want to buy for the garden with our can recycling money: a butterfly box, a birdhouse, or a hummingbird feeder?
- What do you want to cook for the garden party: basil-cream fettuccini or basil-tomato tarts?
- Which do you want to help with next week: filling bird feeders, cleaning and refilling the birdbath, or spraying soapy water on the plants for bugs?
- Did you like or dislike the sage brochette we cooked?

Symbolic graphs should be introduced only after children are confidently and consistently using people, real, and picture graphs. Symbolic graphs use symbols to stand for real things, such as Xs, colored squares, or stickers.

Using Reference Materials

A large part of your job as a teacher involves pointing children in the right direction when they have a question. To assist children in this endeavor, you need to have reference materials available so children can find the answers they seek. Some children will naturally think to check reference materials for added information, while others may need your prompting to seek out these resources. Consulting reference books, seed and garden supply catalogs, gardening magazines, and the Internet provides children with factual information and often leads to further scientific research.

When we had our garden at the laboratory school, our children noticed the hostas were badly eaten. They pointed out the problem to Sara, who helped them to observe and identify slugs as the guilty culprits. Together they consulted one of the many gardening books on the shelf to read about slugs and get ideas for what to do next. They decided to try a recipe for slug repellent that required yeast, water, and sugar. The children followed the recipe and attempted to save the hostas. They wrote about this experience in the garden journal and observed for the next several days to see if the repellent worked. This experience taught the preschoolers the value of nonfiction reference materials and an important lesson on the benefits of literacy.

Technology and the Garden Study

When we began our garden project together, technology as we now know it was in its infancy. We were still using cameras with film, and we couldn't imagine that Internet access for young children could ever be a good thing. Now we see wonderful uses of technology in classrooms across the country. We also see overuse and misuse of computers, tablets, and smartphones. We believe that teachers *can* use technology as they involve children in a garden study, but we advise that they approach cautiously. All early childhood teachers should be familiar with the joint position statement "Technology and Interactive Media as Tools in Early Childhood Programs Serving Children from Birth through Age 8," issued by the National Association for the Education of Young Children and the Fred Rogers Center for Early Learning and Children's Media at Saint Vincent College. In addition, we offer the following suggestions for using technology.

One of the most meaningful and memorable ways to capture the life cycle of any plant or garden is through the use of photography. In today's world, digital cameras, smartphones, tablets, laptop computers, and social media have made taking and sharing photos a national pastime. As a teacher, you can capitalize on this trend by giving children access to digital photography. Digital cameras have become more affordable and easier to operate. You can likely pick up an inexpensive camera or find a family who has an extra one they can donate. Allowing children to use a camera gives them a feeling of ownership. It helps them record the garden as they see it, and it allows them to document their own journey. By the age of three or four, children are fascinated with, and fairly skilled in, taking photographs.

Many schools and teachers have smartphones and tablets, which can also be used to take photos of gardening activities. However, some programs do not allow teachers to use their mobile phones to take photographs. Please check with your administration for permission before moving forward with the use of a personal smartphone or tablet. While there are advantages to using mobile phones, there are also potential liabilities if photos are texted or uploaded online without parental permission. If permitted and handled with caution, photos can be utilized to document learning and share information with parents and community partners through journals, storyboards, and social media. Kate DeRolf, at the Purdue University Calumet–Charlotte R. Riley Child Center, developed a Facebook page for her classroom. She posted photos of the children planting and harvesting items from the garden. This provides a home-school connection and gives parents a way to start conversations with their child at home about what they are learning at school. Teachers could also create a garden blog, where garden photos and stories are posted regularly.

In addition, photos can be used to create science activities and to document the scientific concepts the children are learning. For numerous ideas on how to get the most out of your digital photos, we recommend the book *Picture Science: Using Digital Photography to Teach Young Children* by Carla Neumann-Hinds

Overhead projectors are losing popularity among classroom teachers, and that can be to the advantage of the early childhood teacher. If you can find a discarded overhead projector, you have a treasure. Overhead projectors can

be used to project shadows on the wall. Children can manipulate objects—seeds, flowers, leaves, and other items—and see them oversized on the wall. If you place paper on the wall, the children can then trace the outlines of the objects. You can also print out photographs of the garden on overhead transparencies, and these can then be projected on the wall of various parts of the classroom. For instance, you could project the garden fences and colorful butterfly garden into the block area, inspiring the children to build the garden path and expand on other parts of the garden. Or you could project the sunflowers in the art area near the easels and include sunflower-colored paint to inspire the young artists.

Computers are often used in classrooms simply for children to play games that amount to electronic worksheets. We do not endorse the use of computers for this purpose. Nevertheless, we do find value in computers for other purposes. First, if a classroom has Internet availability, the computer is a wonderful resource tool. When we began gardening with preschoolers, if we had a question or wanted to know more about something, we were limited to the resource books available to us in our classroom. Now those who have Internet access have a wealth of information available. Teachers and children can work together to follow up on questions, find answers, and discover new questions.

Computers serve to connect people in new ways. Classes can join together with others to answer questions and participate in activities, such as the Monarch Watch program (www.monarchwatch.org), which engages children in tracking the migration of monarch butterflies. Teachers may look to find a partner school that has a garden so that students can communicate their experiences to one another. For primary-age children, this could be a good learning opportunity, especially if the partner school is from another region with a different culture, different crops, or different challenges.

Children can also use computers to record their experiences, as we discuss below in the section on documentation. Children can upload photographs they have taken, search for clip art that represents their experiences, or use photographs taken by teachers to tell either factual or make-believe stories. For children who cannot yet write or type, teachers can serve as scribes.

Tablets are popular and are becoming more available to schools. Protective cases are available so that the tablets are less likely to be broken when handled by children. If you are fortunate enough to have access to tablets, you will find that they have the advantages of computers with the added advantage of being mobile. You can actually take the tablet to the garden. You can photograph

the plant on the tablet, do your investigation right there, and also have children write their documentation on the tablet. Tablets, used wisely, offer value to the experience of investigation and documentation. Cassandra Mattoon, at the Illinois State University Thomas Metcalf Laboratory School, uses tablets in protective waterproof, drop-proof cases to document her garden project with children in preschool to eighth grade. She allowed the children to use them to take photos of the plants at various stages. One tablet-based activity she planned involved the children using an app called Educreations to put several photos of one plant in order according to the stages of the life cycle (that is, planting seeds, sprouting, growing taller, producing vegetables, harvest, and so on). They used this same app to allow children to record audio descriptions of the photos they took in the garden.

LCD projectors are available in some schools. Teachers can use projectors to share photos or scanned work of children with groups of children. Photos taken earlier in the day or the day before may be the focus of discussion at class meetings. This can give children a chance to share the work they are

doing or explain something new they have discovered, or it may be an opportunity for the teacher to explore further with children their interests and determine where next to take the curriculum.

Interactive whiteboards have also become available in many elementary school classrooms and are of benefit to visual learners. Laptop computers and tablets can be connected to these devices, allowing information collected outside to be quickly shared with the entire class. Interactive whiteboards can also prove useful when the larger group is establishing common knowledge, creating a topic web, or devising questions for inquiry. This information can quickly be added to or corrected during group discussion and then saved or printed for future use. Google Earth images of the school grounds can be projected and then drawn on as parents, staff, and students collectively plan the garden design. Kinesthetic learners will benefit from actually manipulating, moving, and editing ideas on the whiteboard. The class may conduct research by Skyping with a Master Gardener on a topic of inquiry or taking a virtual field trip via the Internet. Student teams can select a garden topic or question to research and then create an informative presentation for the whole group.

Documenting What Children Learn

As you explore gardening, document the journey the children take in their understanding. Documenting simply means to record, analyze, interpret, and display what children have learned. The children need to investigate their questions, find answers, and represent their learning over and over again to personalize and solidify learning. Children represent what they know about a subject through speaking, singing, writing, drawing, building, and acting out scenarios. Teachers need to find ways to record this process for use in further planning and conveying information about specific children to parents and administrators. There are so many approaches to documentation of young children's learning that we could not describe them all in this book. For more information on documentation methods in early childhood, we suggest the books *The Art of Awareness: How Observation Can Transform Your Teaching*, second edition, by Deb Curtis and Margie Carter and *Building Support for Your School: How to Use Children's Work to Show Learning* by Judy Harris Helm and Amanda Helm. Here we will discuss the two techniques we used most frequently during our years of gardening with children: journals and documentation boards. Remember that the talking and thinking floorbooks and fieldwork follow-up techniques described earlier in this chapter also fall into the category of documentation.

July 15, 1997
We made invitations to our Garden Party.
These are some of the drawings
we created.

A Bee   by Alex

A Flower   by Alex

On Monday, May 20. we noticed an ant hill
in our garden. We quickly noticed another, and
then another! We decided to count all the
ant hills we could find in the garden inside
the fence on our play ground. Sienna and Nyssa
Counted 21 ant hills in all. We decided to
Count again later in the week.

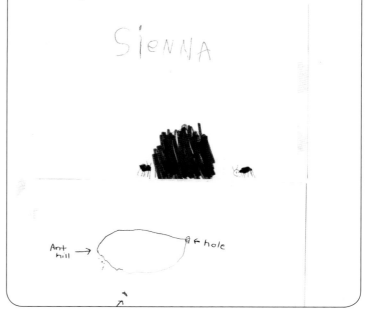

Sienna

Ant hill →   ← hole

June Gippt

I pulled out weeds.
weeds Drnkullof the
wat:

Nyssa

Journals

Keeping a garden journal over the life of a project has many benefits. Children learn to apply emergent literacy and numeracy skills and to record scientific data. They learn that their thoughts, feelings, observations, and experiments can be recorded in various forms and interpreted by others.

Journaling can occur in two formats, either as a group or individually. With preschoolers, we experienced a great deal of success using the group journal format. The first two years we bought a hardcover, spiral-bound sketchbook with blank pages. This allowed children the freedom to draw, create graphs, mount photos, and write stories. Our portable playground shed provided a safe, but accessible, storage place so children could record spontaneous observations, as well as teacher-planned activities. Using only one journal allowed us to compare the interests of the morning and afternoon groups, as well as observe the overall progress of the project. Unfortunately, it also meant that two children or two small groups could not use the book at one time. Therefore, our third year we changed to a page-by-page scrapbook format. A few pages were kept in the playground shed, while a few were kept within children's reach in the classroom. Finished pages were periodically reviewed and added to the journal. This system allowed several children and adults to record information and document garden-related activities simultaneously. Both of these group journal formats fostered a sense of community among the children.

Elementary students can keep individual garden journals if given the time and encouragement to do so. Many elementary teachers prefer to use preformatted photocopied journal pages, and they set aside class time to observe and document plant changes and other garden activities. Others will provide blank journal pages where children can creatively represent their garden explorations through photography, poems, artwork, and stories. If tablets are available, journals may be created through any of the numerous educational apps on the market today, such as iDiary for Kids, Educreations, Evernote, or Notebook. Many of these apps allow photos, electronic drawings, and even a child's recorded voice to be incorporated into the journal.

The teacher plays a critical role here, holding weekly small-group meetings about the journals, providing opportunities for children to explain journal entries to others, and adding challenges as necessary to build developing skills. Some children will eagerly write or draw each day, while others will need to be reminded. Some children need structured assignments, while others perform better with less structure. In *Bringing Reggio Emilia Home*, Louise Boyd Cadwell (1997) writes about a kindergarten class that planted bean seeds and kept bean journals. Each child was invited to draw, write, and record measurements of a specific bean plant as it grew. This project lasted sixty to seventy days, as children fine-tuned their observation, documentation, and representation skills. While some common elements will emerge in all journals, no two journals will be exactly the same.

A successful journal will provide detailed documentation, such as the following:

- dates
- descriptions of major scientific processes
- experiment predictions and outcomes
- key vocabulary words
- observations
- charts and graphs
- photographs at key stages
- poems and songs
- short stories
- favorite recipes
- children's dictation
- children's artwork

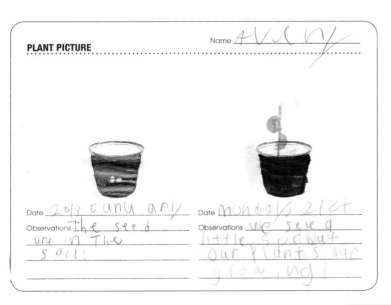

Whatever your combination of the above, journaling will help children remember what happened at various stages, understand the strategies used by people for remembering information, learn from past experiences, and plan for the future.

Documentation Boards

A good way for teachers to share what is happening in the classroom with parents and other visitors is through documentation boards. These exhibits include photographs of the children engaged in play or exploration, along with a written story of what happened. We also include a statement about how the activity relates to the children's learning and development. This statement provides an educational purpose in showing adults the value of play.

Documentation boards have many uses. You can post them in the entry area of your school so that the parents can see what the children in different classes are doing. Visitors and prospective parents will also be able to view them. Parents can stop with their children and read the boards together. Documentation boards can also be displayed outside the facility to show the community what your program is doing.

Documentation boards should be displayed in the classroom so that children can repeatedly refer to them, recalling an activity in which they previously engaged. Sometimes they will be compelled to add to what has been written. As children are exposed to documentation boards, they will probably want to make their own. Teachers can take photos for children to use and take dictation for children who are not yet able to write.

Children can become involved in making documentation boards. Children can use cameras to photograph their work. The teacher can help children become critical thinkers as they evaluate which pictures most clearly represent what they are trying to communicate. The children can use computers to paste these pictures in documents and to add words describing what is taking place. The finished product can be printed and added to a documentation board. Teachers may need to help younger children navigate the computer and may serve as scribes as the children dictate their words. Primary-age children may be able to do this documentation independently. This child-generated documentation is especially effective for documenting the progress of ongoing projects, for instance, studying the growth of a plant over time or studying the birds that visit the bird feeder.

Documentation of the knowledge, skills, and dispositions developed while gardening is important at all stages of the garden study. Careful planning will allow you to capture the children's basic awareness at the beginning of the project by saving lists of what children initially know and say about gardening. You will value this information as you compare it with the learning documented later in the life of the study.

Bringing the Garden Curriculum Indoors

As with any study topic, the garden experience will spill over into most areas of the classroom. By bringing objects from the garden and garden-related items into the classroom, you can enrich the children's play and deepen their understanding in a number of areas. Here we share with you just a few ideas. You are sure to come up with more of your own.

The Art Area

In the art area, items from the garden can be used both as inspiration for art and as the media. Because items from the garden are sometimes precious, in that their quantities are limited and only harvested once a year, we sometimes focus on temporary art rather than permanent art. This way the garden objects can be used many times. For temporary art, we provide a base on which the children can arrange the natural objects, such as seeds, flower petals, leaves, and pods. The base can be a square wooden board or a natural woven place mat. Thrift stores are good places to look for inexpensive items to be used for this purpose. For example, one teacher found inexpensive woven paper plate holders and cut black felt circles to fit them. The artist Andy Goldsworthy is well known for his work with natural materials. His book *Andy Goldsworthy: A Collaboration with Nature* is an excellent addition to any art area, as it is not only beautiful but can also stimulate conversation among children and teachers as teachers encourage children to create their own natural art.

To use your garden products for art, prepare them carefully so that children will use them with care. In fact, if the children take part in this process, they are more likely to have ownership and be invested in treating the materials kindly. Flowers can be kept in a vase until they begin to wilt. At that point, gently pull off the individual petals and lay them on paper to dry. Keep different colors separate. (You can speed up this process for some flowers by using the microwave, but it doesn't work well for all flowers, and different microwaves take different amounts of time. Do an online search to learn more.) The flowers will take a few days to dry, depending on the size of the petal and the humidity level. Once they are dry, we like to store each color in a separate clear jar so the children can see the colors through the glass. Baby food jars work well for this purpose.

Children can collect seeds and pods, and each of these should also be stored in its own container. Avoid mixing the different seeds or petals together. When the children are working, having the materials separated by color and by type allows the children to be very intentional in their work.

Sometimes you will have plenty of yield from your garden, and the children will be able to make permanent art with the flowers, leaves, gourds, and other items. They can use these items alone or combine them with other materials, such as sticks, bark, or tree branch slices (which we like to call "wood cookies") to make sculptures. Using glue bottles can be frustrating, so we like to put glue in cups or small jars and use small brushes. This frees the children up to concentrate more fully on their work. Note that "school glue" is not a heavy glue and is best for paper or light projects. Regular white glue is fine for most work, but for heavy items, such as wood and sticks, we recommend tacky glue, which has a strong hold. The children can use fresh petals and leaves in their collages and sculptures and also in poundings, as we describe later in the "Crushed Kaleidoscope" (pages 192–93) experience.

The flowers, fruit, and vegetables you collect from your garden will also provide inspiration for art, as will the creatures that inhabit the garden. Here are some things to keep in mind as you bring parts of your garden indoors:

- Set a vase of flowers by your easel. Then mix your paints to match the colors of the flowers, and use clear glass jars for the paint so the children can clearly see it. The children will be much more likely to pick up on your cue that the flowers are a subject for painting. It isn't hard to mix paint colors, but make sure you have plenty of white paint. (Some schools buy only the primary colors—red, blue, and yellow—and black and white, and mix everything else. This can really cut down on your paint storage space, and children love to mix paint.)

- Allow children more than one opportunity to represent an object. For instance, if you have brought in a snail from the garden for the children to study and draw, repeat the experience. As children revisit and redraw, they will notice details they overlooked, and their drawing will become more detailed.
- Use different media to represent the same subject. After children have drawn the snail, give them earth clay, and allow them to explore ways to represent the snail in three-dimensional form.
- Provide the colors of the objects in the media you are providing to the children. We explained above how to mix the paints. Also sort your crayons, markers, oil pastels, and colored pencils into containers by color. If you have set out orange and yellow squash for the children to draw, set out the orange and yellow colored pencils and markers.
- Let children choose what media to use. If you have a new branch of forsythia for the children to examine, you could give them the choice of representing it through drawing, by providing markers or colored pencils, with liquid watercolors, or through a tissue paper collage. By allowing the children to select from several types of media, you are giving them a voice to express themselves best through their own language.

Materials from the garden can be used in many different ways. Grasses can be woven together, as can long, thin leaves. Some materials, such as dried gourds, can be used for a variety of purposes, and children can paint them or decorate them in other ways. Children can make rubbings of leaves and petals if you provide them with thin paper and paperless crayons, charcoal, or pastels. Children can also make impressions in clay of roots, leaves, and other plant parts by rolling out the clay and pushing the plant into the flattened clay. The children may notice features of the natural materials in the clay more clearly than they do on the object itself.

If you have a view of your garden from your classroom window, you may want to place the art easel by the window to encourage the children to paint pictures of the garden. And if you have a printed garden design, you can scan and print a large copy of it and display it in your art area. Encourage the children to make their own garden designs by providing sheets of paper, rulers, and colored pencils.

Math Area

Items from the garden make great collectibles for the math area. Children can sort and classify various seeds, leaves, flowers, and other products. To encourage the use of materials in these activities, sort the materials into containers by type. We like to use baskets for larger items and small bowls for smaller items. We shop at thrift shops to find baskets and interesting bowls and containers at good prices. Some items, such as seeds, pods, and dried gourds can take up a permanent home in your math area. You may introduce other, more perishable items, such as flowers or fresh vegetables, for a shorter period of time. For example, flowers will wilt quickly, but pumpkins and gourds will stay fresh for several weeks. Once you have the items from your garden in your math area, highlight them by setting some out on the table in an attractive manner to draw the children's attention, and include the tools the children need to work with the materials. Here are some suggestions:

- For sorting and grouping items, provide bowls into which the children can sort the items. Condiment cups, which are a good size for sorting seeds and other smaller items, are inexpensive and available at discount stores.
- Provide tools for measuring the length of objects, including rulers, tape measures, and unconventional items, such as string, blocks, and so on.
- Provide scales for weighing items. Balance scales work best for younger children, as they explore which item is heavier and will spend a great deal of time testing the cause and effect of adding and taking away items from each side of the scale. As children move into the primary grades, they may be able to use a kitchen scale to weigh and record the weights of produce from the garden as a way of comparing size.
- Include bases for children to build on to encourage counting and patterning. These can be simple small square or rectangular boards or pieces of recycled material such as flooring or cabinet samples.

- Include materials for recording data. These should include pens, colored pencils, markers, plain paper, and graph paper.

For children to gain the best understanding of the materials in the math area, a teacher needs to facilitate the play. The teacher can give language to the connections the children are making and scaffold new learning in the math area. For instance, he can say, "I see you have made a row of two red flowers and two white flowers on your board. I wonder if you can make another row like that." or "I see you have a small leaf and a big leaf. I wonder if you can find one that is even bigger." As the teacher works with the children in the math area, he can pay particular attention to the individual children and engage them in a meaningful conversation about the materials.

Dramatic Play Area

In most classrooms, the dramatic play area is set up as a home living area throughout the year, and props are added to focus on topics of study. This works well with a garden study. Photographs or children's artwork of parts of the garden can be displayed in the dramatic play area. The children can cut fresh flowers and put them in a vase for the table. We like to cut different kinds of herbs for the children to explore as they are cooking and also find that they enjoy working with anything that is plentiful and can be moved in pots, such as seed pods or flower heads. Include gardening magazines and paper and pens with which children can write shopping lists.

As the children gain real-life experience with harvesting, cleaning, and preparing various foods in diverse ways, they carry these themes to the home living area. Adding new cooking tools, such as colanders for rinsing flowers and herbs, small cutting boards with safe knives, and vegetable scrub brushes, can facilitate this type of play by providing motivation and stimulation.

The dramatic play area can also go beyond the home living area to examine other topics the children may be exploring during their garden study. These make-believe experiences allow the children to explore some of the cultural, social, and economic reasons for gardening. For instance, after a field trip to a flower shop, you can provide children with a flower shop prop box for several consecutive days. Plastic vases, silk flowers, tissue paper, florist foam, small pots, receipt pads, play money, cash registers, telephones, and gift cards will allow students to reenact what they saw on the trip.

A greenhouse can be created in the dramatic play area by adding seed trays, small planting pots, seed packets, garden tools, silk or real plants, garden tools, gardening gloves, a watering can, markers and poster board to make signs, and a book with photos and descriptions of various plants.

The children will likely come up with their own play scenarios and will construct their own play objects when you don't provide them. They will print their own money, make telephones from blocks of wood, and create flowers in the art area. So long as you are alert to their cues and give the children some freedom, your children will be inspired to bring the garden into their make-believe world.

Library

Your library area can be stocked with children's literature about gardening, many high-quality reference books on the subject (see appendix 1, "Children's Books about Gardens and Garden Creatures"), and gardening magazines. In this area, you will also want to include samples of the children's writing about the garden. If research teams have created books to represent their learning on fieldwork trips, place them on the shelf for others to read. In addition, you can create handmade class books, such as a garden alphabet book (see "A-B-C You in the Garden" in chapter 7). Books that the children make on the computer or in the writing area can be kept in the library as well.

Also include a variety of puppets related to the garden, such as squirrel, chipmunk, butterfly, and rabbit puppets. You can often find finger puppets of some of the smaller creatures, such as caterpillars and praying mantises. Provide a flannel board with vegetables, flowers, garden tools, and animals. These materials will give the children the opportunity to explore through language and play their experiences in the garden. They will also allow you, as a teacher, to explore themes and tell stories to involve the children further in the garden experience.

Writing Center

The writing center provides children with opportunities to apply emergent literacy skills to the garden study. The garden journal, or blank pages of the journal, can be placed in this area to encourage children to record their daily gardening chores and discoveries and new questions that need answering. Provide a variety of materials to help the children record their experiences. For example, the following materials should be available:

- paper of different sizes and shapes
- colored pencils with colors of nature (available from Nature Explore at www.natureexplore.org)
- regular pencils and pens
- markers
- crayons
- some basic reference books with photos and names of plants and animals in the garden
- a children's photo dictionary
- garden catalogs

- alphabet stamps and pad
- envelopes
- stapler
- premade books
- glue
- scissors
- stencils related to the garden

Also, as part of the writing center, think about putting up a word wall with new words that the children are learning about the garden. These should be words that are important to the children. As they learn new words, the words can be posted on the wall so that they are available to the children in their work.

The teacher can encourage children to use the writing area by guiding them there after key experiences in the garden. For example, after cooking with produce from the garden, children can proceed to the writing center to recall and record the recipe on a poster using invented spelling or by dictating to the teacher about the cooking experience. The poster could then be displayed for parents and visitors to review. The teacher can also set out specific items each day, highlighting them, in order to draw the children's interest to the area.

Science Center

The science center can give the children the opportunity to study different aspects of the garden close-up. Here, you can start seeds, grow plants indoors, and keep a worm composting bin. In addition, you should have a table where children can explore objects related to the garden. Be careful not to overcrowd the science area, but to provide a few objects that you are highlighting along with the tools to study them. For instance, you can bring in a sunflower head, several plants with the roots attached, bulbs and tubers of different plants, or a few creatures that the children found in the garden. Provide tools such as magnifying glasses, balance scales, eyedroppers, tweezers, paper, and writing tools. Record the children's findings.

Locate your science center near a window, if at all possible. This will allow for better lighting for plants, and the children will be able to perform explorations that involve light in the center. Also, if you have a computer, locate it near your science center so that the children can use it as a resource as they ask questions and seek answers. Also include some garden-related reference books in the science area. If you don't have the budget for these, you can check them out from the library based on the topic you are studying at any given time.

Block Area

The block area can lead to many creative building projects if you supply the materials and the inspiration. Post large, interesting photographs on the wall of garden architecture, such as arbors, fences, and walkways. Include pictures that show a bird's-eye view of a garden. If you have a plan that has been drawn of your school garden, enlarge it and display it in your block area. Keep the displays simple and attractive.

Add materials to the block area that will inspire children to draw their own garden design and natural items to encourage innovative building. The following items are suggestions:

- large paper
- colored pencils
- clipboards with graph paper
- rulers
- tape measures
- T-square
- magazines that include garden designs
- smooth, oval rocks in a variety of sizes
- sticks, both thick and thin
- tree bark

- wood cookies (cross sections of a tree or limb)
- small carpet squares, especially in shades of green (available from discarded sample books)
- seashells
- dried, sturdy flower heads
- small, dried gourds
- large, dried pods

Keeping Your Interest Areas Interesting

Change the materials in your interest areas throughout the period of study. When the materials remain the same, they become like wallpaper, and the children fail to notice them. We also believe in highlighting certain materials each day. For instance, in the block area, we may set out the graph paper, the rulers, the colored pencils, and some garden designs, along with the rocks and carpet squares. When the children see these materials on display, they are more likely to be attracted to them and to begin using them in creative ways. Think about how you can set up each of your interest areas each day in an intentional manner to gather the children's attention and inspire their learning. An excellent resource for this is *Learning Together with Young Children: A Curriculum Framework for Reflective Teachers* by Deb Curtis and Margie Carter.

Chapter 3

Planning Your Garden

The plan of a garden should reflect the site and the people who will be using the garden. After you study your site and decide what you want your garden's function to be, the design will reveal itself. With a little creativity and imagination, your garden will be an authentic reflection of the objectives and personality of your school and curriculum.

The approach we suggest will ensure that your garden serves the needs of your program, is flexible, and is suitable for your site. The goal is to create a master plan that may be completed in stages if cost, labor, or time restricts a onetime installation. By installing the garden in stages, you will avoid being overwhelmed, and you will learn with each phase.

As you begin the process of planning and building your garden, you will find that much of the work needs to be done by adults. It's easy to leave the

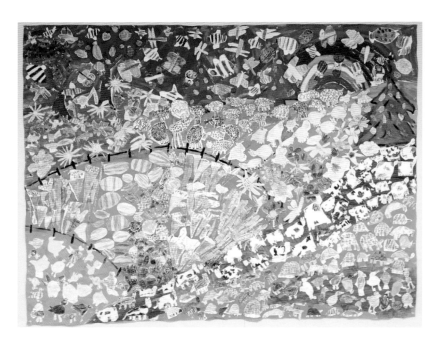

children out of this stage, but we encourage you to include them as much as you can. While you plan your garden, you can continue to explore gardens with the children through books, fieldwork trips, and indoor activities. We have included suggestions throughout this chapter to help you keep the children involved as the adults plan and perform the heavy labor of constructing the garden—they're in the boxes with the grasshopper on top.

There are two tasks to be done before making any other decisions for your garden plan: considering your program and selecting the site. These two components must be compatible for a garden to be successful. Otherwise, you risk building a haphazard garden with activities that do not fit the site, which creates a greater risk of failure.

This chapter discusses the following topics:

- approaches to planning your garden
- factors in selecting the garden site
- advantages and disadvantages of different types of gardens
- ideas for planning theme gardens

Consider Your Gardening Program

A first step in design is to have a clear understanding of your gardening program. Think about each of these questions:

- What do you hope to accomplish through your garden?
- Is your primary focus to help children learn about healthy foods, or do you want to develop an active ecosystem that attracts a variety of wildlife?
- Are you adding a garden as part of a larger outdoor learning environment?
- Is this a project that only one teacher is really interested in, or is it a school-wide project?
- If you are a family child care provider or are homeschooling your children, how will the garden impact your personal space?

Think about the types of learning you want to foster and the kinds of experiences and activities you want the garden to generate. These ideas may come from this book or from other programs you have read about or visited. You may also develop concepts through a brainstorming event with teachers, parents, and others who are invested in the program. Teachers can include input from the children. One successful brainstorming activity is to ask those who are participating to generate as many thoughts and ideas as possible about the future garden, writing each on a separate sheet of paper. After a designated time, categorize the ideas on a large board, then review and discuss common topics. This exercise not only generates ideas but also generates interest in the garden.

Another option is to conduct a survey to evaluate expectations and interest and to elicit appropriate questions to help direct planning. Later, review the outcomes of the brainstorming or survey; consider short-term goals, such as growing lettuce, and long-term goals, such as building a permanent compost bin with worms. While many ideas may not be feasible, this process will start you on the road to making good decisions by discussing and analyzing a variety of options. Take this opportunity to dream big, but avoid being impractical. During this phase, consider your curriculum, age group, time allowed for garden activities, seasons of your school, number of children, and other important factors.

Homeschools, family child care programs, and parent-child collective schools often have the luxury of being a little more flexible than public schools or larger centers. Parents can also have continuity in lessons and experiences over the years with their children/students. If your program is family centered, discover your backyard with your children by gardening, creating niches, and looking for hands-on opportunities.

Dayemi Parent-Child Collective, Carbondale, Illinois

The Dayemi Parent-Child Collective, in the rural town of Carbondale in southern Illinois, was founded by the Sufi religious community as an alternative to public

schools. Their parent-cooperative system is similar to homeschooling except they utilize physical schoolhouses. One schoolhouse serves early childhood students ranging from infancy through kindergarten, and a second one houses first grade through high school students. The Dayemi teaching philosophy includes connecting children of all ages to nature, fostering a work ethic, and being self-sufficient by producing food and other products. The Sufi community also owns a farm, which among other purposes is used as an outdoor classroom for the older students. During the growing season, the students spend Wednesdays working in organic gardens, raising chickens, attending to woodland trails, and learning woodworking and other skills. Students of all ages learn useful skills quickly and have become essential contributors to the functioning of the farm. When the younger children have field trips to the farm, the older children delight in sharing their accomplishments with them.

The school's early childhood playground and garden space, once an asphalt parking lot, had been previously renovated by parents and teachers for gardening,

play, and outdoor learning. While the original makeover was very successful, several years had passed, and the current parents and teachers wanted assistance to further adapt the space. Karen and three of her Southern Illinois University students in the Landscape Design class were requested to help redesign the playground and garden area. Sara joined them as they visited the site to meet with parents and children. One of the objectives in the redesign of the early childhood playground and garden space

was to inspire a love of farming and nature. Sara, the Landscape Design students, and the parents discussed how spaces could best be used and reconstructed, where necessary, to accommodate group objectives. Karen stayed inside with the younger children to assist them in planning their gardens. At the end of the visit, everyone shared his or her ideas. The Landscape Design students created a garden plan to guide parents and children as they made changes to the playground. The drawing called for simple plants in raised beds and the preservation of existing herbs, perennials, and a vine-covered arbor, which created a perfect niche for reading or resting.

Selecting the Garden Site

Another beginning step is to determine the location of the garden, if not yet defined, and evaluate it carefully. Where you decide to put your garden will depend on what space you have available. Some schools have lots of unused land, while others have almost no space at all. Don't despair if you have no obvious gardening area. A container garden can fit on a small patio or even on a rooftop. You can also consider a vertical garden on a fence or wall. If there is absolutely no outdoor space available, you can still garden inside.

Before making a decision about where to put the garden, you will need to evaluate several aspects of your space. These include accessibility, sun exposure, water access, soil quality, drainage, and existing structures and utilities. As you examine the available spaces, you will also want to think about what type of garden will work best for you.

Kid Tip

As you and the children study gardens in magazines and reference books or through an Internet image search, help the children identify the different features: Do the gardens have paths? Are there garden structures, such as trellises, for the plants to climb on? Does the garden include decorations, such as statues or sculptures? Are there birdbaths or other structures to attract animals? How are the plants arranged? Have the children record their findings through drawings or dictation. Post their work in the classroom. You can refer back to these ideas as the children discuss what features they want in their garden.

We suggest you read *Princess Chamomile's Garden* by Hiawyn Oram. Although a bit fanciful, this book describes how Princess Chamomile (a rabbit) designs a garden and how the garden is built over a period of time. Teachers can use the book to lead children into a discussion of what features they would like to have in their garden. In addition, bring in garden catalogs, and encourage the children to look at the pictures and study flowers and vegetables. Children can begin making suggestions about what they would like to plant. You may want to make a simple graph with photographs from the catalogs so children can vote on their favorite plants. Involve children in tasting vegetables and herbs to give them some ideas of what they can grow in their garden.

If you have decided on a garden theme, guide the children in exploring plants that will fit the theme. You can graph this as well with a two-column chart. For instance, if you've decided to plant a kitchen garden, one column can be titled "Plants We Can Eat" and the other, "Plants We Can't Eat." Children can cut photos from catalogs to paste in each column. If adults are involved in the garden design, post plans in the classroom for children and parents to review. Encourage the children to draw similar designs of how the garden should look. Post these in the classroom as well.

Accessibility

Accessibility is the factor that has the greatest impact on the benefits of gardening with your students. If you can't get to the garden easily, chances are it won't become an integral part of your classroom. We strongly recommend putting the garden on your playground, if space allows. In fact, a simple container garden on the playground is probably more effective than an elaborate garden a block away. The greatest benefit of the playground garden is that it allows a few of the teachers and other adults to work with some of the children in the garden even while others are occupied with other types of play. It also provides children the opportunity to interact with the garden alone or with a friend. Since the best gardening experiences happen with individual children or in small groups, the playground garden provides the best opportunities for intense learning.

If you can't put your garden directly on the playground, consider other spaces on the school lot. Again, these will be more accessible than gardens that are farther away. And you may be able to incorporate a landscaping feature to your advantage. For example, one of our local elementary schools used the inside of a circle drive for a garden area, enhancing their landscaping in the process. Finally, if there is no space on the grounds of the school, then look at other nearby areas. Do remember, though, that if you select a spot away from the school, you'll need to have a greater commitment to providing the children with opportunities to visit the garden, and you will also most likely need to work harder to follow through with your maintenance plan.

Sun Exposure

Most vegetables and flowering plants require at least six hours of direct sunlight every day. You will be able to grow a wider variety of plants if you can provide a sunny place for them. Watch sun patterns throughout the day. You may discover areas that are not in full sun all day but receive sun during the morning or afternoon.

If you don't have any space that provides direct sun, you will still be able to garden, but your options will be more limited. Some plants tolerate or actually prefer shade, and these plants can provide you with a cool, lush area for quiet contemplation, art activities, or journal writing. A shade garden makes such a nice refuge during the hot days of summer that you may want to consider planting one even if you also have a great sunny spot.

Kid Tip

Children can become investigators as you examine your area for sun exposure. One idea is to make a simple chart with two columns. Write "sun" at the top of one column and "no sun" at the top of the other. Now place an object in the area you are considering. Once every hour throughout the day, check the area with the children to see if the object is in the sun. (You can use a timer to remind you when it's time to check.) If the object is in the sun, the children place a check mark in the "sun" column. If it is not, then they check the "no sun" column. At the end of the day, add up the marks. If you have six marks in the "sun" column (six hours of sun), the area should be a good place for plants that require full sun. If you have just a few marks, the area will work better for plants that require partial shade. If you only have one or two marks, you should probably look for plants that do best in the shade.

Kid Tip

Children can study the natural rainfall a site receives by using a rain gauge and recording any accumulation of water after a rain. You can also test your sprinkler with a rain gauge. Place the gauge in the area covered by the sprinkler, turn on the water, and check every fifteen minutes. See how long it takes the rain gauge to collect an inch of water. This is the length of time you will need to leave it on to thoroughly water your garden.

Water Access

Your garden must have access to water. Unless you live in an area where consistent rainfall is guaranteed, you will need a water hydrant nearby with sufficient garden hoses, sprinklers, or drip hoses to provide water directly after planting and throughout the season. You will also want to set a schedule to be sure that plants are watered on a regular basis. A deep watering once or twice a week is better than frequent light applications, because it forces the roots to grow deeper in search of water. For this reason, if you let children water, with either a hose or watering cans, you will probably need to follow up with the sprinkler or drip hose to make sure the plants receive enough water. For most effective watering, drip hoses can be laid on the soil before the mulch is laid. This way the water goes directly to the soil and is less likely to evaporate. While watering once a week is usually sufficient in most areas once plants are established, you should talk with experienced gardeners in your area to find out what will work best for you. In very hot weather, small containers, such as pots, need to be watered daily.

Soil Quality

Unfortunately, the soil on many school playgrounds is not the best quality. Years of little feet pushing down on the earth compact the soil so little will grow there. Fortunately, the more you work with your soil, the richer it will become. An ideal soil includes sand, clay, silt, and organic matter in amounts to make it loose, friable (easily crumbled), and easy to work. Such good, loamy soil will provide essential nutrients, air, and water to your plants.

Soil is usually general to the region in which you live. For example, in some regions, the soil may be composed of heavy clay. Other regions may have very sandy soil. If you ask around, you can easily find out what kind of soil is common to your area.

Often you will find that the soil has changed due to development, erosion, or compaction. In any case, you'll want to evaluate the soil in the garden area to see if it is suitable for planting. The best way to do this is to pick up a handful. (If you can't do so, the soil needs work.) Squeeze the soil. If it becomes a tight, sticky mass, you probably have a lot of clay in your soil. If it won't hold a shape at all, you most likely have a lot of sand. The ideal soil will mold to your hand when squeezed, then fall apart when you let go. If your soil meets this description, you are one lucky gardener. Most of us have to work on our soil.

Soil with too much clay in it is hard to work. The small pores in the soil don't let in enough oxygen for the plants. Heavy clay can also cause drainage problems, as it tends to hold water. Sandy soil causes the opposite problem. Water and nutrients run through it so quickly that the plants don't have time to absorb them. Soil with the right proportions of clay, organic matter, and sand takes advantage of the good qualities of each component. The clay and organic matter hold the water and provide nutrients and strength to firmly root the plants, while the sand provides adequate drainage. Good garden soil is easy to work, even for the small hands of preschool children.

If you find that your soil needs help, you can easily improve it by adding topsoil, sand, or organic materials, such as peat moss and compost. For instance, if you have heavy clay soil, you can add sand to it to make it more workable and improve drainage. If your soil is sandy, you can add clay to improve the texture.

Humus improves any soil. Humus is a dark brown or black material in the soil that comes from organic matter—decaying plants or animals. It makes clay soil more friable, improves the water retention of sandy soil, and in the process makes all soil more fertile. Humus-producing organic materials include compost, peat moss, ground-up leaves, rotted sawdust, and straw. If you feel you need assistance in determining how to improve your soil, consult a Master Gardener or your local nursery for assistance. And if the idea of digging up

and reworking your soil seems totally overwhelming, you can avoid the whole ordeal by building raised beds or having a container garden. We'll discuss this in more detail later in this chapter.

Soil pH

When evaluating an area for a garden, you may also need to consider soil pH. Measuring the pH will tell you how acid or alkaline your soil is. Most plants prefer a pH in the neutral range of 6.0 to 7.5, although some plants, such as blueberries, azaleas, and potatoes, prefer a slightly acidic soil. If you have soil with a low pH (high acidity), you can make it more alkaline by adding lime. Or if your soil has a high pH (high alkaline), you can add an acidic-forming fertilizer or pine needles to reduce the pH and make it more acidic. You don't necessarily need to analyze your soil for pH before you start to garden, but if your garden doesn't seem to be growing well, it makes sense to check. Simple testing kits are available at most garden centers. For more advanced testing, you can contact your local extension service. If you need to adjust your soil's pH, we suggest that you consult with a local nursery to determine how much of a supplement you need to add to your specific site.

Drainage

Even with the best garden soil, you can have problems with drainage. The lay of the land or man-made structures can cause water to drain into an area and settle there for long periods of time. This can mean death for plants, which need moisture but cannot obtain oxygen when the roots are covered in water. Carefully check your garden area to be sure that the drainage is sufficient. Consider runoff from rooftops and placement of gutter downspouts. Watch the area over a period of time to see whether water collects there.

If you have an area that would be ideal except for drainage problems, you don't necessarily need to avoid it. Instead, consider building raised beds, which will provide sufficient drainage, or developing a wet area or rain garden with plants that tolerate "wet feet," such as swamp iris, spiderwort, marsh marigold, and royal fern. You can also put in a drainage system, but this may entail more work than you want to do.

Utilities

Be sure to find out whether there are any underground utilities in the desired garden site before you start to dig. You don't want to cut an underground cable or have your garden destroyed because workers have to dig it up to access underground utilities. Call the utility companies before you finalize your plans. They will come out and mark any utilities in the area. Remember, utility lines can be placed at surprisingly shallow levels. Also, be careful not to plant too close to an air-conditioning unit. The hot air from such an appliance will create an unhealthy environment for your plants and the loud noise will be distracting to the children.

Creating a Base Map

Once you have determined your garden site, it's helpful to draw a base map of the area. The base map doesn't need to be perfectly surveyed, but it does need to be detailed enough to aid in making choices about plants and other garden components as you plan. It's easiest to first sketch the layout of the area showing existing features, such as walks and trees. Get the children to help measure the area using a measuring wheel or tape measure and record the dimensions on the sketch. Then convert the dimensions to a scale (for example, 1 inch = 5 feet) and draw the site on grid paper or with a computer program or an architect or engineer scale to a larger sheet of paper. If you know a school family member or other supporter who is a landscape architect or an architect, this is a good time to solicit help. You can also search on the Internet for a satellite map of your site. It's easy to zoom close enough to determine the layout of the

area and existing features. Once you print the site, you may want to enlarge the base map to fit on 24-by-36-inch paper (or larger) if you have access to a printer that can use paper of this size. We suggest using the satellite map to provide the basic layout but not as a substitute for measuring. The exercise of measuring and recording to scale is a valuable experience for the children to observe and be involved in.

Types of Gardens

As you study your site, you should think about what type of garden would be most appropriate for your program. Lack of space for a garden becomes less of an issue because there are so many types of gardens to choose from:

- ground-level gardens
- raised-bed gardens
- container gardens
- green roof gardens
- vertical gardens

Within these five types are several alternatives, ranging from simple to elaborate. You may decide to implement only one type of garden, or you may choose to include several types. For example, you may decide to construct both a raised-bed and a ground-level garden on your preschool playground and a container garden in your toddler area.

Ground-Level Gardens

A ground-level, or in-ground, garden is what most people think of when they picture a garden. In fact, what people often envision is the traditional in-ground garden with vegetables in neatly spaced rows. A ground-level garden takes advantage of the space and soil available. It works well if you have good soil and good drainage. Most of the work goes into digging and enriching the soil. This type of garden may be the most economical because most of the cost is in soil amendments rather than building materials. Another option if space is limited yet the school ground has established landscaping is to incorporate your garden into open areas of the existing planting beds. This works well with annuals, herbs, and some vegetables.

While ground-level gardens have many advantages, the straight-row garden is probably not your best choice. When you plant in rows, you maximize the opportunities for weeds that eagerly pop up in the spaces between your plants. In addition, it's not a very efficient use of your space. We recommend an approach that spaces plants closer together while providing pathways for children to access the garden.

As you plan your in-ground garden, think about where you can put paths and what materials you will use for them. Materials such as bricks, stones, or concrete stepping-stones are durable, but if you are unable to obtain donations, they can be costly. Less expensive choices include wood mulch, straw, sawdust, gravel, or even wooden boards. However, be selective on the quality of the material. Lower-quality wood mulch, sawdust, or gravel may contain undesirable debris or weed seeds. Be aware as well that some woods will quickly rot when exposed to the weather. If possible, select a naturally durable wood, such as redwood, cedar, or Douglas fir. Treated wood is also durable, but you should confirm that the wood has not been treated with chromated copper arsenate (CCA) or creosote. CCA was commonly used before 2003 but is now banned by the Environmental Protection Agency for residential use because it contains arsenic. Creosote is harmful to plants and can cause uncomfortable skin reactions if touched. Contemporary wood treatments use copper borate or alkaline copper quaternary (ACQ) and are reported to be safe for garden usage. You may also use branches and logs along the path's edge. While these materials will have to be replaced from time to time, they work well to define the pathway and keep down weeds.

Because you're working with children, the planting areas need to be narrower than if you were planting for adults. This will ensure that children can reach all the plants. We recommend that the planting space between paths be limited to about eighteen inches if the space is accessible from only one side, or three feet if it is accessible from both sides. If you are planting some perennials at the back of the bed that will require minimum maintenance, you could increase the eighteen inches to two feet. Just remember that children will not be able to reach the perennials without venturing off the path.

The major advantage of a ground-level garden is that it's simple. It doesn't require you to build a frame or to cart in large masses of soil. You have most of what you need right there. The greatest disadvantage of such a garden is that, depending on your soil condition, it may be somewhat labor intensive the first year. However, properly preparing the bed is the key to producing a successful garden with healthy plants. It is well worth the time and effort you take to create good growing conditions for your plants.

Raised-Bed Gardens

A raised bed is a gardening area developed using construction materials, such as landscape timbers or treated wood (see above), to raise the height of the planting area. Raised beds have many advantages. They're easier to reach since you don't have to bend all the way down to the ground to plant and weed. They are also ideal if you want a garden that is fully accessible to people who

use wheelchairs or have other mobility impairments. (For more information on making your garden more accessible to people with disabilities, read *The Enabling Garden: Creating Barrier-Free Gardens* by Gene Rothert [1994].) Raised beds are also easier to maintain because they tend to keep weeds in check better than an in-ground garden. It's easier to control the composition of the soil because you are mixing the ingredients to create your planting medium. And it's easier to keep the children from accidentally trampling the plants because they are above foot level. In addition, the beds usually drain well because they are above the ground level. The disadvantage of the raised bed is that you will have to supply the materials to build the wall of the garden and the soil to fill the bed. This may also be somewhat labor intensive, depending on what you use to build the sides of your beds. Problems with rodents and other pests are typically less since the garden is raised. If your garden is in an area prone to moles or other burrowing animals, simply line the base of the bed with chicken wire or landscape fabric to help discourage their travels into your garden. Mounded bed gardens, or berms, are another type of raised-bed garden. They are like raised-bed gardens without the walls. They can be a good choice if you don't have access to materials for building walls or if you just want a more natural appearance. A berm may be especially pleasing if you have a flat, uninteresting space for your garden. Berms can be arranged in any shape, and the curves that are common to mounded beds make the garden visually enticing, while the height brings the flowers up to a level where they are more noticeable. Improved drainage is also an advantage of berms, although they may too easily shed water from the sides. A deep layer of mulch can help control this problem.

Container Gardens

A container for gardening purposes is any portable item that is used to plant in. This type of garden may be heavy, especially when filled with a soil mix. The main advantage of container gardening is that you can garden in areas that lack a soil base or in small areas, such as a patio or a courtyard. Another advantage is that container gardens are easy to maintain. You have complete control over the soil mixture, and weeds are few and far between. The height of containers makes them easy to work in and increases the visual effect, as they bring the plants closer to eye level. In addition, small- to medium-size containers can be moved to follow the sun or rearranged throughout the season as different plants come into their prime. If you have a long break, smaller containers can also travel home with children for care while the school is closed.

In chapter 1, we highlighted the container garden created at Saint Michael School in a shady courtyard area comprised of asphalt and surrounded by brick building on three sides. This space went from drab to delightful in a few months through the use of window boxes mounted on the redbrick school building, large and small rectangular planters, and a variety of small pots in all shapes and sizes. The school was also able to bring some of the plant

containers indoors, allowing several classrooms to "adopt a plant" and care for it over the winter.

Today's market offers a wide array of container styles and innovative types of containers. Smart Pots (www.smartpots.com) are reusable fabric containers available in several sizes to accommodate a wide range of vegetables and annuals. A nice feature of these pots is that they can be folded up and stored during the off-season without consuming too much space. Another type is self-watering containers. Although the price of these may be higher, the self-watering feature reduces worries over long weekends and may be worth the extra cost. (A good general reference book for planning, planting, and growing ornamental and edible plants in containers is *Crops in Pots: How to Plan, Plant, and Grow Vegetables, Fruits, and Herbs in Easy-Care Containers* by Bob Purnell [2007].)

Green Roof Gardens

The term *green roof* defines a system that supports plants grown on the roof of a building. Green roofs are installed primarily for effectively managing storm water, improving water quality, reducing building energy costs, mitigating the  urban heat island effect, increasing biodiversity, reducing noise, and other environmental benefits. Some cities mandate green roofs on new construction in an effort to reduce environmental problems while also improving the city "landscape." Being able to grow plants on an accessible roof creates new opportunities for urban schools where otherwise gardening space is limited, if available at all. Gardens are popping up on school roofs across the nation. The green roof should be designed and constructed by professionals. Teachers do little garden construction work. The medium for planting is not soil but rather a green roof mix consisting of a lightweight material and some organic material. The depth of the medium will depend on the green roof design. You should work with professionals, if possible, to learn about the depth and content of the medium, irrigation issues, and other limitations and opportunities. The sky is the limit, you might say, on the green roof. It's possible to grow wildflowers, annuals, herbs, fruits, vegetables, and, if the support is there, shrubs and trees.

🍃 Calhoun School—Green Roof Gardens

The Calhoun School on New York City's Upper West Side is a progressive school for children from three years old through twelfth grade. The school added a green roof during the construction of a new addition. The school is located in an area with no ground-level space for a garden, but the roof provides space for gardens and an open grass area. The grassy area provides space for somersaults and picnics and is particularly welcoming because few residents in Manhattan have lawns. The perimeter area of the grass is used by the Lower School classes and their food service chefs to plant herbs and vegetables, which they harvest. Classroom visits by the chefs and an after-school club help children make the connection between the garden and the plate as they learn about nutrition and cooking while sampling their harvests. Besides gardening activities, the teachers and children use the green roof to study plants and discover bugs (yes, even on the roof). The end of the gardening season culminates with a picnic on the roof to celebrate the garden's success with students, chefs, teachers, parents, and visitors. The Calhoun School green roof allows the children to connect with nature, experience growing herbs and vegetables, and develop their awareness of environmental challenges and responsibilities in an urban setting.

Vertical Gardens

A vertical garden, also called a living wall or a green wall, is a garden growing in a vertical position. Typically, the garden is either attached to a wall or fence, either interior or exterior, or is a free-standing tower. Don't confuse the term with vines growing on a wall. The gardens rely on a hydroponic system for water and nutrients as the plant roots are not in the soil but are planted in the wall material or tower. A vertical garden offers gardening opportunities on heavily paved playgrounds and sites with limited space. It's possible to build a do-it-yourself vertical garden from plastic soda bottles, gutters, or other recycled materials. If you're interested in this type, a web search reveals a wealth of instructions. Alternatively, commercial systems offer an array of sizes and styles. Woolly Pocket (www.woollypocket.com) is one company that offers kits for schools to easily install a vertical garden.

As you study your site, you may find that you have an obvious garden space available to you, an area that seems perfect for a garden. Or you may need to spend some time evaluating what is available and choosing the best of several poor alternatives. Under extreme circumstances, where you have absolutely no outdoor space available or where the outdoors is not safe for children, you may choose to plant an indoor garden. Your choice will depend on the location and the resources available to you. No matter what space you select, it is possible to plant a garden that will serve your needs, whether it is traditional with flowers and vegetables, secluded and shady, dug into the ground, built in raised beds, or confined to containers.

Prestwood Elementary School's Vertical Garden

Kristi Draluck's Kindergarten Garden Project at Prestwood School in Sonoma, California:

I started the garden in 2010. I couldn't stand looking at a dead, empty piece of land on campus just sitting there going to waste—empty when outside the fence there was so much life. I imagined a garden—green and beautiful and creatively created by students. I wanted to make that happen. To make something wonderful from nothing, to show my students what was possible if we worked together. And little by little it is growing into what I envisioned. My kindergarten classes planted everything in the garden. Students from past years still consider it theirs; they visit it and see it growing with them. It is a teaching garden where young minds grow! I wrote a grant for picnic tables so students could use them. I try to teach my students a different way of looking at the world and how things can be used, planted, conserved, and taken care of. I do a solar unit and teach about drought-resistant/native plants. We converted the old sandbox into a vegetable garden. Beans climb the playground bars. There is a strawberry pyramid, herb pyramid, and perennial and native drought-resistant plants fill the center of the garden. Succulents are planted in barrel staves planters. The Santa Rosa Iris Society donated irises.

Recently, we planted a rainbow garden in a Triolife Pyramid Planter. There are also two full 275-gallon rainwater collection tanks, which are made from donated recycled liquid food containers. We have two owl-nesting boxes, a bat nesting box, and a solar fountain! We have installed a vertical Woolly Pocket School Garden (which we had the surprise to find nesting juncos in last year) with a drip system as well as a gutter garden with a drip system on the fence! We plant, maintain, observe changes, harvest, bird watch, squirrel watch, have salad parties, sketch, paint, write, read, and enjoy. We have created a wonderful garden from an old, abandoned kindergarten playground at the other end of the school from the main garden! It's been certified as a People's Garden and a NWF Wildlife Habitat. I have funded the garden myself, and I have written and received grants from the Sonoma Valley Education Foundation, Annie's, PG&E, Ledson Winery and Vineyards, The John Jordan Foundation, and the PTO as well as personal donations.

Garden Themes

Almost every garden has a theme. There are vegetable gardens, flower gardens, rose gardens, Japanese gardens, and cactus gardens, to name a few. When you have discussed your garden plans, themes have likely come up in your conversations. As you select a theme, you should consider your goals and the interests of the children in your group. Some groups will be fascinated with cooking and tasting, which could lend itself to herb and vegetable gardens. Other classes will gravitate toward bright colors and new fragrances, which may lead you to develop some type of flower garden. Another group may be enthralled with the idea of winged visitors and other wildlife, convincing you to use plants that will attract birds, butterflies, or rabbits. You will also want to consider your own curriculum goals and objectives as you think about what theme or themes to focus on for your garden.

In this section, we describe six theme gardens in detail and include sample plans. We also include ideas for other theme gardens and lists of plant suggestions for some of these. The names of plants you find in this section are primarily common names. Since common names vary from region to region, we have listed plants by common name in the text and have referenced the common name to the Latin name of many of them in appendix 5. If you know the Latin name, you can be certain that you are finding the plant you want.

Bird and Butterfly Garden

Birds and butterflies are enchanting to children and adults, as well as educational, so attracting them to the garden greatly increases the opportunities for learning. You will probably want a sunny area for this garden since most flowers need at least six hours of sunlight to bloom well.

A bird and butterfly garden should contain a variety of annuals, perennials, and herbs, including clusters of colorful, nectar-producing plants in varieties that provide for successive blooms throughout the season. You should also include one or two bushes to provide the dense branching needed for birds' nests. Possible choices include lilacs and butterfly bushes, which also lend height to the garden. The butterfly bush has the added advantage of growing quite tall in a single season (up to eight feet in our area) and blooming throughout the late summer. And they don't call it a butterfly bush for nothing—it really does attract butterflies. Because the bushes are taller than the children, they also provide private spaces where children can spend time alone or with a friend while remaining within view of adults.

Many flowers and plants will attract butterflies. In our garden, we included bee balm, statice, alyssum, pinks, thyme, basil, sage, and blue salvia. Red salvia has the added attraction of inviting hummingbirds to the garden. A birdbath will help attract birds, especially in dry weather. Additional features you should consider for this type of garden are butterfly houses, butterfly feeders, hummingbird feeders, birdhouses, and bird feeders.

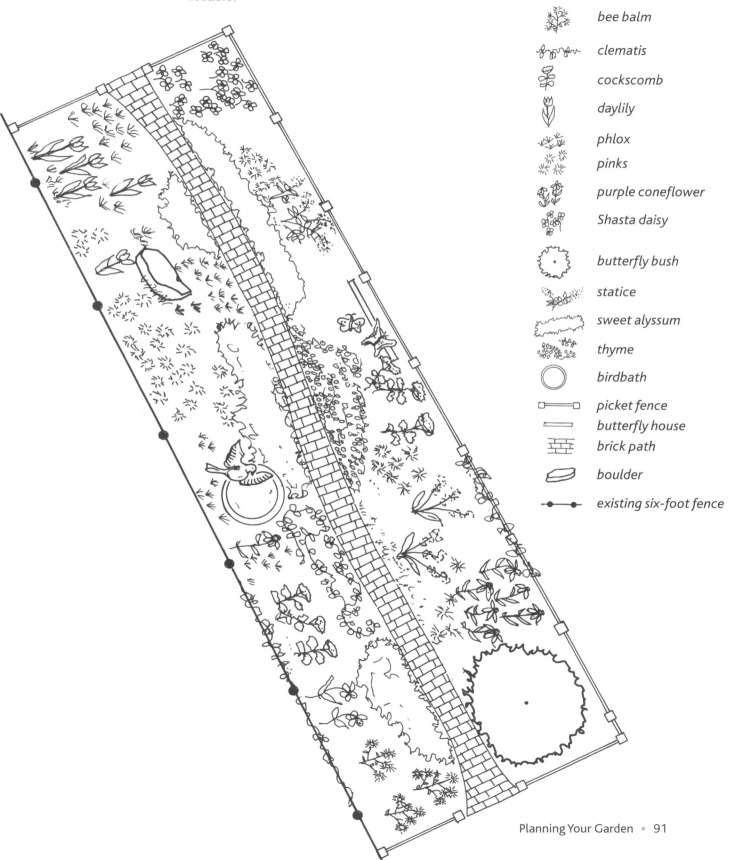

bee balm
clematis
cockscomb
daylily
phlox
pinks
purple coneflower
Shasta daisy
butterfly bush
statice
sweet alyssum
thyme
birdbath
picket fence
butterfly house
brick path
boulder
existing six-foot fence

North American Garden

A North American garden focuses on plants that are native to the North American continent and were grown in the Americas by native peoples before Europeans arrived in 1492. These plants include corn, pumpkins, popcorn, squash, beans, blanketflower, and many types of gourds. To make the most of the space, include some kind of trellis for the vines to climb. While your playground fence can serve this purpose, you may want to use a separate structure that can double for use in dramatic play.

The highlight of our North American garden was a trellis house, which consisted of a wood frame covered with latticework. Each summer the base of the trellis house was planted with climbing vines, which covered the house by the end of the summer. Our favorite plants for this use were gourds because they are so dramatic. They grow quickly and often creep inside the house to grow hanging from the ceiling, much to the delight of the children.

Since most of the plants in this garden are annuals, you can vary the garden design from year to year. Many of the plants take up a great deal of space. If your North American garden space is relatively small, you can use the same small patch to plant something new each year. When we had a North American garden, one year the area contained pumpkins, a favorite of the children, as the vines worked hard to take over the playground and would probably have succeeded if it were not for the intervention of little feet. Other years the same area yielded a patch of closely planted corn, a bean tepee, and a sunflower house.

butterfly weed

corn

gourds on trellis house

pumpkin

purple coneflower

squash

sunflower

stepping-stones

existing six-foot fence

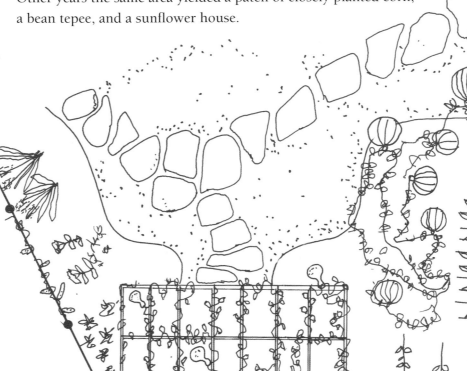

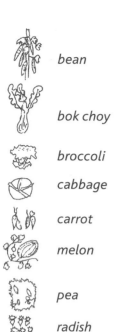

bean

bok choy

broccoli

cabbage

carrot

melon

pea

radish

spinach

strawberry

tomato

Many teachers will want to use their garden to teach how vegetables grow. Vegetable gardens are becoming more important as children need to learn where their food actually comes from. As children watch seeds grow into food, they often develop an interest in cooking and tasting new foods. A kitchen garden fulfills this purpose. To get maximum use out of this area, you can plant several times throughout the growing season. For instance, spring and fall plantings can include cool-weather plants such as lettuce, spinach, broccoli, cauliflower, and radishes. These plants not only can be planted early or late in the season but also develop rapidly from seed to edible vegetables, satisfying the shorter attention spans of some children.

Plants that can be grown during the hot summer, and that you will certainly want to include, are tomatoes, green bell and banana peppers, green beans, and cucumbers. Also try eggplant, potatoes, melons, carrots, and onions. We try to include some vegetables that have edible roots, some that have edible leaves, and some that have edible fruit to expose the children to a variety of plant parts as food. We also like to include produce that can be eaten fresh directly out of the garden as well as vegetables that need to be cooked.

If you have space, you may want to include a small patch of strawberries. These ripen early in the season, and the plump, sweet berries will delight most children. However, strawberries do tend to take over the garden, so you need to periodically pull up the vines to protect the rest of the garden.

Because some of these plants require significant space to grow, you won't be able to plant as closely as you can in some of the other gardens. This can result in more weeds. Heavily mulch this area to control the weeds, as well as to help the plants retain moisture. Materials that work well for this include wood chips, newspaper, and straw.

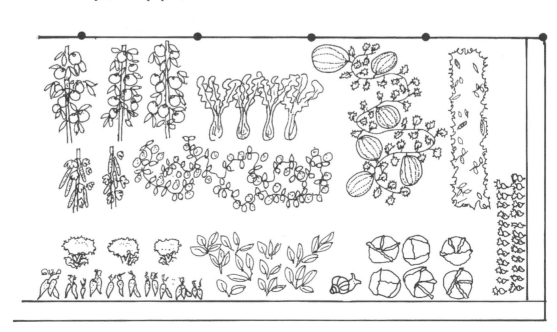

The Elgin Child and Family Resource Center of Elgin, Illinois, serves predominantly Hispanic families. This center houses thirteen bilingual classrooms with children ranging in age from six weeks to five years. In summer 2012, under the leadership of Amy Weimann Collins, one of our former graduate assistants from Southern Illinois University Carbondale, several of the classes decided to plant gardens on the playground. Considering their population, one class decided to plant a salsa garden, which included tomatoes, jalapeño peppers, green onions, and cilantro. Another class planted a vegetable garden, with onions, cherry tomatoes, peppers, zucchini, carrots, and green beans. Yet another class chose a pizza garden, which consisted of Roma tomatoes, onions, green peppers, and basil. The school-age children planted a sunflower garden. They planted several varieties of sunflowers, and as it turns out, weeds, too. They made some beautiful stepping-stones to place throughout this garden. Finally, they developed a sound garden, which consisted of several wind chimes that made lots of different sounds. The children did lots of activities with the gardens. They watered the plants and pulled weeds every day. One day they discovered a huge zucchini. They also found another zucchini with long "hairs." They picked the zucchinis and took them to their classroom, where they measured, weighed, and charted the differences between them. Then they made zucchini bread! They taste tested the vegetables and graphed how many students liked them and how many did not. They also studied the life cycle of the butterfly with live caterpillars in their classrooms, then released them outside.

Sensory Garden

A sensory garden offers many learning opportunities for young children. You may choose to divide a sensory garden into five gardens, each dedicated to one of the five senses: sight, sound, taste, touch, and smell. Or you may prefer to intermingle the plants, since many tend to speak to more than one sense, so that you have one large garden. In either case, a sensory garden can be large, but it doesn't need to be. In fact, this is one garden that works particularly well in containers, one container dedicated to each of the five senses. Half barrels make perfect containers for sensory gardens.

TASTE

The taste garden can contain many of the same plants as the kitchen garden but should focus on those that can be tasted as soon as they are picked. You'll want to include some herbs, since they have strong flavors. Mints are a favorite because they come in many different varieties, which suggest other foods, such as chocolate mint, lemon mint, and lime mint. However, if you plant mint, beware. It grows rampant and will intrude on your other plants if you do not control it. (See sidebar "Dealing with Invasive Plants," page 97)

Berries are also a good choice for this garden. You should find out what plants grow well in your area, but blueberries and blackberries are two possibilities. If you grow blackberries, be sure to get a thornless variety.

Also include some edible flowers. Our favorites are pansies, which grow well in the cooler weather of a southern Illinois spring and fall, and nasturtiums, which we plant during the hot summer.

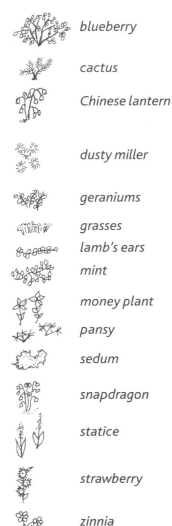

blueberry

cactus

Chinese lantern

dusty miller

geraniums

grasses

lamb's ears

mint

money plant

pansy

sedum

snapdragon

statice

strawberry

zinnia

SOUND

A sound garden is a bit of a challenge because people don't really think of plants as making noise. This garden works best when teachers encourage children to listen for sounds that exist beyond the plants: the buzzing of bees and chirping of birds, for example. However, you will also want to include plants that make a rattling sound if shaken when dried, such as Chinese lanterns and money plant. Flowers that have dryer petals, such as statice and strawflower, also make noise when rubbed. In addition, you can include grasses that rustle in the breeze. Devices such as wind chimes add to the auditory appeal of this garden.

TOUCH

Plants that are fuzzy, prickly, or spongy make up a touch garden. Favorites for touching are lamb's ears, dusty miller, cockscomb, and different varieties of sedum. Also include plants that change when handled. For instance, children quickly learned how to manipulate snapdragons by gently squeezing in the right place to make them open and "snap" shut.

You may want to include a plant or two that has prickles or thorns as well. A small, hardy rose shrub or a cactus plant would serve this purpose. If you include one of these or another thorny plant, place it in the back of the garden where it is not likely to be accidentally bumped, and educate the children about safe handling practices.

Dealing with Invasive Plants

Some plants, such as mint, tend to grow rampant and invade parts of the garden where you do not want them to be. Once they get started, it's hard to stop them. To avoid this problem, you can plant them in containers. You can also limit the space they have to grow by following these steps:

1. Cut out the bottom from a five-gallon bucket or other deep container.
2. Dig a hole in your garden deep enough to hold the container.
3. Place the container in the ground with about one inch protruding above the ground.
4. Fill the container with soil, and plant your invasive plant inside. This will keep the roots from spreading outside the container.

SIGHT

Bright, bold, cheery flowers dominate the sight garden. If you plan well, you can orchestrate a succession of flowers throughout the growing season. In the early spring, tulips are a joy to winter-weary eyes, as are other flowers that grow from bulbs, such as daffodils and crocuses. As summer progresses, flowers such as zinnias, strawflowers, marigolds, hollyhocks, and geraniums can take their place. By including mums in this garden, you will also have blooms as summer turns to fall.

Consider growing plants with interesting leaves. Large-leafed plants, such as cannas or hostas, attract attention. Some sedums actually look like rocks. Colored foliage, such as coleus, provide an interesting visual addition.

Our sight garden was one of our favorites and certainly the one that brought us the most notice. The vibrant plants attracted attention from pedestrians, and the showiness of our sight garden was a sensation from the distant road. It never failed to delight us as we drove past.

SMELL

Highly fragrant plants, such as herbs, are perfect for the smell garden. You may also want to add fragrant flowers, such as scented geraniums or hardy shrub roses. Be careful to select a variety of plants with distinct fragrances.

The scent garden provides for many pleasurable experiences beyond simply smelling plants and flowers. Herbs, such as sage and basil, call for attention and provide new experiences throughout the season. They require frequent deadheading, which involves cutting back the flowers to encourage continued growth, which gives children opportunities to cut flowers. In addition, we have found other uses for the flowers, from tasting them outright to dipping sage blossoms in batter and deep-frying them. We also used these herbs to make food, such as herb butter and basil-tomato tart.

Southwestern Garden

Desert landscapes offer a lesson that gardens can be beautiful and interesting without high maintenance and high water consumption. In fact, xeriscaping—gardening to reduce water consumption by selecting drought-tolerate plants, mulching, and selective irrigation—has become popular across the United States in an effort to be environmentally minded. The concept reflects a desert landscape.

If your school is in a desert region, use native plants that best fit your site conditions. A desert isn't thought of as a formal, symmetrical setting. As you plan, try to re-create natural desert scenery. Offer a meandering path for children to follow with plants of contrasting interests for them to explore. Create a dry creek using small rocks and a few larger boulders where children may sit. Select a few fragrant plants, such as chaparral sage and chocolate flower (*Berlandiera lyrata*). The name *chocolate flower* describes the fragrance and taste of the edible flower, which also attracts butterflies. Other low perennials should add splashes of color and different plant and flower shapes. Desert marigold has yellow daisy-like flowers and reseeds. Children can collect the seeds and small seedlings to study. The white or pink flowers of gaura grow on spikes, and the flower shape resembles a butterfly. Mexican hat has a fun cone-shaped flower. Group several of each perennial together, leaving open spaces, as you would see in a desert landscape. Along the edge of the dry creek, plant trailing gazania and fragrant creeping rosemary in spots. Use succulent plants for added interest and to simulate a desert landscape. There are numerous agaves and aloes to choose. However, many have sharp tips, which could be dangerous to a young eye. If you select smooth agave or another plant with sharp tips, place it to the back of the landscape. For added character, add features such as small sculptures of desert animals or pots for a few seasonal vegetables.

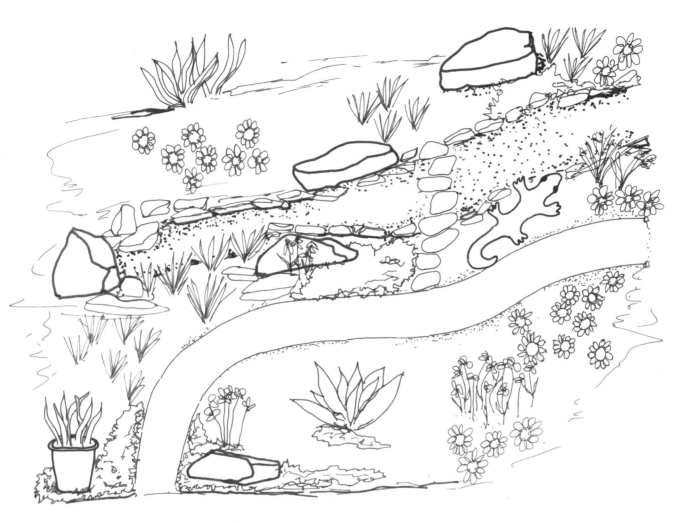

 aloe

 sage

 Mexican hat flower

 agave

 gaura

 desert marigold

 creeping gazania

 boulders and stones

 lizard sculpture

 container

river gravel

Dinosaur Garden

Dinosaurs fascinate many young children, so a garden designed with dinosaurs in mind is a natural attraction. Our dinosaur garden was inspired by some sculptures we had from previous classroom experiences. One of our parents, who taught art, had his class assemble two large dinosaur frames from rebar. These were initially overlaid with chicken wire and covered by the children with papier-mâché. However, by the time we built the garden, the papier-mâché and chicken wire had been removed, and only the frames remained. These seemed to be perfect for garden trellises, so we decided to use them to suggest a dinosaur theme in an area that was in deep shade.

Both sunny and shaded areas work well for the dinosaur garden. We chose plants with large leaves to give the garden a larger-than-life feel that would give children the experience of lush, junglelike vegetation. Especially appropriate to this type of garden are plants that tower over the children. If you live in a warm, humid climate, it should be easy to find plants that meet these requirements.

You may want to combine plants from ancient families, such as *ginkgo biloba*, large southern magnolia trees, or ferns, with more modern plants that have a "Jurassic" look. Love-lies-bleeding and elephant amaranth may be appropriate. For our purposes and with our climate limitations, hosta and astilbe worked well. We also included New Guinea impatiens, which added color to this garden.

To extend the dinosaur theme in our garden, we made dinosaur stepping-stones for the pathway. Karen used a photograph of an actual iguanodon footprint from one of our reference books to make patterns for right and left feet for the stepping-stones. The father of one of our children used this drawing to make the molds, which were filled with concrete to make the stones. If you don't know anyone who has the resources to do this, you can dig a hole the shape of a dinosaur foot in a box of wet sand and use this as a mold for the concrete.

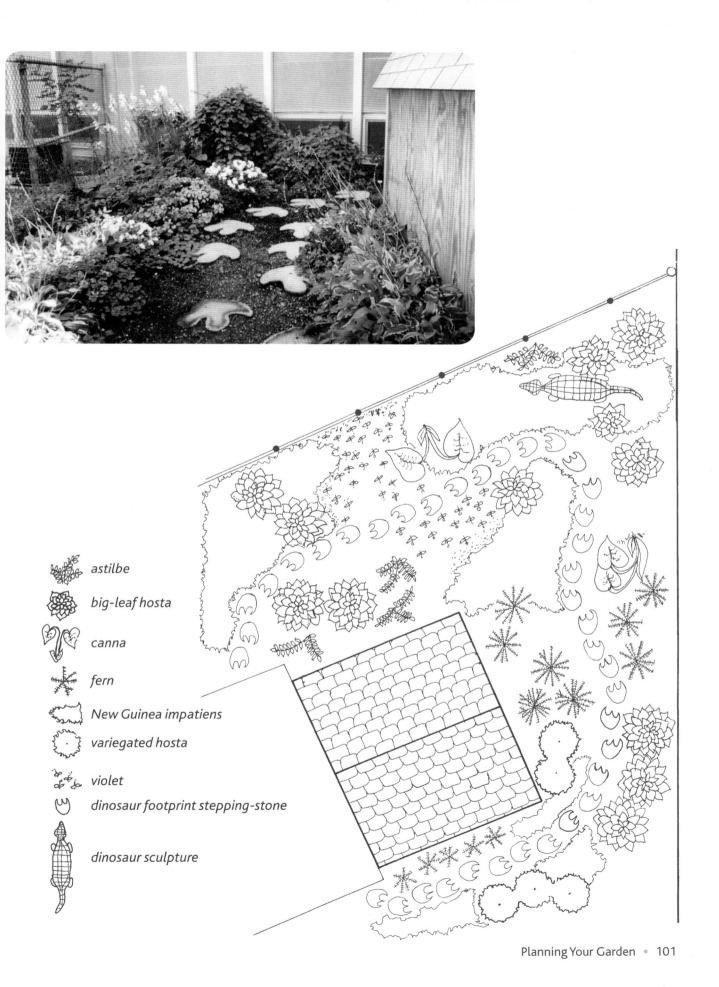

astilbe

big-leaf hosta

canna

fern

New Guinea impatiens

variegated hosta

violet

dinosaur footprint stepping-stone

dinosaur sculpture

More Ideas for Themes

Let your interests and those of your children be your guide as you explore different types of gardens. Also, look to your community for ideas. You may want to select a cultural theme, especially if you have a significant number of children who come from a particular culture. For example, you could plant a Chinese vegetable garden or a garden with foods specific to Mexican cooking. Japanese gardens are beautiful additions and can take advantage of small spaces. These tranquil spots can encourage children to slow down, observe, and think. Parents are good resources if you decide to focus on a specific culture. They will be able to help you decide what to grow and may be able to lead you to sources for seeds that are less common in this country.

A crazy colors vegetable garden can be fun for older children who are familiar with traditional vegetables. You will find lots of vegetables in new colors if you search garden catalogs or check out companies online. Here are some ideas from Totally Tomatoes (www.totallytomato.com):

- Indigo Rose Tomato—a purple and deep red tomato
- Aunt Molly's Ground Cherry Tomato—a golden-yellow cherry tomato
- Tango—a bright orange sweet bell pepper
- Purple Beauty—a dark purple sweet bell pepper
- Panther—lime-green cauliflower
- Cheddar—orange cauliflower, rich in beta carotene
- Graffiti—deep purple cauliflower
- Bright Lights Swiss Chard—stems of many colors in orange to red range
- Watermelon Radish—a radish with a green rind framing pink flesh to resemble a watermelon
- Rainbow Hybrid Carrots—carrots in yellow, white, light and dark orange, and coral
- Yellow Mini-Tiger Watermelon—green, striped rind with deep yellow flesh inside
- Faerie Watermelon—yellow rind with pink flesh

Another suggestion is a dye garden. This would include plants that can be used to make dyes, such as marigolds, coreopsis, zinnia, cosmos, dahlias, tansy, indigo, and blackberries. Children may choose to dye cloth but can also make paints out of the plants in this garden. You'll want to locate this garden near a shady spot with space for activities. You could include large boulders for sitting (or for pounding berries) and old crates to use as tables.

An excellent source for suggestions for theme gardens is the 4-H Children's Gardens at Michigan State University (http://4hgarden.cowplex.com/Virtual_Tours), which has an excellent website that includes plant lists. Whatever theme you choose, you shouldn't feel you are stuck with it forever. Many

plants need to be replanted yearly, and perennials can always be removed if they are no longer wanted. New groups of children will have different interests, so you should consider your garden a constantly evolving learning center. As you gain experience, you will find there are some plants you would never be without and some that are so much trouble you don't want to mess with them. This is part of the joy of gardening.

Jessica Chambers designed our garden at the Southern Illinois University Child Development Laboratories as a graduate student in the Plant, Soil, and Agricultural Systems department. Currently, Jessica serves as the director of the Horticulture Center at Illinois State University, where she has developed an extensive twelve-acre themed botanical garden. Some of her themed gardens include the Herb Garden, the Bird Garden, the Butterfly Garden, the Grain Garden, the Nutraceutical Garden (plants with healing qualities), the Gardens of Ill Repute (poisonous plants), the Native Gardens, the Pinetum (evergreen collection), the Prairie area, the Children's Garden, and the Trial Gardens, which are used for faculty research.

In fall 2012, Marla and Sara were able to tag along on a field trip to the Horticulture Center with teacher Cassandra Mattoon and her preschool class

from the Thomas Metcalf Laboratory School at Illinois State University. The trip served to expand on what the children had already learned by creating a garden on their playground. On the trip, the children listened to books about gardening, walked through a corn maze, learned about "cucurbits" in the pumpkin patch, participated in a scavenger hunt, and toured the various themed gardens. Our favorite section by far was the Children's Garden, which had many subthemes. We were thrilled to discover the Garden Library area, where a glass-enclosed, waterproof bookcase housed numerous children's books related to gardening and nature. The children opened the case, selected books, and cuddled up on a butterfly-shaped bench with Cassandra to read. We thought this was a great way to encourage children to take some peaceful downtime away from the hustle and bustle of preschool life.

Chapter 4

Building Your Garden

Once you have decided what kind of garden you want and where to build it, you are ready to start the process of selecting plants and building the garden. Now it's time to get organized. Spending time planning and preparing for your garden pays off in making the physical work go more smoothly.

Make a plan for preparing the area, obtaining materials, and securing labor. If you are on a tight budget, this is the time to solicit volunteers and donations. Use your garden design as a tool to build interest among staff, parents, local nurseries, and garden centers when asking for their assistance. A drawn plan and list of plant and construction materials will show that you have a plan, and it will help you obtain the materials needed.

Gathering Resources

The thought of building your garden may seem overwhelming. A school garden can be a costly venture both in terms of time and capital. Fortunately, most schools find willing partners close by. We recommend that you begin by building a garden team. Many people share a passion for gardening. As you form your team, look for teachers, administrators, family, and community members who are active or experienced in gardening. We also recommend that you involve whoever is responsible for maintaining your outdoor area. Success of your garden will often depend on the cooperation of this person.

Local Resources

Once your team is formed, evaluate the resources that are available to you. What can each person on the team contribute? How can you involve the families in your program? What organizations do you belong to that could contribute to the garden? Do you have connections to businesses that could make donations? Examine your community. If your school or center is part of a university or corporation, think about what is available within this organization. Can you gain access to a greenhouse to start seedlings? Are there groups looking to do service work that could help you in building or maintaining your garden? Is there a museum or are there art students that would be willing to contribute sculptures or build stepping-stones or mosaics? Does someone know where you can find some discarded bricks to build a walkway? The more you get to know your community, the more resources you will find that are available to you.

Acquaint yourselves with garden centers and nurseries in your community. Loyal customers can sometimes arrange donations of plants or seeds. In one case, we purchased a number of plants, and the nursery donated several bushes and plants in return.

Look for professional assistance from garden clubs, extension services, and botanic gardens. Grants may be available through local organizations, such as a rotary club or women's organizations. The National Gardening Association shares information about grants for school gardens through its Kids Gardening website (www.kidsgardening.org). You can sign up for their newsletter to keep you updated on new grants, curriculum ideas, and professional development opportunities.

One of the best examples we have seen of school and community collaboration is the school gardening project at the Indianapolis Public Schools/ Butler University Laboratory School. This preschool through second-grade magnet school features a curriculum that is inspired by Reggio Emilia early childhood education principles. Initially, the project work of students in Marissa Argus's K–1 classroom sparked interest in developing a school garden. That same spring, Argus learned that Dr. Catherine Pangan, from the College of Education at Butler University, was teaching a Leadership in Education course, where the students were looking for ways to learn about grant writing. This sparked a collaborative effort between the two groups. The college students applied for and received a $750 grant award of garden supplies and plants from the National Gardening Association, as winners in the Midwest Adopt a

School Garden competition. An additional $2,100 was raised through an on-campus bake sale. The school's teaching staff, with the strong support of Principal Ron Smith, engaged the children in selecting vegetables and herbs of their own choosing and planting them in three raised beds. Then, in an effort to expand what had been started, the College of Education faculty and students collaborated again to write and receive a $12,000 Dow Promise Grant, which developed the pilot garden into a full-scale outdoor classroom. In October 2012, forty-five local scientists from Indianapolis-based Dow AgroSciences volunteered their time and expertise to work alongside school staff, K–2 students, parents, Butler faculty, and education majors to install six new raised beds, build a storage shed, plant flowers and native grasses, refurbish the school's courtyard, and spruce up neglected landscape areas. Marla was able to witness and photograph the work-day, which was extremely well coordinated by Argus. The children were brought outside in teams to fully participate in removing dead plants and weeds, filling raised beds with soil, and planting fruit trees. This also allowed the children to observe the rototilling, building, digging, and tree trimming involved in the transformation of the barren school yard. Three chickens, named Dottie, Thelma, and Louise, were donated by a local business. Their eggs are now used to make cupcakes for the children's birthday celebrations, and their waste products are incorporated into the school's compost system.

Involve Families

Plan days when family members can help work in the garden. Select times that work for your families, and consider whether they will need child care in order to participate. One school planned Saturday workdays that included extensive physical labor. Families whose schedule did not allow attendance were invited to provide refreshments. One father who was unable to attend the workday tilled the garden while the children were in session. This gave the children the opportunity to observe some of the work being done.

Every family can donate to the garden. Once you have decided what you need for the garden, you can post a list, and families can sign up to donate different items. When we did this, we made sure the list provided a wide range of price options, from a six-pack of marigolds to a more expensive lilac bush. You can also set out a jar to collect pennies or involve the children in fund-raising efforts.

State and National Programs

Another place to look for resources is at the regional, state, and national levels. There are a number of programs to tap into if your school is interested or feels limited in terms of resources.

For excellent advice specific to your region, try to find a Master Gardener in your area. The Master Gardener program is coordinated through universities in the United States and Canada. Individuals receive extensive home horticulture training and then serve as volunteers in their communities, teaching workshops, creating gardens, doing research, and many other projects. To find programs in your state, check online for contacts for Farm to School programs (www.farmtoschool.org), Cooperative Extension services, and the Department of Conservation (some states may call this department by a different name).

Andrew Pense is the coordinator of the Farm to School program of the Office of Child Nutrition in West Virginia. When we first talked to Pense, he was working for AmeriCorps in West Virginia on projects that were components of the Farm to School program. He explained that their goals included not only educating students about nutrition and where food comes from but also encouraging school cafeterias to buy locally grown food. He expressed his enthusiasm by sharing the success of a sampling of his work with two elementary schools. "It has been a lot of fun working with kids developing gardens, working mainly with K–4th graders. At one school, we (the kids, teachers, parent volunteers, and I) built and planted ten raised beds, built compost bins from pallets, built a shed, and planted fifty berry bushes (fifteen blueberry, fifteen blackberry, twenty raspberry). We also planted garlic there. At the other school, we got started later, in March. We built and planted six raised beds, and planted eighty-five pounds of potatoes in a tilled patch, planted 200 strawberry plants, peppers, watermelon vines, and some tomato plants." Pense continued visits to the schools throughout the season for maintenance and harvests with the children. He shared his references with us too. "I've used the Junior Master Gardener books *Square Foot Gardening* by Mel Bartholomew, *Lasagna Gardening* by Patricia Lanza, and *The Complete Book of Composting* by J. I. Rodale as the basis for the lessons I've taught. I've always tried to keep things as hands-on as possible."

As part of the program, Pense also arranged for farmers to conduct workshops with the kids and has taken the children on field trips to two farms. He felt this experience completed the children's experiences of bringing food to school and fostering an appreciation of gardening and farming. Although these projects involved children from kindergarten through fourth grade, preschool children could also participate in aspects of these projects and reap fruitful benefits.

One of the pioneering programs we discovered was Grow Northwest Indiana, which unfortunately is no longer in operation. This program promoted community pride and empowerment through hands-on teaching. The program brought together the resources of the farming and gardening communities with other community members who were learning new life and work skills. The program offered free workshops for children through adults, taught by Purdue University Master Gardeners, local farmers, and volunteers. Additional goals of the organization involved food production, health and nutrition education, community involvement, and job creation. The program was simple. It built as many high-quality raised beds as possible, then gave them free to as many community and faith-based groups as possible. The program even provided schools with a variety of vegetable and herb plants to get started.

Children's Role in Building the Garden

As you begin the actual construction of the garden, the children will want to be involved. And you will want to involve them as much as possible to ensure that they feel ownership of the garden. Some of the construction work will need to be completed by adults, but children can participate in their own way as you begin your work.

When you begin laying out the plan, if you are creating an in-ground or raised garden, the children can assist in staking and flagging the area. They can observe as adults build the beds and can keep track of the progress in their garden journal. Be sure to take photographs of the site before you begin and at various stages of development. These will be valuable as the children recall the sequence of the garden installation. If the children keep a running record of how their garden was built, the photographs, drawings, and dictation can be used for documentation that will inform others about your garden.

Children can also assist in moving soil and added amendments, such as organic matter, to help improve the soil quality. They can fill small wheelbarrows with these materials and move them to the garden area. If you take time to prepare the bed, children can also assist in mixing the materials in the beds. If you are going to be gardening in containers, the children can mix soil ingredients in a large container or wheelbarrow and then help fill the containers with potting mix. Children can also spend time exploring the soil and examining living creatures that are stirred up in the process of building the garden.

Constructing Different Types of Gardens

Once you know what kind of garden you want to build and you have secured the needed materials, you're ready to start. Next you will find basic instructions for preparing each type of garden (see chapter 3 for explanations of the different types of gardens):

- ground-level gardens
- raised-bed gardens
- container gardens
- green roof gardens
- vertical gardens

We have also included some suggestions for indoor gardens.

Ground-Level Gardens

There are three approaches to choose from as you consider preparing your planting area. If the area is full of invasive weeds or aggressive grass (such as nutsedge or Bermuda grass), you may want to spray a chemical herbicide to kill the growth. If you decide this is necessary, identify the plants and seek professional advice on the type of herbicide, the amount to use, the timing of the application, and precautions to take. Be sure to let the professional know that you are dealing with a children's garden. Following proper precautions is critical for the safety of the children, the environment, and any adults involved in the project. Plan ahead. Most chemicals take ten days to two weeks to take effect, and a second application may be necessary. Do not apply the herbicide when children are present. You will probably want to spray at the beginning of a weekend or a long break to give the herbicide time to break down.

The second approach is to skip the spray application and either remove the sod manually or begin turning soil over as is, leaving the existing vegetation to be used as a green fertilizer. This is preferable if you aren't worried about existing plants invading the garden. To remove the sod, use a flat-tipped spade to separate it from the soil an inch or two below the surface of the grass.

Planting along Pathways

If you are building an outdoor nature playscape, you may want to have plantings along your pathways. When children are able to walk directly alongside the plants, they feel closeness to the plants, and the plants become a real part of their everyday world. It also encourages them to observe details of the plants' characteristics. When you plant along pathways, choose the plants and plant them carefully.

Select plants that require little care and that will grow high enough to make a clear pathway so that children will not step on the plants. However, make sure that adults supervising the children will be able to easily see over the plants so that supervision will not be compromised. Avoid buying plants that may grow tall, consequently blocking the view or flopping into the pathway, or you may have to trim or remove them. Plants native to your area are ideal for planting on pathways. They should do well with little maintenance. Consider sensory characteristics and seasonal interest as well. Early spring bulbs, fragrant blooms or herbs, and furry leaves will draw children along the path. You can also consult experts in your area about other plants that survive well with little care.

Plant the plants close together so that they will fill in quickly and discourage weeds from growing. You should protect the plants the first couple of years while they take hold, so involve the children in this process. The children can make signs reminding people that the plants are small, using their own words to ask people to use caution. Children may also want to make some barriers to protect the young plants while they mature. We find that the more children are involved in the process, the more likely they will work to help the plants survive.

The third approach will work only if you can plan ahead, because it requires time—an entire growing season. You can get rid of weeds by placing clear or black plastic weighed down with logs or bricks over the area in the spring. Leave the plastic over a growing season to allow heat to build up underneath the plastic to kill the weeds. This is called solar sterilization.

After you have decided which approach to use and after the weeds or grasses have been eliminated, it's time to turn over the soil. (This is a good time to invite families to a workday.) Outline the area with string or spray paint. Using a shovel or spading fork, dig down twelve to sixteen inches. Turn the soil over, leaving it in large clods if you have clay soil. The purpose of this procedure is to loosen the soil, allowing plant roots to penetrate, and to improve water drainage. Continue working this way until the entire outlined area is turned over. This will go much faster if several people work together.

The next step is to add organic matter to the overturned soil to a depth of six to eight inches. Many schools and universities are now stockpiling grass and leaf clippings and other materials throughout the year to use as compost. Check around to see if someone locally can provide you with compost. If not, you can purchase peat moss to add to the soil. Also add any other supplements your previous research has determined you need. Do not use compost that includes fresh manure. Pathogens such as *E. coli* could be present and could cause illness to children and teachers who eat fresh produce grown in it unless serious precautions are taken. Additionally, fresh manure typically is high in weed seeds, which will flourish in your garden, and soluble forms of nitrogen, which can lead to salt buildup in your soil.

Once the organic matter is roughly spread over the area, use a rototiller to break up the large clods and to work the organic matter into the soil. (You will likely be able to find someone who has a rototiller that you can borrow, but if not, you can probably rent one at a local rental store.) Go over the bed twice, the second time at a right angle to the first. Don't be concerned if the rototiller blades do not reach to the depth of the overturned soil. By following this procedure, you will create an environment where healthy plants can grow and children can plant using hand trowels.

When you are finished tilling, your bed is ready for planting.

Raised-Bed Gardens

Proper preparation of a raised bed is similar to that of an in-ground garden. First, select the material for the "wall" of the bed. The material may be chosen for aesthetic reasons or because it fits your budget. For instance, native stones are attractive, and you may be able to get them for free or at a low cost. Other materials you could use include concrete blocks, landscape timbers, and pressure-treated wood. Many gardening companies even sell kits to make raised beds. Scrap lumber can be used if more durable materials are not available, but it will not last as long as treated wood. If you use scrap lumber, watch out for splinters and old nails. Do not use new railroad ties for your raised beds. The creosote with which they are treated is toxic to plants and may irritate skin. If you use old timbers, be sure they won't easily splinter. We recommend using pressure-treated wood, since it contains compounds that will seal out moisture and inhibit rotting (refer to chapter 3 for the discussion of wood durability and treated wood). You can use untreated wood, but it will need to be replaced within a short period of time. There are many commercially available raised-beds kits, which come precut with corner supports and ground anchors. These systems are convenient but are more costly than building your own. You could check with a local store, or shop online. You should consider the safety and longevity of any material you use.

No matter what material you select, think seriously about the height and width of the bed before construction. Avoid building a bed that is too high for children to reach into or for you to observe over. The maximum height should be twenty-four inches. There are several things to consider. The decision may be based on available material and cost. Also consider that children will need to kneel or sit while working in a low bed, whereas they will need to stand when working in a higher raised bed. The height may be as low as six inches—just high enough to define the planting area, provide better drainage, and add soil amendments. But typically you reap greater advantages from a raised bed (such as weed control and discouraging rodents) with greater height. If you are planning accessibility for children who use wheelchairs, the height becomes very important in relation to the child's reach. As suggested by the "Americans with Disability Act (ADA) Accessibility Guidelines for Buildings and Facilities: Building Elements Designed for Children's Use," determine the height by the age group (ADA 1998). The guidelines specify thirty-six inches (high) and twenty inches (low) for ages two through four, and forty inches (high) and eighteen inches (low) for ages five through eight. While these guidelines are for mounting controls and storage elements, the height applies to appropriate reaching heights for children in wheelchairs. We suggest using the lower heights to accommodate children who are shorter as well.

The width of the bed is also important. For young children, the best width for a freestanding bed is no more than three feet (and that's pushing it for very young children), since children have such a short reach and will need to reach the middle of the bed. If the bed is accessible from only one side, don't exceed eighteen inches. These widths may vary with age groups, and exceptions may be made if the plantings are shrubs or perennials with a wide spread. If the bed is much wider, the children will need to be able to get in the garden, and a shallower frame will work better. If you have a low (eight-inch raised bed), children could step into the bed to reach the vegetation if the design requires a bed wider than three feet. In this case, space the plants to allow open areas for children to go into the garden. If you have children who use wheelchairs, you can also let them sit in these beds if you leave open space.

You should till the soil to improve the texture before you start building your bed. However, you won't need to turn over the soil, since you're raising the height. After you till and build the walls to the bed, fill your bed with a combination of topsoil and organic matter. One suggestion is to add two parts topsoil to one part peat moss and one part compost. You may want to check with local gardeners or your garden center before deciding what mixture to use. You may find a "ready to purchase" topsoil-compost mix available at a

reasonable price at a local landscape supply company. One of the advantages of the raised bed is being able to control your planting medium, so this is your chance to mix up a soil that will be most favorable for your plants.

Fill the bed so that the planting medium comes to within two inches of the top of the bed after it is raked and lightly compacted. This will ensure that the soil won't spill out, and you will still have room to add mulch to the bed. Once the bed is filled, you're ready to plant.

Container Gardens

The possibilities are endless when it comes to container gardening. Obvious choices are flowerpots, troughs, and window boxes, which are available for purchase in a large range of sizes and several different materials. (If you use pots, buy plastic rather than terra-cotta. The moisture in terra-cotta pots evaporates too quickly to make them a good choice for school gardens.) Also consider some of the new fabric-based containers, such as the Smart Pots mentioned in chapter 3 (see page 86). However, any container can be used for gardening as long as it is strong enough to hold the plants and soil, is safe for children, and has sufficient drainage holes. Pots, pails, watering cans, and even coffee cans make good small containers. If you want something larger, try used car or tractor tires, wooden crates, or half barrels. Be aware that the use of tires is somewhat controversial because of concern about toxic substances potentially emitted from the tire. Tires are not banned by the Environmental Protection Agency or other safety organizations, and the practice of gardening in tires dates back many years. A tire is a convenient and durable container (but not the most aesthetic choice), yet you should consider safety concerns. An old but solid plastic swimming pool that leaks (to allow drainage) is a good choice. If you're lucky, you may even come across a leaky or unused old canoe or other small boat that can easily be transformed into a garden. Your only limit is your imagination.

If you're going to place your containers on a patio or permanent surface, select containers that have bottoms. If you convert objects from other uses to gardening, be sure to drill drainage holes. A drill with a half-inch bit will work for drilling several holes in smaller containers, but if you have large containers, use a one-inch hole saw, which can be attached to a drill. You want the water to drain easily so that your plants don't sit in wet soil. Otherwise you risk root rot and unhealthy plant growth.

To make your garden the most interesting, select a variety of containers in different sizes. This will also help you find the right-sized receptacle for each plant. Match the size of the pot to the plant, and remember to consider the mature size of the plant. For instance, while a young tomato plant may fit into a small pot, the mature plant may be six feet or more in height. You'll need a big container to hold a plant that size. A large, twenty-inch pot or a half barrel works well, as do two or three stacked car tires. Tires also work well for potatoes, which need depth to grow. Start out by planting them in one tire. As they grow, add additional tires, filling them with a mixture of straw and soil. You'll eventually have a tower four or five tires tall. You may wish to start with a larger tire on the bottom to lend stability as the tower grows along with the potatoes. Whatever containers you use, ensure that they are stable and won't topple over if a child leans on them to smell a flower or pick a vegetable.

One of the disadvantages of containers is that the soil dries out much more rapidly than in other kinds of gardens. In very hot weather, small containers may need watering twice a day. We recommend adding a mulch, such as wood chips or small pebbles, to containers to slow down evaporation. Remember that the larger the containers you use, the less you will have to worry about the plants drying out.

If you need to use containers and have no way of watering over long weekends, consider installing a simple irrigation system. Drip water systems are available at most discount stores and garden centers and are surprisingly easy to set up. These can be attached, using a hose, to a timer that will regulate the watering over the weekend. You should also consider using self-watering containers, making sure that the water level is adequate before a long weekend.

Most experts recommend using a potting mix for containers. You can buy potting mix already made at any garden center, or you can make your own. If you buy potting mix, avoid the kind with fertilizer mixed in, as it should not be handled by children. The fertilizer could be poisonous if consumed, or irritate some children's skin or eyes. If the children want to help, provide gloves for them to wear, and don't allow them to put the fertilizer in their mouths or rub their eyes. If you are planting a large container, such as a boat or swimming pool, you can use the same kind of mix you would use for a raised bed.

When planting a container, place pieces of broken terra-cotta pots or large chunks of gravel in the bottom of the container before adding the soil mix. This will increase the effectiveness of the drainage. Fill the container to about one inch from the top so you'll have space for watering. If the container is large, place it in the location where it will remain before adding the soil mix and plants. If the location of your container garden is on a patio, consider that water will run onto the surface underneath. So you may want to place the container away from an entrance or popular path.

Green Roof Gardens

As mentioned in chapter 3, your preparation for a green roof garden will mostly be concerned with the plants. Note: A green roof system should be installed by professionals. You need to learn the depth of the medium and what the limitations may be for plants. Find a person who is knowledgeable about the roof system to guide you with plant decisions. You will be amazed at

what you can grow on a green roof. Basically, you can plan it as you would a ground-level garden. If you have the space, consider a mix of gardens. An area of native plants can be used for lessons in sustainability as children observe the butterflies and bees throughout the spring until early autumn. It's also possible to plant other perennials and annuals; just beware that temperatures are harsher on the roof, as are wind conditions. You can have cool- and warm-season crops as you would in a ground-level garden. Many vegetables do very well on the roof, although root crops, such as potatoes and carrots, may be limited if the medium depth is shallow. A drip irrigation system on a timer is a simple solution to watering concerns, although hand watering and sprinklers work too. They are more time consuming and may require weekend visits. If you use sprinklers, beware of water going over the edge and showering pass-ersby. This has happened!

There are a few additional critical points you must be attentive to when gardening on a green roof:

- You do *not* want to puncture the moisture barrier of the roof. Although a drainage system and other layers will separate the medium from the barrier, it's best to be overly cautious. Therefore, do not use rakes or pointed tools. The medium is loose and easy to plant in, so use rounded hand trowels.
- If you are working on a hot day, be aware that the temperatures on a roof rise faster. Be sure to keep yourself and the children hydrated to avoid dehydration.
- Lastly, don't think you won't have rodent and insect problems. Squirrels, raccoons, and annoying insects, as well as beneficial insects, can find their way to the roof to share your produce.

Vertical Gardens

Most vertical gardens do not require soil but use either a recommended soil-less medium or are strictly hydroponic, meaning plants are cultivated in a water-nutrient solution. Vertical gardens can be very successful if carefully planned and maintained. Systems attached to the wall range in design and materials but share a critical common feature: they avoid moisture contacting the wall. A waterproof membrane is essential to separate the garden system from the wall to avoid moisture damage to the building wall and structure. The system in the College of Agricultural Sciences that Karen and her students installed employed three layers to discourage moisture penetration into the existing wall. First, they attached a sheet of marine plywood, which is specially designed to be a premium panel of wood suitable for uses needing moisture control. A thick sheet of black plastic was adhered to the plywood, and then a sheet of PVC. PVC is a thermoplastic and does not allow water

penetration. The rest of the vertical garden system and plants were installed onto the PVC layer.

A vertical garden inside a classroom needs to be carefully planned to have proper lighting and to accommodate a hydroponic system to water and fertilize the plants. Numerous commercial systems are available, and we recommend you use one of these if you wish to have an interior vertical garden. Commercial systems include the freestanding towers and systems that attach to the wall. Follow the instructions provided by the company, or hire a professional to install it. Most indoor attached wall systems are planted with tropical plants and not treated as a garden. If your school or center has the resources for this type, especially in an infant room, you will have the opportunity to reap the therapeutic benefits of plants with the infants and the staff. Plants create a calm effect by softening the architecture and bringing life into the room or area. Each plant will grow, possibly bloom, adding interest, mild stimulus, and personality to the vertical garden. Children may also touch the plants, learning to be gentle while gaining a sense of wonderment and appreciation for plant life. Most of these systems are expensive to install, but once they are installed and the automatic watering system is regulated, there is very little maintenance. The towers accommodate producing lettuce, strawberries, cherry tomatoes, and many other crops. The children can plant seeds directly into the medium in the tower openings, but you may have greater success planting seedlings. An advantage of towers is the accessibility for the children. They are freestanding, and children are able to reach all sides. The top openings may be too high for children, but a teacher can assist in planting and harvesting what the children can't reach.

For outdoor vertical gardens (not the tower style), evaluate the sun exposure carefully, because the garden will have a back side. The placement may be dictated by the structures available to attach it to, but try to select a site where plants will receive at least six hours of sun a day. Determine what plants you can use based on the location's sunlight and temperature. As you and the children determine the plant placement, think about the form of each plant to avoid hanging plants shading out the plants below. Work with the children to create a "to scale" outdoor vertical garden out of construction paper and other materials to select and place the plants.

Indoor Gardens

Teachers should consider an indoor garden if an outdoor garden seems to present too many obstacles. Although the experience will be different from that of studying an outdoor garden ecosystem, indoor gardens can be rewarding for the children to study plants in any environment. One advantage of indoor gardening is that you can grow plants year-round. This may be of particular benefit to preschool programs that are on a nine-month calendar or in very cold climates.

Indoor gardens are usually container gardens, and the previous instructions for planting containers apply to indoor gardens as well. The exception is that you need to provide trays to catch the water runoff. Trays made specifically for this purpose are available in the garden section of most discount stores, but you can improvise and use any flat object with a lip that will hold the container. You may also choose to install a vertical garden system, as described previously.

The major difficulty in building an indoor garden is providing enough light for the plants. If you have sunny windows, you may be able to grow some herbs and flowers on the windowsill. However, if you are going to be gardening on a larger scale, you need to devise an indoor lighting system using fluorescent lights. If you choose to go this route, we

Hollyhock Dolls

To make hollyhock dolls, you need a hollyhock bloom that is in full flower for the skirt and a bud for the head. When you pick the flower, be sure to include about a half inch of the stem. Set the flower aside while you select and prepare the bud. Choose a bud that is just beginning to open up and is showing some color. Carefully remove the green covering from the bud. Pull the stem and attached green off the bud. Where the stem was, there should be a small hole. You can enlarge this with a small stick. Now retrieve the flower. Place the hole of the bud on top of the stem of the flower, and you have your doll.

recommend that you consult *GrowLab: A Complete Guide to Gardening in the Classroom* by Eve Pranis and Jack Hale. The book contains illustrated instructions for building an extensive lighting system that will sustain a number of plants. *GrowLab* was written specifically for teachers who want to garden in the classroom and includes information that will be helpful in establishing an indoor garden.

Plant Selection

One of the most important parts of the gardening process is selecting the plants you will grow. You should consider this during your planning stage, but you can focus on details after the major decisions have been made about the garden type. Children should be actively involved in choosing which plants to include in the garden. However, the adult should have a basic understanding of plant hardiness and how plants are affected by climate.

The best resource for finding out what plants do well in your area is local gardeners and gardening experts. Select a variety of plants that will provide diversity to your garden. Think about what you can do with the plants that will maintain the children's interest. For instance, flowers are beautiful to look at, and some varieties are edible. By including edible flowers, you increase the appeal of your garden. Herbs can be dried or can be used for cooking and making such things as teas, flavored vinegars, and potpourri. In addition, the flowers of many herbs are attractive and can be used for decoration as well as cooking.

Some plants provide materials for future activities. Gourds are easy to grow and will cover an entire fence or trellis, and the gourds they produce can be used for making birdhouses and bird feeders. Job's tears is a fun plant that produces bead-like seeds that children can string. Hollyhocks can be used to make hollyhock dolls, and snapdragons draw a child's interest because they can be manipulated to snap open and shut. Sunflowers can be planted in a circle or rectangle so they will eventually grow into the walls of a house or a fort.

One book that we prize is *Plants for Play: A Plant Selection Guide for Children's Outdoor Environments* by Robin Moore. Moore includes lists of plants that can be selected for fragrance, texture, wind effects, hiding places, play props, and many other attributes. For teachers who want to grow and cook vegetables, we recommend *Early Sprouts: Cultivating Healthy Food Choices in Young Children* by Karrie Kalich, Dottie Bauer, and Deirdre McPartlin. This book gives specific information about six target vegetables and a number of recipes and includes a twenty-four-week curriculum with information on how to involve families.

You need to consider several factors before making your plant selections. These include

- the climate in which you live,
- the hours of sunlight on the site,
- the drainage of the planting area,
- whether you want an annual or perennial garden, and
- whether to start with seeds or purchase transplants.

When trying to decide what to grow, first consider if you want to have an ornamental garden with mostly flowers, or if you will include fruits, herbs, and vegetables. Once you decide this, consider whether you want to grow annuals or perennials. Annuals are plants that grow for only one season; perennials come back year after year. Most vegetables are grown as annuals, with the exception of asparagus and a few others. Many gardeners prefer annual flowers because they tend to bloom continuously throughout the season, providing constant color to the garden, while most perennials have a shorter blooming season. Another advantage of annuals is that you can change your garden easily every year. The old plants die off, leaving space to put in new ones in the spring.

Perennials, however, have the advantage of lasting. Though they cost more to buy initially, in the long run you'll spend less money. Not only that, but perennials multiply. By dividing your plants, you can make new ones to plant or share. Also, you may find people who are willing to share their perennials with you. Perennials take less time because you don't have to plant them every year. However, to maintain their health, you need to divide them every two or three years.

The decision of what plants you choose should be based on your objectives for the garden, the type and size of the garden, and the time and resources available for maintenance. Areas planted with annuals can change each year and can change with the seasons. In early spring and early fall, plant cool-season crops, such as pansies, lettuce, and broccoli. For hotter months, plant warm-season crops like sunflowers, tomatoes, and zucchini. You can change themes each year based on color, ethnic produce (herbs, vegetables, or fruits typically grown and consumed by a culture that define their cuisine), attracting butterflies, or other interests. It's nice to combine perennials and annuals, reducing your annual labor and the cost of replanting all of the plants. If you choose a perennial garden, plan to interplant early-blooming spring bulbs with later-blooming flowers to provide successional beauty in the garden.

Garden catalogs and nurseries generally separate annual and perennial plants, so it's easy to learn which is which. Some plants are annual in cold climates and perennial in warmer climates, so if you live in a warm area, you may have more perennials to choose from. Your local experts are the best people to guide you as you determine what plants are perennial in your area.

Native Plants: The College School

As you consider what plants you want to include in your garden, give serious consideration to native plants, plants that live or exist naturally in a given geographic region. In fact, some grant programs require that you select native plants. Native plants offer many benefits. The first is simplicity of care. Once a native plant is established, it requires little care. Because it is native to the area, it shouldn't need to be watered or fertilized. And native plants have built up resistance to diseases and insects common to your area, so they are likely to flourish in your garden. If you plant the plants close together, you may have few problems with weeds. In fact, many native plants are considered weeds when they grow wild.

Another important reason to consider native plants is that you will be building habitat for native wildlife. Often when areas are developed, the native plants are removed, which destroys the habitats for birds, butterflies, and other creatures. When you use native plants, you are restoring some of this habitat.

The College School in Webster Groves, Missouri, a Reggio-inspired program serving preschool through middle school, with a deep history of environmentalism and sustainability, has developed a gardening program with a strong

emphasis on growing native plants. The school has a large greenhouse where the children harvest seeds in the fall and grow their own plants. The native plants attract and provide habitat and food for birds and butterflies. The students have developed a monarch waystation and are active in Monarch Watch, a program that tracks the migration of monarch butterflies. As part of this program, the children capture, tag, and release the butterflies, then track the monarchs on the Monarch Watch website.

According to Tim Wood, sustainability coordinator at the College School, first- and second-grade children have the dexterity and the patience to plant many small seeds and transplant small seedlings when too many have been planted in one pot. Preschool children will likely overplant if the seeds are small, so it will be necessary to either remove the extra seedlings or transplant them to a new space. If you want to harvest and grow native plants, do be aware that some need to be stratified or put through a cooling-off period. This may involve putting them in sand or peat moss and refrigerating them for a period of time. Some seeds may also need to be scarified, or nicked, if they have a very hard shell. If you are going to grow from seeds you have harvested, do some research first to determine if your seeds need any pretreatment.

Climate

The climate is the prevailing weather conditions for a particular region. Climate affects planting and harvesting times, as well as plant selection. You probably already have a good idea of what your climate is from having lived there, but you will now need to think about how your climate affects the plants in your area. You should consider the average high and low temperatures for summer and winter, the general wind direction, and average yearly rainfall. You also need to consider the microclimate of your site: average hours of sunlight, soil moisture, whether your area is prone to early frost, and other observations specific to that area.

For example, southern Illinois has a temperate climate with moderately cold winters and hot summers, so most of our suggestions are based on having a garden that experiences changes throughout the seasons. In this book, we have included lists of plants for specific types of gardens and some sample garden designs. These plants do well in our southern Illinois climate and will grow in most temperate climates. We have also included a plan for a Southwestern garden. Do take into consideration where you live and consider your local climatic conditions. If necessary, consult a local plant expert about plant choices.

Temperature

Temperature affects the length of the growing season. If you don't already know, find out the typical dates for the last and first frosts of the year in your area. These dates determine what plants can be grown and when you can safely plant them. You'll also need to find out what zone your area is in from the U.S. Department of Agriculture's Plant Hardiness Zone Map, which is based on the average low temperature for the area. This map is available in almost every garden catalog, and you should also be able to find out your zone by consulting your local nursery. When buying seeds or plants from catalogs, be sure to check for the zone in which the plants will grow. Most catalogs will include this information in the plant listing. Nurseries and garden centers usually sell plants appropriate to the zone in which they are located. Remember that some plants that are perennials in warmer climates may still be grown as annuals in colder climates.

If you live in an area where the winters are severe and the growing season is short, choose plants that either survive deep cold or that have a short growing season. Hot temperatures can be as limiting as cold temperatures since some plants are not heat tolerant. If you're not sure if a plant will do well, consult your local nursery. Most nurseries offer plants that do well in the area in which they are located. For that reason, local nurseries are a better place to buy plants than are garden companies located far away.

Plants to Avoid

There are some plants you'll definitely want to avoid. These include plants that require a great deal of maintenance, such as most hybrid tea roses, which need to be sprayed regularly to prevent disease. In addition, some plants need to be placed carefully. If you plant a less fussy rosebush, a barberry, or any other plant with thorns, be sure to put it in an area where children are not likely to fall into it during their normal play. Thorns can cause a great deal of damage and emotional distress.

You also need to avoid plants that are toxic. We have included a list of poisonous plants in appendix 6, but this is only a partial guide. If you are unsure about the safety of a plant, call your local Poison Control Center. They are very helpful and have the most current information. Again, the book *Plants for Play* by Robin Moore offers advice in this area. Moore argues, and we agree, that not all poisonous plants need to be banned from school gardens. In fact, he stresses that children need to learn about poisonous plants, as they will come across them in their lives and need to be able to identify them and understand the dangers involved. He suggests the school yard can be a place where, under careful supervision, children can learn about some toxic plants. Moore also points out that different poisonous plants have different levels of toxicity. The plants he lists are divided by level of toxicity: highly toxic, moderately toxic, and slightly toxic. Highly toxic plants, such as castor bean, belladonna, and angel's trumpet, can cause serious illness or even death if ingested.

Moderately toxic plants, such as foxglove, English ivy, and columbine, can cause illness when ingested or serious contact dermatitis if touched. Slightly toxic plants, such as bleeding heart and buttercup, may cause mild illness or contact dermatitis.

Consider the level of toxicity of the plant and the age and maturity of your children, as well as the educational value of the plant, when deciding whether you want to include it in your garden. You may also need to alter your plant selection if you have children with serious allergies. In addition, think about what part of the plant is toxic and how likely children are to come in contact with that part. You should be extremely cautious if you have young children who are prone to putting objects—including fingers—in their mouths. If infants and toddlers have access to the area, avoid all toxic plants and plants with small berries or seeds that they could choke on. Above all, be sure that any staff and volunteers who are supervising children are well aware of any plants that could cause problems. Also, be sure to keep the number of the closest Poison Control Center next to the phone in case of emergency.

Seeds or Transplants

Before the planting season arrives, start thinking about whether you want to grow your own plants from seed or to purchase plants ready to transplant into your garden. The teacher in you may think that planting seeds is the way to go if you want children to have the full experience of seeing how plants develop, and you would be right to a point. Certainly the experience of growing plants from seed is fascinating for children. Some plants grow easily from seed, and some plants are only available to you if you grow them yourself. Others need to be directly seeded because they do not transplant well. However, many plants are more difficult to grow from seed and are most practically purchased as transplants. Also, the space available in many classrooms limits the number of seedlings that can be sustained during the late winter. We suggest that you use a combination of both methods. Grow some of the easier seeds in the classroom in the late winter and also use some transplants that have been purchased or donated.

When we were working together, we were fortunate that we were able to use a campus greenhouse to grow many of our plants. We were also able to entice volunteers to monitor and care for the plants in the greenhouse. Check around for greenhouse space available in your area and volunteers to monitor and care for the plants. For instance, you could look for a family-owned organic farm or garden center nearby. The children could take a field trip to plant the seeds and later to observe the germination and plant growth. If you have the classroom space or find a greenhouse, you can save a lot of money growing your own plants, especially if you are also able to get the seeds donated.

A greenhouse can be useful for protecting tender plants from harsh weather and is especially helpful for programs that have a shorter growing season. Although large, heated greenhouses are expensive, small greenhouses are available in many forms that are quite economical. These smaller greenhouses can be used to give a start to early crops or to give plants a head start. Cold frames can extend the life of cold-weather crops, such as members of the cabbage family and leafy greens.

Programs that are able to secure funding for a greenhouse will find the investment greatly enhances the garden experience. Dimensions Early Education Programs in Lincoln, Nebraska, has a greenhouse that is fully integrated into their Nature Explore classroom. The greenhouse measures twenty-two by twelve feet and includes three picnic tables and a worm bin, which is a large galvanized tub. Clipboards and colored pencils are always available to sketch the plants, which are available year-round, including a selection of herbs and plants of different sensory qualities. The greenhouse is usually open as a play space during outdoor playtime, when sufficient supervision is available. Teachers can reserve the greenhouse for small-group activities during the school day.

The Dimensions greenhouse is heated and is used throughout the year for a number of projects. In the spring, the children search the assortment of seed

catalogs, mapping out their garden plot for the spring. Each group is responsible for a portion of the garden, and after completing their garden plan, they start the seeds in the greenhouse. Children also grow lettuce in flats in all but the coldest weather. In the fall, the children are able to observe the cycle of life as plants begin to die and go dormant for the winter. They take cuttings of some plants and root them in perlite in the greenhouse. They remove the dried, spent flowers, called deadheading, carefully sorting and saving the seeds and labeling the packets. At Dimensions, children grow gifts for special days, such as Mother's Day or Christmas, in the greenhouse, and the children consider these the most prized gifts of all. While plants the children have grown are wonderful gifts, an extraspecial gift is a supply of the nutrient-rich worm castings, a fertilizer valued by gardeners, which the children carefully gather from the worm bin and place into bottles.

If you decide to grow plants from seed, consider where you will get your seed. Seeds are available at many discount stores and garden centers, with an even wider variety available online. You may be able to obtain donations of seeds from local merchants or mail-order companies. We recommend that you purchase seeds packaged for the year you are planting them. Look on the seed package to determine if they are the current year's supply. Seeds from previous years may germinate, but the success rate increases, as do the chances of a healthy plant, with fresher, properly stored seeds. If you store seeds from year to year, be sure they are stored in a cool, dry space and are labeled with plant name and date for identification.

If you are going to grow seeds yourself, check the package to see whether they should be started indoors first or directly seeded into the garden. You'll want to start those that need to be planted inside early enough so that the seedlings will be ready to plant in your garden by the frost-free date. Each packet of seeds tells how far ahead of time you should plant the seeds, and this varies depending on the plant. Determine the frost-free date and then count backward to come up with the right day to plant. For instance, the date after which we are usually frost-free in southern Illinois is April 15. If seeds take six weeks from planting time to mature, we would need to plant them the first week of March. Since different seeds need different lengths of time to develop, you need to come up with a timetable for planting. (You can even use a large calendar and attach seed packets to the dates on which you plan to plant.) This process can be fun in a classroom, as you will have many planting opportunities, and

seedlings will be springing up over a period of time. This helps sustain the children's interest as they wait for the actual planting time to come.

Many methods can be used to start seeds. You can purchase flats or peat pots intended for starting seeds, but you can also start seeds in milk cartons, egg cartons, or other used containers. If you reuse containers, be sure to disinfect them with a bleach-water solution. And no matter what type of container you use, buy new, sterile seed-starter mix. Your mix and containers must be free of bacteria if you are to have healthy plants.

Provide the proper amount of water to new seedlings. They need to be kept slightly moist, but too much water encourages fungus and root rot. If new seedlings start falling over and dying, you likely have a fungus that causes what is called damping off, which must be avoided as it spreads to other young plants and can mean death for your seed-starting efforts. Our experiences with growing seeds in the classroom have taught us that children often overwater and that it is also difficult to keep seedlings moist over weekends. Because of these problems, we often use a self-watering seed-starting system that transfers water to the soil by means of a capillary mat, which is submerged in water at one end. This ensures that the soil remains consistently moist even when we are gone. Children still have the experience of watering the seedlings by filling the reservoir. These systems are now becoming more available at large garden centers and from mail-order companies.

For best results with seeds started indoors, use fluorescent lights to help the plants grow. It's easy and surprisingly inexpensive to set up a lighting system. A forty-eight-inch fluorescent light fixture can often be bought for under ten dollars, and bulbs for such fixtures are reasonably priced. You can buy special plant bulbs, but these are more expensive and not necessary. Most experts suggest that you use one cool bulb and one warm bulb in a two-light fixture to provide an appropriate light range for plants. Use lightweight chain to suspend the light fixture so you can change its height to keep it about three inches above the plants as they grow. As previously mentioned, a good source for information on growing plants inside is *GrowLab: A Complete Guide to Gardening in the Classroom* by Eve Pranis and Jack Hale (1999).

SELECTING TRANSPLANTS

Flats of transplants can be purchased from nurseries, garden centers, discount stores, roadside stands, and even grocery stores. A large selection is available in early spring, and sometimes it seems impossible to go to a store that doesn't have plants for sale. Most plants will be healthy and ready to grow if you get them soon after they arrive at the store. However, some stores have better strategies for caring for plants than others. Some seem to take the tactic of buying the plants, selling what they can, and letting the rest die. Therefore, if you get to the store early, you can get some real bargains. But if you wait, you will find mostly sick, wilting plants.

Look for healthy plants with bright, firm leaves. Feel free to pull one out of the pack to examine the roots. The root ball should simply lift out of the tray. The roots should be white and healthy looking. The soil should be moist if they are being well cared for. Avoid plants with roots that look as if they are rotting.

Avoid plants in full flower or with vegetables already developing. If they are already blooming strongly, they won't transplant as well. You want small, compact, healthy plants, perhaps with buds starting to develop. Such plants should perform well for you.

Don't purchase the plant if it looks distressed, even if the price is reduced. Chances are it won't do well, and it could carry a disease that will affect the rest of your garden. Healthy transplants are critical to getting your garden off to a good start.

Preventing Vandalism

One concern of many teachers is the threat of vandalism in the garden. In some areas, teachers may be worried enough that they will want to limit the access to the garden with a fence or other barrier. We were a bit anxious when we built our first school garden because a large part of it was outside the playground fence along a busy sidewalk. We were especially concerned that if the college students got a bit rambunctious at night, our garden would be in their path. We wanted to protect the work of our children.

One of the first steps we took was making a sign for the garden, which we posted in a prominent place. It said, "This garden is planted and cared for by the children of the Child Development Laboratories. Please be gentle." This did the trick for us. However, Jessica Chambers at the Horticulture Center at Illinois State University was not so fortunate. In fall 2012, vandals drove a truck through her twelve-acre garden, causing a tremendous amount of damage. Sadly, the Children's Garden, which was nearest the busy road, sustained the most harm. Fortunately, through local news coverage, Chambers was able to raise funds to repair most of the damage and to enlist the watchful eye of many sympathetic supporters in the future.

If you are concerned about vandalism, start by posting signs, as we mentioned above. You may also want to alert neighbors and the local police department to help you by keeping an eye on the garden when you're not around. Be sure to let them know who to call if they notice suspicious visitors. Consider involving community members with your garden. The more people who feel ownership, the less likely harm will be done. Our experience has been that people often respect the work more when they know children are invested in it. The more you can spread this message, the more likely you will be to avoid problems. Another way to prevent theft or damage is to install motion sensor lights or solar lights near the garden area. Troublemakers are more likely to avoid a well-lit area. One school we know posted a sign near their garden area that read, "Smile, You're on Camera!" If your school has a video surveillance system, inquire if your garden area can be added to the list of monitored areas. If not, you can always purchase fake security cameras and mount them near the garden. These cameras look surprisingly real and even have the option to install batteries so that a bright red light adds to the authenticity.

Chapter 5

Working with Children in the Garden

This is the moment you have been waiting for. Now that you have planned your garden, gathered resources, and involved your community, it is time to get your hands dirty. In this chapter, you will discover tips on involving children in the planting process, supervising students in the garden, managing garden maintenance, welcoming and deterring animals, harvesting plants and seeds, and sharing your garden project with others.

Planting the Garden

Once you have prepared your garden beds and obtained your seeds and transplants, it's time for you to plant the garden. Be sure to wait until your area is free of frost, or you will risk losing all your plants. You need to plan carefully for the actual planting of the garden, and your strategy will differ depending on the size of your garden and the types of plants you are including.

As you think about how you will plant the garden, consider what you will do to ensure that the children feel ownership of the garden. If a number of adults come in and take control, children will likely miss out on much of the planting process. To ensure they perceive the garden as their own, include them in the planting as much as possible.

A small, simple garden with only flowers and vegetables can be planted over a period of a few days or a week, a few plants at a time. This technique works well because it gives teachers an opportunity to work with small groups of children. The teacher can provide a rich experience as children examine the roots of the transplants or compare the size, shape, and texture of seeds. Often there is a temptation to plant the entire garden at once, but the process of spending time with children should not be sacrificed for the benefit of getting everything in the ground quickly.

If you are gardening on a larger scale or if you will be doing heavy work, such as moving large boulders, installing stepping-stones, or planting shrubs or trees, you may need to arrange a more organized event. As we wrote previously, this is a good time to engage your garden team if you have one, including parents, extended family members, and interested community members. You may also recruit volunteers, such as a college class that is studying landscaping, a sorority or fraternity, or a local gardening club. Nevertheless, be careful that you don't have the adults do all the work. The first time we planted a garden together, we found that sometimes the children were left out in the hurry to get all the plants in. We learned to take a more leisurely approach to the actual planting of the garden and use our extra help (a class of college students) to concentrate on doing the heavy labor or working one-on-one with the children in planting.

If you decide to involve a large number of people, think carefully about each person's role and communicate this to them. Devise a plan that will be easy for them to follow. If the work is extensive, some will need to be done prior to the planting day. For instance, all of the hard construction—such as building retaining walls, raised beds, fences, paths, trellises, and playhouses or moving large boulders—should be completed before planting. If your work crew is going to perform any of this work on the planting day, have those who will be involved come early so that it will be finished before the actual planting begins.

While the children will not be able to participate in this heavy labor, they will enjoy watching and asking questions as others do the work. Our children were fascinated when Sara's husband, Charles, brought his rototiller to prepare the soil in one bed. After watching him work, they decided to include a photograph of him tilling in their garden journal.

Once the construction is complete and the planting area is prepared, you are ready to plant. Well before your planting day, prepare markers or flags with the names of the plants or seeds you will be planting. Before anyone begins to plant, place the markers in your garden in the exact place you want the plant or seeds to go. Then place the actual seeds or plants as close as possible to the space where they will go, without blocking the planting area.

Next, get all your tools ready. Children work best with hand tools. Our experience has shown us that preschoolers and kindergartners often have difficulty handling long-handled tools safely. They have an incredible urge to swing hoes up over the shoulder, and this can be disastrous if other children are standing behind when it happens. After a few nerve-wracking experiences, we started using hand trowels and cultivator forks. If the soil in your garden is easy to work, these are sufficient. If you have older children (second or third graders, for example), you may want to experiment with long-handled tools for bigger jobs, but carefully instruct the children in their use and closely monitor them. In addition to trowels, we also keep a large supply of gloves in both adult and child sizes. Many adults prefer to wear gloves, and we like to give children the same option. Children's garden gloves are easily obtainable at discount stores and garden centers.

Explain the planting procedure to teachers and volunteers who are helping. Be sure they understand how to plant the seeds or transplants they will be dealing with. This won't be a problem if you have experienced gardeners, but novices will need basic information, such as the following:

- Some seeds are broadcast over a general area, and some are planted in holes. Read the package directions carefully to find out how to plant each type of seed.
- Most seeds need to be planted at a depth no greater than two or three times their size. If planted deeper, they may not come up. Again, seed packages should give clear directions about planting depth. Children may be tempted to dig deep holes to bury seeds. They will need assistance to avoid this common mistake.
- Care is necessary to remove transplants from their packaging. Sometimes the best way to do this is to gently squeeze the container around the roots. As much as possible, avoid pulling on the stems of plants, as they are very fragile. If you simply pull on the plant to remove it, you run the risk of breaking it apart. Special attention should be given to showing children how to do this.

- If plants were grown in biodegradable pots, such as peat pots, they can be planted directly into the ground without being removed from the pot. If the pot is formed of peat, be careful that it is entirely covered with soil or it may dry out easily. You may want to tear off the top part of the pot if it protrudes above the soil level, because the soil should come to the same level it did in the original pot.
- Dig holes slightly larger than the root ball of the plant. (The root ball includes the roots of the plant and the surrounding soil.) Plant the transplants so that they rest at the same soil level as they did in their original containers.
- Before planting transplants, gently tease the roots apart at the bottom. Children love doing this. This helps the roots grow deep into the ground, rather than continuing to grow around in a circle, as they may have done in their original container.
- Once the plant is in the ground, gently pat the soil around it to stabilize it. If you are planting shrubs or trees, get specific planting instructions for them when you make your purchase. You'll probably want to plant these larger plants first.

Once you have given instructions to your assistants, assign children to specific adults. Because this may be the first day the children have actually worked in the garden, they are apt to be enthusiastic, so it is best to keep groups small. Sometimes we have been able to assign each child to a single adult, but this is not always possible. Two preschool-age children per adult is ideal, and four children is workable if the adult is experienced working with groups of children. Keep your groups small, and let children go in shifts rather than overburdening a volunteer with more children than can be handled easily.

Once all the plants are in the ground, you may want to mulch, although it is not necessary to do this right away. If you choose to mulch, instructions for mulching are given later in this chapter (page 138). You will certainly need to water the garden thoroughly as soon as you are finished planting. This is crucial for transplants as well as for seeds, which need moisture to germinate. Be sure that the garden remains moist over the next few days to ensure germination and allow plants to establish themselves in their new environment.

Once you've built and planted your garden, you're well into your garden project. Now you begin the best times of all, as your garden becomes a part of every school day. The next sections cover the following information:

- supervising children in the garden
- maintaining the garden
- animals in the garden
- harvesting plants and seeds
- sharing your garden with others

Supervising Children in the Garden

If children have regular access to the garden because it is located where they play, many garden activities will occur informally during the time children are playing outside. However, sometimes more formal activities need to take place that require closer attention from an adult. Examples of these activities include planting, weeding, deadheading, and harvesting. Supervising a large number of children in these activities can be difficult, especially if your garden is located away from the space where the children normally play outside. We find it is best to limit the number of children involved in these activities so that an adult is able to keep a close eye on what the children are doing and provide appropriate guidance. For preschoolers, the optimal number of children seems to be four or five, depending on their ages. Since few programs have ratios of one adult to four or five children, it may be helpful to enlist volunteers to assist during these times. Parents are often happy to help. (We have had more parents volunteer to help with gardening than with any other activity.) Many communities have garden clubs whose members would jump at the chance to involve children in their favorite hobby. And if you are near a college or university, you may be able to recruit student volunteers. Many fraternities, sororities, and other campus organizations are often looking for service projects. All you have to do is ask.

Consider separating children into pairs and assigning specific tasks to each set of partners. By providing each child with a partner, you also set the stage for negotiation and problem solving as children learn to cooperate to accomplish goals.

When you're working in the garden with children, inevitably someone is going to make a mistake. Sometimes a child trying to pick a flower will pull up the whole plant. Or a child will pull up a cherished plant, mistaking it for a weed. Sara had a hard time holding her tongue the day she learned that a volunteer, who was helping the children weed, had pulled up the Job's tears Sara had carefully nurtured from seeds. But learn to take such actions in stride. Sometimes the plant can be placed back in the ground with little harm done. Even if the plant is past saving, the damage done to it is less than the damage you could do by overreacting. Remember that the garden project is a learning experience. In this case, the children learned that sometimes when you pull a plant up, roots and all, it dies.

If your garden is located on your outdoor play space, the children have access to this section anytime they are outside. You will need to watch the children carefully, and if they move into the garden area, always position a teacher nearby. Children are natural explorers, and they will often be tempted to pick unripe vegetables or flowers that are being saved for a special activity. This can be disappointing to other children when the group has made plans for harvesting. With a teacher nearby, watching and redirecting, problems are less likely to occur. The teacher will also be more likely to optimize teachable moments, because she will be more aware of the children's interests.

Because children do like to dig and explore, give them some space where they can do this without damaging the plants in the main garden. Set aside a small plot where children can dig and plant seeds, and plant and dig up plants as much as they like. You can label this area with a sign that says, "Digging Area." Keep a crate or other storage unit with trowels and gardening gloves near the area so children don't need to ask a teacher for tools. You may be able to pick up plants for this area by asking a store with a garden center to let you occasionally go through plants they plan to discard. You can often find a few healthy plants among the dying.

Some areas of a garden may require props if the children are to get the most out of them. For instance, we built a trellis house that grew over with vines every summer. We wanted children to get the feeling of being inside this wonderful environment, where gourds hung down from overhead and vines crept over the windows, but the empty house had limited appeal. By allowing the children to bring boards and crates inside and to build tables and chairs with them, we opened up many opportunities for dramatic play. One year the children didn't seem to be moving into the house to play at all, so we placed a table and chairs inside and added dishes. Immediately children began to play inside the trellis house. After this we periodically changed the materials inside to keep the children interested and motivated.

We had a similar situation occur the year we built our first sunflower house. At first the children didn't seem to notice the open area inside. By adding a blanket and books, we were able to show children the possibilities of this area. Soon they were inside, snuggling up with a teacher or a friend as they read together. By varying the materials, we were able to expand the interest in the sunflower house. From these experiences we learned that if the children are not as interested in the garden as we would like them to be, we need to modify the environment to introduce new forms of play.

Maintaining the Garden

Once your planting is finished, you should devise a system for maintaining the garden. You need to ensure that plants receive adequate moisture and that weeds are kept in check so that your plants flourish. You may also need to fertilize the garden to be sure plants receive plenty of nutrients. If you want flowers to continue to develop as long as possible, you need to deadhead, or cut away, old flowers. In addition, think about ways to help staff and volunteers identify the plants.

Mulching

Mulching the garden is one of the wisest steps you can take to retain moisture in the garden and reduce the weed population. Many types of mulch are available. In selecting one, consider your budget, as well as appearance. Also, in some regions certain mulches are readily available, but other mulches are difficult to find. You may want to use several mulches so children can observe and compare the effectiveness of each. One of the most common mulches is bark or wood chips. You can purchase these by the bag at garden centers and discount stores, but it is more economical to buy in quantity from a nursery. Beware of wood chips donated by a utility company. These can contain substances—such as herbicides, insecticides, and poison ivy—that you don't want in your garden. Sometimes sheets of black plastic or landscape fabric are used as mulch, but be aware that water will not penetrate the plastic. Other mulches include grass clippings, newspaper, straw, leaves, pine needles, and sawdust.

Mulching is always an appealing experience for the children. When we gardened together, we used shredded bark mulch, which the university grounds staff dumped in a large pile by our garden. The children filled child-size wheelbarrows with the mulch and wheeled it to the part of the garden where they would be working. Amazingly, some children would spend a couple of hours on this task. Supervise carefully when children are applying mulch, because it is easy to inadvertently bury tender young plants.

One important practice when mulching is to first check that the soil has warmed up from early spring. Mulch helps the soil maintain a cool temperature, which is beneficial in the hot summer but not desirable when you are planting seeds or young seedlings in the spring. Maintain a mulch depth of two to four inches around annuals, perennials, and shrubs. You may apply mulch as deep as six inches around large trees. But do not mulch closely to the stem or branches of any of the plants. Leave a little breathing room (about an inch). The stems and branches need air circulation to avoid rotting or being weakened. It is okay if some of the mulch touches the plant—just avoid tightly mulching around the plant.

Weeding and Watering

Set up a schedule for watering and weeding. In our area, we water once a week unless it rains. Depending on your climate, you may need to water more or less. Find out what is recommended for your area. Because we want to give plants about an inch of water a week, we use a rain gauge to check rainfall. If we get an inch of rain over a week's time, we don't water. By monitoring a rain gauge, children gain an understanding of how we need to supplement nature in caring for our garden.

The biggest chore in gardening is weeding. The best way to keep weeds under control is to teach the children how to identify the weeds and make it a habit to survey the garden daily, removing any weeds that are cropping up. Weeds are much easier to tackle when they are small. Also, make surveying for weeds a weekly event. Controlling weeds is why you need to keep your garden a manageable size. If your garden is small, you may be able to keep the children interested long enough to weed your garden regularly. Children quickly learn to identify weeds and remove them.

If you have a large garden, the children cannot be expected to do all the weeding. You will need to come up with a plan to keep up with the weeds. Perhaps you can select a weekly weeding day and invite parents and community gardeners to join you for the fun.

We like to pull most of our weeds by hand. This is easier if the ground is damp, so water the day before you weed. We like pulling weeds because the weeds are less likely to come back if they are pulled, and it also gives us an opportunity to examine the different root systems of plants with the children. However, if you have large areas of weeds, using a hoe is much quicker. If you are going to hoe, having an adult do the work is safer for the plants and the children. If you let children hoe, monitor them closely.

Feeding Your Plants

If you start out your garden with rich compost, it may do well the first year without any additional fertilizer. However, for the healthiest plants, especially after the first year, you'll want to add nutrients to your garden. If you garden in containers, you need to feed your plants, as repeated watering washes nutrients out of the pot. Many good fertilizers are available, and your choice will depend on the age of the children and how you use the fertilizer.

For the children's use, we prefer natural, organic fertilizers, because they pose less risk for children than chemical fertilizers. You have many choices here, such as blood meal, bonemeal, seasoned manure, cottonseed meal, fish meal, seaweed, and fish emulsion fertilizer. While many adults balk at the disagreeable smell of fish emulsion fertilizer, children seem to have a special affinity for anything adults find disgusting. They also enjoy using substances such as manure, which appeal to their sense of humor. If you use manure, make sure it is well aged. Fresh manure may have undesirable weed seeds and potentially have pathogens, such as *E. coli*, or parasites, such as tapeworms. Additionally, fresh manure can burn the plants, causing them to weaken and possibly die. This damage occurs because fresh manure—the same is true for freshly made wood chips and sawdust—is high in nitrogen. As it decomposes, the manure may rob nutrients from the plants and soil and may cause dehydration, thus leading to weakness or death. You can buy manure at your local garden store or nursery, or you may be able to find a farmer who would be happy to share some aged manure that would be safe to use.

Deadheading

If you want your flowers to keep blooming throughout the season, you'll need to remove the spent flowers. Herbs will quit producing as well if their flowers are allowed to go to seed. Once the flower of a plant dies, the plant begins to make seeds in order to reproduce. Seed production is a signal to the plant to quit making flowers. You can interrupt this signal by removing the flower so

the plant will make more flowers in its determined effort to reproduce. This process is called deadheading.

There are many opinions about the best way to deadhead, but for your purposes the process is simple. Simply cut the flower off. We try to cut flowers in time to use them for decoration or activities in the classroom, but the flowers often bloom faster than we can work. Sometimes we take the children out with scissors and let them cut to their hearts' content. Pulling the spent bloom off is acceptable but not as clean and somewhat risky. Many flower heads are tough to pull off, and if not done carefully, the plant can be damaged or completely pulled out of the ground. It's also important to remove the entire seed pod and the petals (not just the petals). This is an easier task for children if they use scissors, plus it helps them focus on carefully removing one at a time. If you have mums in your garden, you should cut them back a couple of times over the summer before they bloom so you'll have compact, healthy blooms in the fall. If stems are very tough, children's scissors may not be sufficient for cutting. In this case, we use pruning shears and either deadhead ourselves or closely supervise one child at a time with the shears.

Labeling

Label plants if you have a number of people spending time in a garden. While you may have a clear idea of what you planted and where you put it, other visitors to the garden may have trouble identifying what plant is which. Also, plant labels add to the children's literacy as they begin to match the spoken with the written word. We have experimented with a number of labels over the years and found that most have both positive and negative attributes. Do you want labels that are easy to read, that will last, or that the children can make? Think about whether the labels have sharp parts, how well they will

stay in place once you put them in the garden, and how well they will survive the weather.

There are many ways to make labels. For instance, children can cover seed packets with clear self-adhesive paper and attach them to a stick. They can also use Popsicle sticks or other pieces of wood to make labels, writing the name of the plant with a marker. Homemade labels are great for helping children feel ownership of the garden. You will find many innovative ideas for making labels available online. Some use flowerpots, wooden spoons, or rocks and are attractive additions to the garden.

Plant markers are also available for purchase. The least expensive kinds are simple plastic sticks with pointed ends that you push into the ground. We haven't found these to be effective for use with children, since the name of the plant is sideways once the marker is in the ground and children have to turn their heads to read them. This is confusing for children who are just learning to read. We use these to label seed trays, but we do not use them in the garden. Some markers are plastic with space to write horizontally at the top. These are somewhat expensive, and the writing must be small, but they are easy to read. Experiment with different types of markers to see what works for you. Let children work with a variety of materials to come up with their own plant labels. They may surprise you with some of their ideas.

To Bug or Not to Bug

We use the word *bug* throughout this book to refer to small insects and other creatures, such as spiders, pill bugs, millipedes, and the like that are found in the garden. This is common usage, but we do want to point out that these are not true bugs. Technically, a bug is an insect that belongs to the order Hemiptera. Cicadas and aphids are true bugs, but many of the creatures we refer to as bugs are not. Some experts suggest that we refer to these other insects, arachnids, arthropods, and so on as small animals or small creatures instead of bugs. We think this is a terrific idea and encourage you to do so. However, like the individual who believes in vegetarianism as a principle but can't quite seem to carry it off, we will continue to use the word bug. It expresses what we want to express in easily understandable terms without confusion.

Garden Creatures

No matter how small your garden, you will find that it attracts animals. These may be miniscule insects and other bugs or mammals, such as rabbits, squirrels, chipmunks, and deer. One question you'll have to ask is whether these animals are friend or foe—a more complex question than it seems at first glance. For instance, some gardeners spend many hours devising methods to keep squirrels out of their gardens and bird feeders. Indeed, squirrels will steal from the garden, and they will eat food intended for our feathered friends. But in the children's garden they offer much opportunity for study. One fascinating experience occurred when a mother squirrel built her nest in the hollow of a tree just a few feet outside our playground fence. The children and teachers enjoyed following the growth of the two babies and observing their antics as they chased each other around the trunk of the tree. We would not have traded this experience for a better harvest or more food for the birds. In fact, the university campus was so heavily populated with squirrels that it would have been impossible to discourage them from inhabiting our playground, even if we didn't have a garden. We learned to live with them and to grow a little more so there was enough to share. Establishing such an attitude toward wildlife is an important part of managing a garden when children are involved. Advantage must always be weighed against disadvantage.

In addition, the safety of the children is of utmost importance. Chemical pesticides should never be used in an area that is to be inhabited by children. We have found that by choosing hardy plants we are able to maintain a healthy garden and that pests are rarely so destructive that they completely kill a plant. In the cases where a plant does die from pests, we use the opportunity as a learning experience and may eliminate that plant from the garden the next year.

If you notice that something is damaging or stealing your crops, the first thing you should do is find out what is happening. Involve the children in the process. This is a good time to bring out their investigative skills. When you notice the problem, ask the children what they think could be causing it. Accept all their answers. Write them down so you can follow up with further investigation. Some steps you and the children can take to determine who the culprit is include the following:

- Look at the plant carefully. Do you see any insects on it? Get out a magnifying glass. Now can you see anything? Shake the leaves over a piece of white paper, and examine again with a magnifying glass. Very small creatures, such as spider mites, that aren't apparent on the leaf may be visible against the white paper. If you find something, consult a reference book, the Internet, or a gardening expert to help you identify it. Be sure to include the children in this process.

Homemade Insecticides

Garlic Bug Spray

5 cloves garlic
1 quart water
cheesecloth

1. Mash garlic cloves, and remove skin.
2. Add garlic to water. Let sit overnight.
3. Strain garlic water through cheesecloth. Pour into spray bottle. Use to spray pesky insects.

Soap Bug Spray

½ cup liquid soap or detergent
1 gallon water

1. Gently mix soap with water, so as not to make too many bubbles.
2. Pour mixture into spray bottles, and spray on pests.

Garlic and Soap Bug Spray

1 quart hot water
4 cloves garlic
2 tablespoons liquid soap
cheesecloth

1. Crush and peel the garlic.
2. Add the garlic to the hot water. Gently stir in the soap so that it doesn't bubble too much.
3. Let sit overnight.
4. Strain the mixture through cheesecloth, and pour into spray bottles. Spray on bothersome bugs.

- If you can't find anything on the plant, spend some time observing the plant in its environment. Encourage the children to watch carefully while they are in or near the garden. They may spot a rabbit, bird, or other animal going into the garden.

- Do some research if you still can't figure out what is happening. You can start by looking through reference books or searching online, or you may want to involve the children in some active investigation. Children can start by interviewing their parents. Most schools will have some parents who have a lot of gardening experience and can come up with the answer. Another possibility is to call in a gardening expert. You can usually find someone through your extension service or at a garden center. If you can't get someone to come to you, take a piece of the damaged plant to a garden center for analysis.

Once you have determined what is damaging your plants, you'll need to decide what to do about it. Decide on a safe way to tackle the problem if you decide you want to eliminate the pest. The children should be instrumental in making this decision. Consider the following options:

- Leave it alone. Sometimes the culprit has caused minimal damage, or is so interesting that you don't really want to discourage it from coming to your garden.

- Research different ways to deal with the pest. For instance, if birds are stealing from your garden, have the children interview family members to come up with ways to keep the birds out of the garden. Since there are many ways to keep birds away, the children will probably come up with a variety of ideas. (If you don't really want to keep the birds away, then relax. Although many gardeners use scarecrows or models of owls or snakes to get rid of birds, these methods aren't terribly effective. If your birds aren't scared off by children running and yelling, it's doubtful they'll be bothered by scarecrows. Chances are you'll still have plenty of birds to study.)

- Use a pesticide spray, but avoid using chemical pesticides. Soap sprays are particularly effective, but applications need to be repeated regularly. Some recipes include pepper, which can be effective. Even so, we prefer not to use pepper sprays with children since they could get it in their eyes or mouths. Oil can also be effective, as it sticks to the bodies of the pests, but it can be harder on the plants, particularly in extreme heat. Spray

Plants That Deter Insects

Some plants are believed to keep away insects. Try planting the following among your other plants to see if they repel pests:

asters

chrysanthemums

geraniums

marigolds

onions

calendulas

cautiously at first, testing one leaf to see how the plant reacts. Spray in the cooler part of the day so that the plant will be less stressed. If all is well, you will want to spray thoroughly, making sure you get the undersides of the leaves as well as the tops, once a week. Children seem to have an undying enthusiasm for spraying plants with squirt bottles, so getting them involved is usually easy. If your children are less interested, you can use the opportunity to inspect plants when they are not sprayed and compare them to when they are. Here we have included some recipes for safe sprays that can be used by children. You can find other recipes online.

- Use insects to get rid of insects. Many people know that ladybugs eat aphids, and ladybug releases are becoming increasingly common. However, ladybugs are not the best insect predators. Other insects, such as green lacewings, have more voracious appetites. Beneficial insects are now being used more than ever in controlling garden pests and can be purchased from a variety of sources. Some of these are listed in appendix

- By introducing predators into the garden, you can help the children gain a concrete understanding of the food chain. *Good Bug, Bad Bug: Who's Who, What They Do, and How to Manage Them Organically: All You Need to Know about the Insects in Your Garden* by Jessica Walliser is a good reference book to help you learn more about both beneficial insects and pests.

- Remove the plant. This may be the best option if the plant is diseased and there is no cure for the disease or if the only cure would be dangerous for the children. If the disease poses no threat to the rest of your garden, you may also choose to leave the plant and let the children observe the progress of the disease.

Animals in the Garden

As you involve children in studying and making decisions about the garden ecosystem, they will begin to understand the interdependence between the plants and animals. As a teacher, the more you learn about the animals you encounter, the more you will be able to foster the children's awareness. The following are descriptions of just a few creatures you may find in your garden. This information is included to give you an initial understanding. If you do encounter these animals, you will want to involve the children in further study. Reference books are valuable in this process, and in the appendixes you will find a list of some excellent books about these creatures.

The Good Guys

You will definitely want to invite some animals into your garden. Many adults sometimes have difficulty discriminating between beneficial creatures and pests. Here are some insights into attracting and studying just a few of the animals that are helpful to the gardener.

WORMS

Worms are wonderful! Worms are great! Worms till the soil, bringing oxygen to the roots of plants. They eat organic matter and turn it into fertilizer. If you want to check the health of your soil, count your worms. The more worms you have, the better the soil is likely to be. Also, consider starting a worm composter. You can purchase worms by the pound, and they'll eat your left-

over fruits and vegetables. The resultant castings can be put in your garden to help your plants grow. What other creature does so much?

Worms are also great subjects for study. Give them a choice between a damp and a dry environment, and watch them scurry over to the damp. Give them the opportunity and they will choose to be in the dark rather than the light. On pages 203–7, you'll find some experiments you can try with worms. Our favorite activity with earthworms is simple in design. We simply put worms out for the children to explore and make sure a teacher is available to guide their interactions with and observations of the worms. To do this, we use cafeteria trays, but any trays or pans with a lip will do. We put moist paper towels on the trays to prevent the worms from drying out and dying. This is essential anytime you take worms out of their environment for a period of time. Then we put several worms on each tray. The worms are a virtual child magnet. We have had children spend an entire hour exploring worms in this manner. We also do this with pill bugs, or roly-polys, which can be found under rocks or rotting wood in the garden or other natural areas. In chapter 7 we describe some more-sophisticated experiments.

BEES

Bees are some of the most fascinating insects around. Most children know that bees make honey. Some people think they do this by collecting pollen. Actually, bees collect nectar from flowers to make honey. As they do this, they pick up pollen and carry it from flower to flower, performing the essential job of pollination. Bees are so essential to agriculture that farmers often pay bee-keepers to keep bees on their farms or in their orchards. As common as these insects are, many misconceptions exist. Help children understand some facts about bees.

The bees you see in the garden are worker bees. These are all females. The only job the male bees (drones) have is to mate with the queen bee, so they stay back at the hive. Only female bees sting. The male bee has no stinger. (Therefore, if you have been singing "I'm Bringing Home a Baby Bumblebee" and including the words, "Ouch, he stung me," you are scientifically incorrect!)

Bees sting only when they are afraid or feel threatened. Bees die once they have stung, so they don't go around looking for opportunities to attack. Teach children how to behave properly around bees to avoid stings. Some adults are terrible role models for this. As soon as they see a bee, they start swinging their arms and flailing around. The message to the bee is clear: this person is trying to kill me. This is the likeliest way to be stung. Teach children to move slowly around bees. If children stand still or move with caution, the bees will not feel threatened, and they will not sting. In fact, bees will often land on people and walk around on them without posing a threat, so long as the person remains quiet. If you can teach yourself to remain calm around bees, you will be a great role model for children.

Some children are highly allergic to bee stings. If you have such a child in your program, you may want to avoid plants that draw a lot of bees. You should also work with the child's parents to develop a plan of action in case the child is stung.

LADYBUGS

Ladybugs, also known as ladybird beetles, are favored garden predators. Few children can resist picking up a ladybug and letting it crawl across their hands. These are gentle creatures, and their hearty appetite for that unwelcome garden pest the aphid makes them welcome visitors to a garden. If you want to introduce ladybugs to your garden, you can often buy them from commercial suppliers. You can increase the likelihood that the ladybugs will stay in your garden by dampening the plants before releasing them and choosing a release time early in the morning or late in the day. Also, be sure to place them at the base of plants actually infested with aphids, rather than simply letting them go anywhere. If they have food to eat, they'll be less likely to flee. Be sure to do some research about ladybugs so that you will be able to identify the larvae. Though not as attractive as the mature beetles, the larvae have more voracious appetites and are the key to maintaining a population of ladybugs in your garden.

PRAYING MANTISES

An impressive creature with bulging eyes and long legs, the praying mantis is often found in gardens. The name comes from the way the mantis positions its front legs, as though it is praying. The praying mantis is the only insect that can look over its shoulder, giving it a rather quizzical appearance. These insects are often hard to spot, as their protective coloration serves them well in the garden environment. They have big appetites and will eat even large insects, such as grasshoppers and bees. Their only drawback is that they're as likely to eat beneficial insects as they are pests.

If you don't have any praying mantises in your garden, you can purchase egg cases from commercial suppliers. To provide for closer observation by the children, these can be hatched inside. You'll need to do this in the early spring, usually late April or early May. (You can buy the egg cases earlier than this and refrigerate them until your area is frost-free.)

Place the egg case in a jar. Be sure to place a couple of layers of cheese-cloth or pantyhose over the top of the jar before you put on a lid with holes punched in it. The hatchlings are tiny, and we have heard stories of them escaping through the holes in a jar lid. An egg case holds up to two hundred eggs, so this could result in more excitement than you want!

Release the nymphs soon after they hatch, because they'll be hungry, and newly hatched nymphs may eat each other if they don't have sufficient food. However, you may want to keep one nymph to observe indoors. You likely won't see the ones you release outside. They're very small, and they may leave the area or be eaten by other predators. It takes five months for a nymph to grow to full-size.

SPIDERS

Spiders are not only good garden predators, they are fascinating subjects for study. Their intricately designed webs are marvels of geometry, and their penchant for wrapping their prey with silk before feasting makes them especially engaging to young children. Be sure to let children know that spiders are not insects but arachnids. Children can learn to tell the difference by counting legs. Insects have six; arachnids have eight.

You should be cautious about handling spiders. While most poisonous varieties do not hang out in the garden, some spiders will bite when provoked, so most varieties are best observed without handling. The only exception we make to this rule is with daddy longlegs, which technically are arachnids but not spiders. They are gentle, harmless, and easily identifiable.

If you let children hold a daddy longlegs, supervise closely, since their delicate legs are easily damaged. We require that children hold them with open hands only and return them immediately after examination to the place where they were found.

Trevor saw a daddy longlegs outside by the climber. He tried to step on it, but I stopped him. I showed Trevor and Marquis how to hold the daddy longlegs gently. I explained to them that the daddy longlegs isn't a spider but is an arachnid and that spiders are arachnids too. We looked at how delicate and long its legs are. The boys were a little frightened at first, but they became braver as they spent more time with the arachnid.

They dropped it a few times, as it tickled their hands and arms, but the daddy longlegs was all right. The boys picked it up and tried again. They took turns holding it. We talked about what to do with the daddy longlegs. Trevor thought it should go in the garden where it would be safe away from the children. After a while, Trevor and Marquis put the daddy longlegs on a sunflower. The arachnid dropped to the ground and crawled away.

I felt proud of Trevor. He had wanted to kill the daddy longlegs because he was afraid of it, and he almost did. If I hadn't caught his foot before it hit the daddy longlegs, this experience would not have happened. But with just a little guidance, Trevor was able to refocus and study the arachnid. He realized that the arachnid wouldn't hurt him, and he and Marquis became the protector of the daddy longlegs when they found a safe place for it in the garden.

FROGS AND TOADS

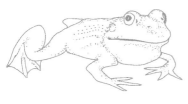

Frogs and toads are voracious eaters and will help keep down the insect and slug population in your garden. If you are lucky enough to have these amphibians near your garden, the children will enjoy capturing and studying them. Just be sure to release them at the end of the day at the same spot where they were found. You can make a home for a toad by partially burying a terra-cotta flowerpot on its side. If you plant a hosta or a daylily in front of the opening, the plant will provide extra protection for the toad.

SNAKES

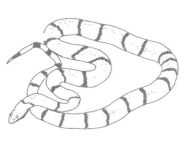

That's right, snakes are good guys in the garden. One of the most maligned animals in history, the snake does more than its share of the work in keeping down the pest population, feeding on insects and small animals, such as mice and rats. Many adults react with panic when they see snakes, passing their prejudices and fears down to the next generation. Since young children don't come with preconceptions about these reptiles, an adult who can model respect and appreciation for snakes can go a long way in building positive attitudes.

Few species of snakes in the United States are poisonous, and these are not likely to be attracted to a garden in temperate regions such as ours. (Of course, if you should find yourself with a poisonous variety, call animal control to remove it immediately.) In addition, snakes are shy creatures and usually flee when they encounter humans. You may have to be warier of snakes if you live in a region where poisonous snakes are common, as are rattlesnakes in the Southwest. Also, if you live in Florida or nearby, you may need to watch out for nonnative species of snakes that have been released into the wild either accidently or purposely by pet owners and reptile enthusiasts. Pythons have invaded the Everglades to the point that they are seriously threatening the mammal population. Such snakes thrive in the warm, humid climate, and their threat should be taken seriously (U.S. Geological Survey 2012).

Still, if you are lucky enough to have a snake visit, use the opportunity for a learning experience. Let the children observe from a distance. If you feel the snake absolutely must go, find someone who knows how to handle snakes and have the snake humanely removed and relocated. If you do this, the children will learn that all animals deserve respect.

The Bad Guys

You'll have the opportunity to get to know a lot of insects and other bugs in the garden. Many of these will enjoy chomping the leaves of the plants you have so carefully nurtured. You will probably want to rid the garden of some of these pests. Some of them can be handpicked or simply washed off the plants with a strong stream of water. Others will need to be sprayed with safe insecticide—a soap or other safe spray. You may even want to try using beneficial insects (see ladybugs and praying mantises, above) to control the population of damage-causing bugs. Listed below are some common garden pests.

APHIDS

Aphids are small, soft-bodied insects that feed on the sap of plants. They can often be found clustered around the buds and stems. Aphids can be white, black, or green. If you have them, you may notice deformed buds or flowers or stunted growth. Plants with aphids will be more susceptible to disease. The simplest form of control is washing them off the plant, but you may also choose to use a safe spray to control them. Ladybugs and ladybug larvae like to eat aphids, so you may want to bring some aphids and ladybugs into the classroom to observe.

SPIDER MITES

Spider mites are tiny arachnids that are almost invisible to the eye. They suck the sap out of leaves, and the first sign that you have them may be that your leaves begin to "bronze," or take on a brown discoloration. The leaves will eventually die and drop off the plants. Another sign of spider mites is fine webbing between the leaves and stems of your plants. Spider mites are most prevalent during the hot, dry days of summer. To check for spider mites, shake the damaged leaves over a sheet of white paper. Observe carefully, using a magnifying glass if possible. If you see tiny spots that move, there's a good chance you have spider mites. The safest control is to use a strong, fine stream of water to knock them off the plants.

BEETLES

A number of beetles like to eat plants, but some beetles, such as the ladybug, are good for the garden. Be sure to identify beetles to learn if they are friend or foe. Some beetles, such as cucumber beetles and Japanese beetles, can do a great deal of damage in a short time as they chew on your leaves and flowers. The simplest control is to pick them off by hand.

CATERPILLARS

Caterpillars can have voracious appetites and can cause a great deal of damage to plants. Fortunately, they are easy to spot and can be picked off plants easily. However, don't be too quick to remove caterpillars. While some can do a great amount of damage in a short period of time, you don't want to get rid of a caterpillar that could become a beautiful butterfly. Reference books on butterflies and moths will help you identify which caterpillar you have, and you can also do an Internet search to identify your caterpillar. If you decide to capture a caterpillar and bring it inside to observe, be sure to find out what kind it is and what it eats. Some caterpillars are very particular and will die if they don't have the exact food they require.

ANTS

Keep an eye out for ants. Our children became fascinated with the ants in our garden and worked hard at counting anthills and documenting their experiences with ants. While ants don't do any harm to the garden themselves, they are attracted to honeydew, which is a substance excreted by insects such as aphids, mealybugs, whiteflies, and scales. Ants sometimes even carry aphids to healthy plants to keep up the production of honeydew. While we don't advocate trying to rid your garden of ants, if you have ants, you should check to see if they are an indication of other insects.

SLUGS AND SNAILS

Slugs and snails make fascinating research subjects for indoor study. These slimy creatures (which are related to clams and oysters) can be interesting pets if kept in an aquarium. They're easy to tell apart, since snails have a hard shell and slugs are soft-bodied. Because they leave a shiny trail wherever they go, children enjoy searching for them in the garden.

Slugs and snails must remain moist at all times, so they usually hide in damp places during the day and come out at night to feed. For this reason, you

Slug Trap

1 tablespoon dry yeast
¼ cup sugar
3 cups warm water

1 Mix the yeast and sugar in the warm water.

2 Place a shallow can or pan with straight sides in the problem area of the garden. (Tuna cans or old baking pans work well for this. The goal is for the slugs to be able to get in but not out.)

3 Fill the pan with the yeast mixture. Check the next morning to see if you have caught any slugs.

may not see them eating your plants, but the signs that they have been around are often clear.

You should avoid snail bait, as it is dangerous for young children; and beer, the favorite bait of many gardeners, is probably not appropriate for most early childhood programs. We have included a recipe for a yeast-based bait that you can try. Our children, who were annoyed that slugs were decimating our hostas, became enthusiastic in their quest to drown the slugs in this mixture (see sidebar). We can't vouch for its effectiveness, as we didn't catch any slugs, but the experience of making it was worthwhile. Our slug problem was solved once our hostas grew and became healthy enough to withstand some munching.

BIRDS

Okay, we don't really think birds are pests. We love them and want them to visit our garden, and children will spend many hours observing, drawing, and recording their observations about birds. However, if the birds are consuming your blueberries or carrying off your sunflower seeds before you have a chance to harvest them, you may find the birds annoying. If you do, discuss the problem with the children, and determine together what you want to do.

MAMMALS

Depending on where you live, you may have a variety of species of mammals that visit your garden. Squirrels, rabbits, and chipmunks visited our school garden. There are also raccoons and deer in our area, and Sara saw both a coyote and a fox checking out her home garden after her husband deposited some rabbit manure on a raised bed. Because we have enjoyed our encounters with animals in our school garden, we haven't made any serious attempts to keep them away, even though we have been frustrated at times by their intrusion.

For example, it took us three years to grow a sunflower house because the squirrels kept stealing the seeds. The chipmunks were blamed for eating all of the ferns we planted in the dinosaur garden and for uprooting our morning glory seedlings. (We can't be sure this is what happened, but these were the conclusions the children came to after studying the situation. In fact, slugs may have been at fault for the disappearance of the ferns.) In the case of the sunflower house, we simply kept trying new techniques until one worked—planting three packets of seed and hoping at least some would come up. In other situations we gave up—ferns are expensive, so we decided we would have to do without. You will also want to evaluate any damage mammals do to your garden and determine what, if any, steps you want to take to deal with them.

We do want to caution you in two areas. First, be aware that some mammals carry rabies and other diseases. Whenever you see a sick or strange-acting animal in or near your garden, you should call animal control. This happened to us only a couple of times during more than a decade, but it is important that children be kept away from sick animals, which are likely to bite if disturbed.

The other concern you may need to deal with is children chasing the animals. The squirrels on our campus were accustomed to people and very brave. Because of this, they came close to the children. Children delight in chasing squirrels, so we spent a great deal of energy curbing this behavior. We were aware that a child could corner a squirrel, which then could bite out of fear. We believe that children should be taught that chasing any wild animal is unacceptable behavior.

Harvesting

Once your garden is established, you can reap the educational benefits of harvesting with young children. Much learning occurs through picking, preparing, and using flowers, produce, and herbs. Again, you play a vital role in the learning process through modeling and guiding in small groups. Programs with summer sessions will find harvesting to be a perpetual source of joy to

the children. You can do many things with your harvest, some of which are presented in the sections that follow.

Picking and Cleaning

The children may need help identifying when a particular fruit, vegetable, or herb is ready for harvest. You can facilitate this process by providing a variety of reference books with color photographs of the plants in the garden. Then, if children are unsure about the readiness of a particular plant, they can be referred to these resources. Key words such as *green, unripe, ripe, overripe, rotten,* and *spoiled* should be emphasized. Coaching may be needed for harvesting techniques for various plants. Some require clipping, while others lend themselves to snapping, digging, cutting, or pulling. Use these terms with children to build vocabulary and understanding.

We suggest you also incorporate various math skills into harvesting. For instance, when we harvested our green beans, we asked each child to look at the bowl full of beans and to estimate how many were there. Then we counted the actual number of beans, which turned out to be much higher than predicted. Next, we snapped the beans into smaller pieces for cooking. At this point, the children wanted to guess and count again. We did, with some guesses getting much closer the second time. Similarly, the weight of pumpkins can be predicted and measured with a scale, and the length of carrots can

---

July 23, 2012

8:47 PM — Avery helped pick tomatoes today. We decided we hit the jackpot because we had been on vacation and we found a lot of ripe tomatoes. We counted them. There were 8 Early Girls. 17 were rotten. We had so many cherry tomatoes that we decided to count them by fives. We used cupcake tins to sort them by fives. We counted by 5's to 130, then added the one more. We harvested 131 in all! We are going to make salsa tomorrow with the tomatoes plus the basil from our garden.

counting by 5's

---

be estimated and determined with a ruler. Children can also learn to classify and sort while harvesting. For example, peppers can be sorted into piles of red and green, hot and mild.

Produce should be rinsed thoroughly under running water after harvest and before cooking. We used large colanders at child-size sinks so children could become fully engaged in this process. Be sure you use food preparation sinks and not hand-washing sinks for washing the produce. Take photographs at all stages of picking and cleaning, and record children's comments and reactions in group or individual journals.

Cooking

Gardening leads to cooking, and cooking leads to wonderful learning opportunities. Children read recipe charts, measure ingredients, learn about sanitation and safety, observe changes in matter, and experience the nutritional benefits of gardening firsthand. Many parents are shocked to find out that their children ate raw broccoli or red leaf lettuce at school, when they have never done so at home. The key here seems to be motivation. When children feel invested in something, they are more willing to take risks to reap the benefits of their labor. The act of gardening exposes the children to the taste, smell, and texture of many new vegetables and herbs.

Teachers can incorporate literacy skills into cooking by providing various cookbooks and gardening magazines for children to explore. All recipes used for cooking in small groups should be printed on recipe charts. Recipe charts for younger children can include the use of cutout magazine pictures or drawings to facilitate emergent literacy and the awareness of environmental print. We like to read each step of the recipe aloud as we cook, calling attention to key words and mathematical concepts. We recommend laminating your favorite recipe charts.

Recipe cards can also be used to create a workstation for children to use individually or in pairs during work time. For this technique, one step is written and illustrated on each card, beginning with the most basic step of washing your hands and sanitizing the work space. Each of the required steps is then provided on the following cards, including instructions for cleaning and preparing the work space for the next student. This strategy works well with older, more independent children.

When creating recipe charts or cards, be sure to use pictures and symbols in the rebus format to aid children in developing reading skills. Clip art or an Internet search will offer a wide variety of symbols to choose from for your recipe charts. In fact, older preschoolers can assist teachers in making these charts. You can laminate charts that will be used repeatedly. Always use actual cooking terminology to provide the most realistic experience and expose

Journal entry

We invited our parents to a picnic at Child Development Laboratories. We made Purple Pansy Pumpernickel Sandwiches for appetizers. The following dictation was taken:

"We picked the pansies. Then you get some bread. Then you get some cream cheese. You wash the pansies in water. Then you put the pansies on the sandwiches. Then you eat them." Kasey

"You couldn't really taste the flower. It looked like flowers. Half the bread was white. I ate about three." Neil

"I ate the flower. It didn't taste good, but the cream cheese and the bread taste good." Hodge

"They are called pumpernickel pansies sandwiches. It tastes good. It had all good vitamins in it." Dorsey

"I ate a pansy pumpernickel sandwich. It felt soft and fuzzy in my mouth. You can hardly taste the flower." Marla (teacher)

children to new vocabulary. For instance, recipes and charts can require them to *dice* tomatoes, *shred* cabbage, *simmer* green beans, or *marinate* cucumbers.

Children also learn a great deal from preparing one food in a variety of ways. Boil and mash potatoes, bake them whole and as fries, and shred them for potato pancakes. Roast pumpkin seeds, and use the pumpkin to make cookies or pie. Eat cucumbers raw, dice them into a salad, or make them into pickles. Herbs can be dried in open air or in a dehydrator, or they can be used fresh. We used some herbs at school, sending the remainder home with children in clear, labeled storage bags for family cooking.

Remember that experimentation is good and that not every recipe will be a huge success. Once, after our children found three large green tomatoes that had fallen from the vine, we decided to make fried green tomatoes, which was a first for all of us. After the activity, we took dictation from the children. They described the fried

Mint Tea

Cut the mint with scissors.

Wash the mint. Clean it well.

Put the mint in a clean jar.

Fill the jar with cold water.

Set the jar in the warm sun. Leave it there for about six hours. When it is done, it will taste like mint.

Journal entry

Michelle and Kati cut flowers outside. They cecided the flowers would be great for a wedding. Michelle was the bride.

"I was the bride and Jo was the priest."

Kati was the sister who held Michelle's dress.

green tomatoes as "sour," "yucky," and "not so good." The learning experience, however, was wonderful.

We suggest looking for recipes that call for several of the items you have grown in the garden. This reduces your grocery bill and allows the children to see the full potential of the garden. For example, we made salsa, which used tomatoes, red peppers, and green peppers from our garden. We also used these same ingredients later to make mini pizzas on English muffins. Our coleslaw recipe combined carrots and cabbage, and a tossed salad incorporated lettuce, cucumbers, radishes, and tomatoes. Another favorite combination recipe, Basil-Tomato Pie, paired fresh basil with tomatoes. The Internet makes finding recipes easier now than ever.

Many adults and children in our program were especially surprised by the use of flowers as edible ingredients in various recipes. Nasturtiums can be added to salads to make them prettier. Sage flowers can be cut, dipped in batter made from a purchased fritter mix, and fried to make sage brochette. We also created masterpieces such as marigold cheesecake and purple pumpernickel pansy sandwiches. These make excellent recipes for garden parties, picnics, and other festive celebrations, such as birthdays and end-of-the-year events.

Creative Use of Garden Products

In addition to cooking, you can use items harvested from the garden in a variety of ways. You can either leave your gourds in the garden to dry or hang them to dry indoors. Once dry, they can be used to make vases, birdhouses, and maracas, among other items. Zinnias, strawflowers, asters, and marigolds can be used in both fresh and dry flower arrangements. You can also dry herbs and flowers to make sweet-smelling potpourri sachets to give as gifts. Hollyhock dolls (see page 121), created on the playground, can spark creative

dramatic-play scenarios. We suggest you subscribe to garden magazines or ask parents to donate old ones. They are full of creative recipes, ideas, and projects. You will also find hundreds of ideas online on social networking sites, such as Pinterest.

Harvesting and Saving Seeds

When you think about harvesting, don't forget to collect seeds from your garden to plant next year. Children can learn a great deal from identifying, col-

lecting, and saving their own seeds. The seeds of annual plants lend themselves to this process since they fulfill their life cycle in one year. Seeds from biennials and perennials can be salvaged as well. However, seeds from hybrid plants (many vegetables, for example) will not usually grow true to form. This is one good reason to grow heirloom varieties of many vegetables.

Encourage children to take seeds from only healthy, thriving plants and to remove all pulp or fiber from the surface of each seed. The best time to harvest each type of seed will vary from plant to plant. Generally, seeds should be allowed to dry naturally on the plant as long as possible. We suggest you try harvesting seeds from vegetables, such as beans, peas, peppers, pumpkins, and tomatoes. You could also collect seeds from annual flowers, such as zinnias, sunflowers, marigolds, and cosmos. We encourage you to be creative

and experimental in this process. For example, you could take seeds from plants you know are hybrids to allow the children to see whether they breed true.

With help from parents or other volunteers, your class could harvest and sell seeds as a fund-raising project. We know of a class of third and fourth graders who worked with their classroom teacher to harvest seeds and enlisted the supervision of their art teacher in creating marketable seed packets. These students counted seeds, labeled packets with planting instructions, and sold seeds to community members. This clearly provided a valuable lesson in science, math, economics, and communication.

Sharing Your Garden with Others

Throughout the life of your garden, children will use various means to represent what they have learned. When closing a study, children will need assistance in finalizing these representations as they apply and articulate the new concepts they have learned. You can facilitate the final representation of new knowledge by helping children to review garden journals and other records and select their best work. At this point, some children may even want to consolidate their learning by adding dictation to sketches or redrawing them completely to fill in previously missed details. Others will want to write a few final pages in their journal or prepare a presentation using digital media to summarize their thoughts and feelings about the overall gardening process. Children will be motivated to engage in these tasks if they are working toward meaningful goals, such as planning a culminating event or creating a classroom display.

Culminating Events

Culminating events are a great way to bring closure to a study by providing opportunities to exhibit the work of the project to an audience. The active planning of culminating events provides children with the motivation to consolidate and apply newly acquired information. This can be done in a variety of ways, depending on the children's developmental level and individual interests. The teacher needs to guide the children in making decisions about the type of event to plan. The younger the children, the more you will need to lead. For instance, you can suggest an event to younger children and then invite their full participation in the preparations. On the other hand, you can interview elementary students about their ideas for ways to present and communicate their learning to others.

Parties, open houses, and a visit from another class are examples of excellent culminating events. Regardless of the type of event selected, you should think about the audience. Would your children feel comfortable presenting their learning to parents and community members, or would they rather invite another class from your school? Would they like to do an oral presentation with a slide show, perform through drama and song, or provide tours of the garden and other classroom displays? These are decisions that each teacher must make based on the confidence and skill levels of her students.

Our favorite culminating event occurred at the end of summer the first year we had our garden. It was a garden party for families, contributing community members, and other classes at our preschool. The teachers suggested this event to the children and then solicited their ideas and involvement. One of our major concerns in planning this event was to ensure that the children felt ownership of the party and the process. We wanted the party to be full of their ideas and to clearly represent their learning. We started by asking the children how to plan a party. Many of the children knew that invitations were necessary, while others suggested food and games. Some children mentioned wearing party clothes and listening to music at parties they had attended.

Based on the children's prior knowledge of parties, we embarked on the process of planning our culminating event. First, we invited the children to draw garden-related pictures for the invitations on business card–size slips of paper. This allowed for several children's artwork to be used in the final copy. Another way we ensured child ownership was to allow the children to select their favorite recipes, based on the cooking experiences we had previously provided and the current available herbs, flowers, and vegetables in the garden. Our final menu was indeed festive, including marigold cheesecake, basil-tomato pies, chive potato pancakes, and purple pumpernickel pansy sandwiches.

With the party fast approaching, the children prepared to provide guided tours of their favorite sections of the garden to partygoers. One way that we prepared them for this was to hold a garden scavenger hunt, as described in chapter 7. The children were given small cards with the picture and name of a certain plant. In this way, they learned to locate and name the herbs, flowers, and vegetables very quickly. On party day, many guests and parents were impressed by the preschoolers' ability to discriminate between plants such as basil and sage.

To incorporate music, the children selected a favorite song from our new repertoire of songs and poems about gardening to perform at the party. A note was sent home to parents asking for volunteers to play live music in the garden during the event. One parent played the flute, and others agreed to play their guitars. Other festivities included the making of party hats from newspaper, glue, sequins, and feathers, and bubble blowing at the sensory table. The teachers created a program to be used on party day that explained the various sections of the garden and included quotations from the children about each.

For a week before the event, the children harvested produce and prepared food for the party. They weeded the garden, filled bird feeders and birdbaths, and picked up litter from the playground. We also prepared a guest book where visitors could sign in and provide feedback. All of these activities helped children develop social skills and experience a sense of community while working toward the shared goal of hosting a party.

Displays

Displays provide another avenue for children to reflect on and communicate to others what they have learned. Teachers can encourage children to review all relevant sketches, journal entries, and other records they have kept of their work. The children can then form small groups to create murals with clearly labeled details. Some children may choose to represent the various plants in the garden. One way to do this is to transfer the color from each plant onto a large white sheet by pounding it with a rock (see "Crushed Kaleidoscope" activity in chapter 7). Other groups may want to make a mural about the tools and techniques used while mulching, watering, weeding, and deadheading. Yet another group may want to create a mural of a fieldwork site, such as a water garden or flower shop, based on photos, videos, and sketches from the trip.

Photographs taken over the life of the project also lend themselves to beautiful and meaningful displays. In preparation for our garden party, we created four large posters with the following headings: "Before and After," "Planting," "Tending," and "Harvesting." Photographs were mounted on each poster, and then various children were asked to tell what they were doing in each picture. The children's statements were then typed on a computer and printed for mounting on the posters. This was another way for the preschoolers to share what they had been learning with their parents, peers, and visitors.

Displays can be three-dimensional, such as a collection of garden tools, seed packets, soil types, vegetables, reference books, and measurement instruments, like a rain gauge and thermometer. Try preparing one tray full of garden products to stimulate each of the five senses (see "You Fill Up My Senses" in chapter 7). Other displays could involve a collection of matted artwork and handwritten stories created at various stages of the project. Charts and graphs could be included with children's written anecdotal accounts of the scientific processes used. Finally, don't forget to display any concept webs you have created showing the topics covered or any work showing questions that the children have asked and answered during the study, so that families and children can compare beginning knowledge with what the children have learned.

Chapter 6

Gardening with Infants and Toddlers

Relationships are key for infants and toddlers. To learn, they must feel secure in their relationships with the primary adults in their lives. These youngest children are especially vulnerable. Initially lacking the ability to communicate or move freely, they depend on adults to listen to subtle cues, respond to their needs readily, comfort them when they are sad, and celebrate with them when they are joyous. To meet the needs of an infant or toddler, the adult needs to engage in a sort of dance, a warm, responsive, reciprocal relationship through which the child builds trust and learns about the world.

Because infants and toddlers bond strongly to their primary caregiver, the attitude you have toward nature becomes critical. Sometimes nature is messy. Some of nature's creatures are less appealing than others. How do you feel about spiders and worms? Most young children greet small creatures with great curiosity. However, their connection with nature is dependent on their relationships with the key adults in their lives. The dance continues in the garden, and if the children see you responding with fear or disgust, they will pick up your cues. To succeed in helping young children learn to love nature, it is critical that you first build a trusting relationship with nature yourself. Take time to sit quietly outdoors. Study the creatures that you are nervous about. Watch a spider on its web. You don't have to touch it, but notice the details of the spider, how delicate it is. Study the intricacy of the web. Marvel at what the spider can do. Think about picking up the worm. It isn't really slimy, you know. It feels cool, and it tickles when it wiggles in your hand. It can't hurt you, but you could hurt the worm easily, so return it to the earth where it will be safe. When you are working with children in the garden, you will encounter these creatures and others as well. You don't have to love them. But learn to accept them for the children's sake, and learn to appreciate their place in the world, because these creatures offer young children opportunities for deep study.

Infants and toddlers are sensory learners. Watch how closely an infant examines her world. She notices every little speck. She picks it up, inspects it thoroughly, looking at it, feeling it; now she puts it in her mouth to taste it, rolls her tongue over it to feel the texture. Everything is new to infants and toddlers. Curious, they respond to color, shape, sound, and texture.

We took some daffodils and pansies into the infant room and set them on the floor next to where the babies were playing. The daffodils had been picked that morning, but the pansies had been pulled from a six-pack, the soil still clinging to their roots. The infants immediately reached out to examine the flowers. A boy in a green shirt grabbed a pansy by the roots, closely inspecting the soil that clung there, picking some away with his left hand. Another infant picked up a yellow daffodil and waved it around, exploring the balance of the flower at the end of the stalk, moving the flower closer to her face, touching it to her cheek, then waving it around some more, following the motion with her eyes. A third infant picked up one of the long, slender leaves from a daffodil. He grabbed each end with a hand, bending and straightening the leaf over and over, studying closely the movement of the leaf as he moved his hands. For almost fifteen minutes, several of the children studied the flowers and leaves, putting one down and picking up another.

Taking Infants and Toddlers Outside

American infants and toddlers rarely run free these days. We most often see them carried in car seats or pushed in strollers. When did this happen—this movement to safely contain our youngest children—so adult hands and minds can be free? What do we know about how infants and toddlers develop? We know that they explore the world through their senses. They listen carefully, they look closely, they reach out to touch, they smell, and they taste. They also need to move, to become aware of balance and spatial orientation and where their body is in space, to develop their vestibular and proprioceptive systems. The vestibular and proprioceptive senses tell a person where his or her body is in space and how much their muscles should react to different inputs. Movement is critical to young children. The domains are closely connected. When an infant develops physically, when he is able to move to new places, his world expands. He experiences new discoveries that were not available when he could only stay in one place. He can find new objects to explore on his own, no longer dependent on adults to provide them. When he learns to stand, he can see the world from a new perspective. The world looks different, and now he can reach things that before were out of grasp. Soon he can walk and touch those things if he wishes. Exploring new objects with his senses, he learns about them and is able to enlarge his knowledge of the world. Mobility expands the cognition of the infant and toddler. When we keep children immobile by keeping them in swings, bouncy seats, strollers, and car seats, we are limiting their ability to learn and to grow.

Infants and toddlers want and need to go outside but are dependent on adults to take them there. Sadly, sometimes adults are reluctant to take the youngest children outside. Often infants and toddlers cannot express their

desire to go outdoors in words, but they do give cues. They stand banging at the door or window or looking outside. It is up to the adult to pick up on these signals and make sure that infants and toddlers spend ample time outdoors exploring the natural environment. One way you can assist nonverbal infants and toddlers in this area is to teach them some basic sign language so that they can clearly let you know when they want to go outside.

The outdoors also has a calming effect on infants. Many times we have seen a crying infant calm upon being carried outside. In fact, this strategy was so effective that it was repeatedly used at the Child Development Laboratories at Southern Illinois University Carbondale, where we had an open-door policy for outdoor play (meaning there were always adults available to go outside, and children could choose to play inside or outside). When an infant was crying, the lead teacher would frequently say, "Take her outside." And when the infant was taken outside, the crying would usually stop. Why does this work? It could be that being in an infant room is noisy and therefore stressful, and the outdoors is less stressful. But there is something about being outside that is fundamentally different from being inside. Infants, in all their newness, respond to this difference.

Try this. Go to the door, open it, and step outside. Notice the difference in how your skin feels, in what you can see, and what you smell. Being outdoors is a whole-body experience that awakens all your senses. You notice the air, whether it is cool or warm, dry or humid. You can see farther than you can indoors. New smells greet you. If you are in a natural area, this is all amplified. It is what Richard Louv (2011) refers to as Vitamin N (for nature) in his book *The Nature Principle*. This connection with nature is critical to young children's physical and emotional health.

Even small infants can go outside. Either hold the infants on your lap or put them on their backs directly on a grassy or other comfortable garden surface. If infants are old enough to sit on their own, you can put them in a sitting position. Put them close enough that they can see or reach (if they are old enough to grab) the flowers or plants nearby. You may want to cut a few pieces of a plant or some flowers and place these within the infant's reach. Avoid restraining infants by placing them in devices such as baby carriers or those that hold them in a seated position. Freedom of movement is a "basic need and a path to learning" for infants (Gonzalez-Mena 2007, 22). When a child can move freely, she can focus her energy on learning and exploring what her body can do. Outdoors, the child can feel the grass under her legs and arms, wiggle around, and explore the garden on her own terms.

Wait for children to respond. There is no need to rush. Remember that your relationship with nature is the foundation of the child's relationship with nature. The children will respond to your appreciation for the natural setting. Sometimes the children will be in awe of something they have discovered—bees buzzing or ants crawling, a flower dancing in the wind. These are times to sit quietly and watch. Avoid breaking the spell with too much talk. There are times for silence in the garden, times to let nature do its work, times to be inspired and just soak in the wonder. Be alert for these times so that you do not miss them. They are critical times.

There are also times for sharing words, for expanding knowledge and filling minds. Before you speak, listen to the children. Even if they are nonverbal, they are speaking in their own way. Notice what they are reaching for, looking at, what interests them. Use mirror talk to reflect what you see the child doing. "Lan, I see you pulled so hard you pulled that sage blossom right off the sage plant." "Kyle, I notice you are rubbing the lemon balm leaves between your fingers. Have you tried smelling the leaves?"

Use a rich vocabulary even with infants and toddlers. Avoid talking down to the children. As you have conversations, use the names of plants and animals. Don't be afraid to use technical terms, such as *trowel* and *cultivator*. Children are capable of much more than most adults give them credit for, and if you see children as capable, they will rise to the challenge.

Have discussions about things that are happening in the garden. Ask the children questions that have meaning, and build on their experiences. For example, "Remember when we planted the bulbs in the bench. What do you think that is poking up there?" Avoid talking down to the children because they are small. Questions that are restricted to color, shape, size, and the like are limiting and fail to help children build the dispositions required to retain their curiosity and desire to solve problems.

Allow children to struggle, to have the moment, before you decide to intervene. What is worth having does not always come easily. It may be hard to pull the flower from the plant, but let the child try to do it himself. If necessary, hold the plant firm, so that he doesn't pull it up roots and all. Look for the learning that is occurring in the moment. When a child is trying to figure out how to carry a big stick or a sunflower stalk, this is visual-spatial learning. If you take the stalk away before the child figures out how to balance it or how to walk with it, you are taking away the opportunity for learning. If she wants to bring the stalk back to the classroom, help her figure out how she can do that.

Toddlers can work in the garden. They can plant seedlings. Help them dig the hole, then assist them, if necessary, in separating the plant from its container. Show them the roots embedded in the soil, and talk to them about how the roots will deliver water and food to the growing plant. Teach them how to place the plant in the ground and gently cover the roots with soil. Toddlers can also cover plants with mulch if you give them a little at a time and teach them to place it around but not on the plants. Toddlers especially enjoy moving things around, so having the opportunity to carry buckets of mulch or push wheelbarrows of mulch can be particularly satisfying for them.

Toddlers can water plants, and they can feed plants with organic fertilizers, such as fish emulsion. If you have a worm bin, they can sprinkle the rich worm castings on the plants. Many of your flowering plants and herbs will need to be deadheaded to keep them blooming. Toddlers can cut the blooms with scissors, using tools in a nonconventional way.

Talk to the children about respecting nature. They can search under rocks and logs to see what is living there. When they find a snail or pill bug, teach them to be gentle and to return the creature to its home. Toddlers have a tendency to get excited, squealing with delight at a new discovery. Help them slow down and watch in the garden. Teach them to be still when they want to hold something live. Use words such as "respect" and "careful" to help them understand that these creatures must be treated well.

Working with Families

Some families will be hesitant to let their infants and toddlers go outside, particularly when the weather is cold or rainy. They may feel uncomfortable having their infants or toddlers touching soil or small animals. You can help by educating parents. Help them understand that going outside is healthy for young children. The viruses that cause colds and the flu are more likely to spread when children are inside. Going outside does not increase the chance of getting sick. In fact, the germs that cause these illnesses are less likely to survive outdoors. If children are healthy enough to come to school, they are healthy enough to go outside.

Also, take time to teach parents and other family members about what the children are learning through their experiences. Show them how the children are exploring science concepts as they dig in the soil or search under rocks and unearth small creatures. Talk to parents about the dispositions the children develop as you allow them to exercise their curiosity and sense of wonder, to ask questions and solve problems, and to practice persistence when something doesn't work out the first time.

Invite family members to join you in your garden project. As your relationship with nature is critical to the children's relationship with nature, so can it influence the attitudes of parents of your children. If you model care and reverence for nature, others will notice and respond.

Outside Every Day

If possible, take the children outside every day. They can go out even when it is cold or raining. Collect extra rain boots and raincoats so you will always have some for children who don't bring them from home. Playing outside on a rainy day is great fun. In the garden, the children can see if the plants are getting wet, notice how the water beads up on some plants, and watch water collect in the birdbath. They can study what animals do. Have the birds come out? Are worms coming to the surface? Inclement weather is just one more thing to study.

Planting Bulbs

We had an old plastic deck bench with the seat broken off. Rather than sending it to the landfill or attempting to recycle it, we decided to reuse it as a flower garden. We filled it with topsoil and planted bulbs and a few pansies. We tore open the bags of soil and dumped them in (a few children had to get in the bench first just to see if they fit inside). We opened the package of bulbs and began to look at them.

"There's long things on this one," said Owen as he touched the roots.

Oakley was peeling off the papery outer layers. "Squirrels eats this," she said.

We had daffodils and tulips, so I showed the children the tops of the packages so they could look at the flowers.

"This is what they will grow into," I said. "We have to plant them in the dirt, and then after the wintertime they will sprout."

We talked about putting the roots down and the little stem part up. As we were working, Kate was patting the dirt around the bulbs. She and Oakley were working side by side.

"Tuck them in, Oakley, like this," she said.

"Good night," said Oakley.

After this exchange, we were all "tucking in" the bulbs and telling them, "Good night, sleep tight, see you in the spring."

As the bulbs began sprouting up out of the earth this spring, we went looking to see how many we could find.

"Look, they are waking up," said Aaron.

Nicholas put his face down to the dirt and shouted, "Wake up!"

—**Barb Meraz,** Southeast Missouri State University

How to Take a Walk with Infants and Toddlers

Taking field trips with infants and toddlers may seem more difficult than with preschoolers, but a walk around the neighborhood can lead to the same kinds of investigations older children may make on a field trip. Survey your neighborhood for plants that could be interesting to the children. Note a few thought-provoking places to stop and look at bushes or flowers. See if you can find a destination spot that is particularly interesting. Destination spots that we have known to be popular with this age group include grassy hills, large sculptures, large rocks, a bridge, and a small garden. If you are in an urban setting, you may be able to visit a garden or even someone's yard. Take advantage of bushes and trees that you pass on the way.

If the children are old enough, give them a choice about how they want to travel. Do they want to walk, ride in the stroller, or ride in a wagon? Wagons with high wooden sides are good for pulling children on walks as long as the children are able to sit well on their own. You do need to be careful on turns so that the wagon remains balanced. Walks should take a long time. As you are walking, linger when you see something interesting. Stop to study the plants and flowers or an interesting insect. Let the children touch and hold the object whenever possible. Get the children out of the stroller or wagon to observe more closely. If you see a squirrel or a bird, encourage the children to watch it quietly while you stop the procession. Be alert for verbal and nonverbal cues. If you see a child pointing or hear a child noticing something by making sounds ("uh, uh, uh"), stop and pay attention. These are teachable moments. Let the children build the curriculum.

Special places require special attention. A wooden bridge is a place to act out stories the children know, such as "Three Billy Goats Gruff," and to inspect the plant life under and above the bridge. A grassy hill is a place to run up and roll down, further developing the children's vestibular and proprioceptive systems, while building connections with the grass beneath them. In the garden, the children can sit quietly on benches experiencing the calm of the garden, or they can explore, examining the plants up close or searching for creatures among the plantings. Teachers may want to take clipboards, paper, and pencils or other writing implements so that the children can make sketches while on the trip. Toddlers are capable of making representations. Revisiting the same site and giving the children repeated opportunities to sketch the same object will lead to more sophisticated observations and more detailed representations in the children's sketches.

The walk should give infants and toddlers the opportunity to discover the natural world outside their classroom and outdoor play space. By knowing the area, planning ahead, taking time, and paying attention to the children's cues, the teacher can make the most of this experience for the children.

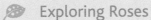

"The pink ones smell the best," exclaimed Kate as she reached for another rose.

"I like this one," said Willow, putting a bright pink and white rose up to her face.

"It's soft!" said Oakley as she rubbed a petal on her cheek.

Nicholas and Willow began placing roses on black felt circles.

"Here's one, and one and one," he said.

"That's my favorite," said Willow, picking up another black circle and putting her rose on it.

We carried the box of roses outside, and Willow gathered up the circles. She spread them out on the hillside, and the children began a one-to-one correspondence of roses to circles. As the roses wilted and dried out, we pulled off any remaining petals and put them all into a wicker basket. It sits on our shelf under a lamp and still smells good when we stir it up!

—**Barb Meraz,** University School for Young Children, Southeast Missouri State University

Choosing Plants for Infants and Toddlers

We believe the best choice for infants and toddlers is a sensory garden. Children in their first three years observe closely with their eyes, then smell, touch, and taste as they explore their world. They listen carefully. Herbs are a particularly good choice for this age group because they are edible and sturdy. Most of them need to be deadheaded, so if the children pull the flowers off, it won't hurt the plant. Fuzzy lamb's ears are good for touching, and colorful flowers catch the eye of an infant or toddler. The flowers of nasturtiums and pansies are edible, so they are good choices. Quick-growing greens and vegetables are also good selections.

Container gardens work well for this age group because of their ease of maintenance. Toddlers are unlikely to be able to spend long periods of time weeding and may not be able to determine the difference between a wanted plant and a weed. Toddlers are also likely to become overzealous when given the task of weeding, and pull up the lettuce with the weeds. They are usually enthusiastic, however, about watering, which they can do regularly with a container garden. Short containers, such as window boxes, work well for infants, who may not be able to reach taller containers.

If you choose raised beds for infants and toddlers, make them low raised beds, ten to twelve inches in height. This way the children can reach them easily and even sit on the edges of the beds. You may want to put pathways between the beds. Toddlers who are used to walking indoors on even flooring will find new challenges when walking on a pathway that is uneven. You will see the children taking extra caution, paying more attention to their steps, and adjusting their bodies as they navigate the uneven surfaces of a garden pathway.

With infants and toddlers, *always make certain* that the plants in the garden that they can access independently are nontoxic. These children will put things in their mouths, and they will want to taste the plants. Always supervise them to make sure they do not put large pieces of the plants in their mouths, as they can be choking hazards. Be clear as you let children taste herbs that not all plants are safe to eat and that they should always ask a teacher or parent before tasting a plant. Teach them to pinch off only a tiny piece to taste.

Bringing the Garden Inside

You may also want to bring the garden inside for the children to explore. You can do this in a variety of ways by growing plants inside, by worm composting, and by bringing flowers and plants from the garden inside. Initially, let children explore items by placing them on the floor, in the sensory table, or on

a regular table. The children will need to become familiar with the items by feeling, observing, smelling, and perhaps tasting them. Help the children explore the items. Show the infant or toddler the object you are focusing on, gently touching the part of nature you want to address—roots, petals, and so on. Help them understand when gentle care is needed. "You need to hold the roots at the bottom. If you pull the plant from the top, it will break."

Remember that everything is new to infants and toddlers, so repeatedly bring the same materials in for them to explore, or keep plants or animals in the classroom for the children to observe over time. This is what Barb Meraz did when she introduced herbs to her class of two-year-olds and got surprise visitors along with the parsley.

After a request for some plants to care for in the classroom, it was decided that herbs would be the best choice for our two-year-olds in case they should explore the plants with their mouths. In my past experience, I found that caring for herbs that could be added to lunchtime foods enhanced our mealtime and encouraged the children to try new foods on other occasions. Adding the herbs also got many children to eat certain foods more heartily that they had only "tasted" on other offerings.

When the pots of plants arrived on a Thursday afternoon, we were delighted to discover five or six caterpillars on the parsley. After some investigation on the Internet, we found them to be yellow swallowtail butterfly larvae, or "calerpillars" as the children came to call them. The caterpillars were content to hang out on the parsley and munch away as we positioned the pots near the glass window by the door to the playground. The children watched them with interest, and some tried to "pet" them as they crawled around on the parsley leaves. When we left for the weekend on Friday, they had made a real dent in the amount of parsley in the pot. Our "herb donor" promised to bring another pot of parsley on Monday so they could continue to feed.

Monday morning arrived, and as the opening teacher began to put the classroom together for the day, he noticed a caterpillar on the rug by the doorway. He found another one crawling up the curtain covering the doorway when he went to slide it open. We put

the caterpillars back in the parsley pot, but one of them did not move; we thought maybe it had dehydrated as it was trying to get outside. The parsley in the pot was completely stripped bare, so perhaps they were looking for more food. The new pot soon arrived that morning, and we transferred the remaining caterpillars—we could only find three. The children continued to watch with curiosity as we looked through books with photographs of chrysalises in anticipation of what our caterpillars would do when the time came to make their "little houses."

We put a branch in the pot in hopes of them choosing to transform on it. By Tuesday the caterpillars had stopped eating and began crawling around and around the edge of the pot. The next morning one of them had attached to the edge of the pot and made its chrysalis. We placed the pot on an activity shelf where the children could take turns standing on a chair to get a good look at it and at the same time give it some protection. The other two caterpillars were still crawling round—we put one back in the pot twice during the morning hours. After naptime that day we went to look at the caterpillars but could only find one . . . we searched and searched. Later that afternoon as we were putting blocks away, we found the caterpillar! It had crawled down and attached itself to the underside of the top shelf! The chrysalis was hanging inside our shelf. We placed a piece of clear Plexiglas on the front of the opening and used clear packing tape to secure it. We could now observe the butterfly without fear of accidental bumping. For the next week we watched for signs of hatching butterflies.

The next week as we prepared to go outside, I noticed something near the top of the curtain on the door. In the top right-hand corner, where the curtain gets bunched up as we slide it open, was a butterfly! I said, "Look! There's a butterfly!" The children got very excited and ran to the doorway. We grabbed the camera and began to take pictures. "How can we get it down?" asked Paxton. "It needs to fly," said Aaron. We took the branch we had stuck in the pot of herbs and offered it to the butterfly. "It has to dry its wings and get strong," I said. "Let's help it down." The yellow swallowtail butterfly stepped onto our stick. As we lowered it down toward the table, it flew off and landed on the wall.

"Yikes!" shouted Willow. We retrieved it from the wall with the stick, and this time it stayed there.

"It's a butterfly," said Paxton.

"Fly!" Aaron said.

"We need to take it outside," said Kate.

"Yep, that's where it lives," said Aaron.

We agreed it should go outside, so we opened the door to the playground and took it out. The breeze caught it, and it fluttered down to the hillside. There were other toddlers already outside, so

we got it onto the stick again and lifted it up high. This time when it flew, it went up into the air and flew over the building.

"Bye, Butterfly!" shouted Oakley.

"See you tomorrow," shouted Kate.

The next morning the chrysalis on the edge of the pot began to wiggle. We were able to take some video of it, and a parent dropping off her child watched for several minutes with us. It stopped moving again, but we were sure we would get to see a butterfly hatch that day. However, nothing ever came out. The chrysalis under the shelf did not ever mature and hatch either. We wondered if our air-conditioned climate had anything to do with it.

The herbs continue to be an important part of our classroom environment. There is a small bench near them that faces the window. Children often sit here and pick the leaves, smell them, and rub them between their fingers. We take turns watering them and observing their growth. One child in our classroom has special learning abilities. He does not use words to communicate but will sometimes make loud vocalizations. One morning after spending a long time on the housekeeping center's couch, he walked over to the bench and sat down. He put his hands into the lush leaves of one of the pots and swished them around. Some of the leaves came off; he put them up to his face and smelled them. He smiled and stuck his hands back into the leaves. He stayed for several more minutes before getting up and walking off.

We occasionally have canned potatoes for lunch that are peeled and sliced. They are not much to look at, and only two or three children out of twelve eat them on average. We began making "parsley potatoes" on these days, and now everyone eats them! The specks of green mixed with the white potatoes look appetizing, and parsley gives them a new exciting aroma and flavor—one that we grew ourselves!

With young children, as in Meraz's classroom, repeated exposure is important. Having the herbs for one day would have been interesting, but having the herbs day after day is what makes for real learning. This is how indoor experiences can become powerful. Tammy Davis tells of a similar experience in building a worm composting bin with her children, ages twelve- to twenty-four months, and with one boy, Connor, in particular at the Center for Child Studies at Southeast Missouri State University.

I opened a can of worms, figuratively speaking, when I followed the suggestion of the director of my program to introduce a new composting system to the toddlers. I was not sure how the children would react to the worms or how I would feel about them. The worms arrived on a late fall day. They came by mail, a big ball of worms in a cloth bag inside the cardboard box, mixed with just a bit of vermicompost to keep them safe. I would later learn the vermicompost is the rich castings (or "worm poop" in kid language) that the worms make from eating everything in sight. The toddlers were full of excitement and wonder as I showed the worms to them. Some were a little uncertain as well. We made a home for the worms in a large plastic storage container about ten inches high with a vented lid. The toddlers helped tear newspaper and dampen it with water. Then we mixed in a cup of soil from outside. This gave the worms both a home and food, as they eat paper and need to be kept moist.

I made sure to introduce the worms to the toddlers' parents as they came in that day. I knew that I would not be able to cultivate a community of respect for the worms without engaging the parents, so I wanted to show them the worms and explain the composting to them. The support of the parents was critical in making the worm composting a central part of our curriculum.

The worms were available for the children at all times. If children were nonverbal they could walk over and pull on the lid to let me know they wanted to work with the worms. Every day the children would explore the worms.

Connor became especially invested in worm composting. He and his mom would arrive every morning with coffee grounds. Connor would take her by the hand and guide her over to the worm bin. She would hand Connor the bag full of coffee grounds, and he would dump the grounds into the compost, a look of pride on his face. He and his mother took this time to share precious moments. Caring for the worms gave Connor and his mother the opportunity to discover the value of caring for animals, sharing time sitting on the floor together, exchanging smiles, laughter, and simple words ("Worms, Mom") in the complexity of a relationship between Connor, his mother, and nature. This time of transition also allowed for a stress-free way for Connor's mom to say good-bye.

Connor would spend much of his mornings playing in the compost with the other toddlers and me. He would frequently dig with small shovels to find the worms or use his hands to dig through the compost. Together we would find very tiny, almost transparent baby worms. The toddlers marveled at "the baby worms," which were so small they would fit on the tip of even a toddler's finger. Often Connor would find a magnifying glass so that we could have a closer view of the "baby worms." We studied the baby worms frequently in silence, sometimes exchanging worms from hand to hand while talking to one another. We had to be much gentler with the baby worms because they were so tiny and fragile. Finding the baby worms became a part of our daily routine. The toddlers seemed to feel a sense of responsibility toward the baby worms. Connor wanted to make sure each baby would become a "big, big, big worm," and he would stretch his arms out wide to demonstrate how big they would grow. Through the transparent, tiny baby worms, I was able to cultivate in the toddlers the disposition of love and respect for the natural world.

The toddlers knew that we had to shred paper for the worms to eat. Finding newspaper became a part of our routine and the opportunity for a perfect toddler field trip. I would ask who wanted to go to find the university paper for shredding. Sometimes a few toddlers would join me and other times the entire group. Conner knew that we had to give the worms water by using the spray bottles. He learned to take turns, developing a sense of time as he learned to wait, and visual spatial learning as he struggled to figure out how to point the spray bottle down into the compost bin rather than at another child or teacher. Having to wait and take turns to use the spray bottles helped the children begin to understand that everyone had the right to give the worms water. Allowing each child to have the opportunity to water worms became an extremely important part of the process of taking care of the worms. Connor had made mutual agreements with the other toddlers sitting next to him. Taking turns for toddlers can be a very difficult and frustrating process. The worms allowed this process to happen with ease. Connor gave the worms our scraps from lunch. He knew without food and water the worms might die. The worms were as important as the train, cars, blocks, books, paint, or any plastic toy I could bring into the room.

I gave the children many opportunities to learn about the worms through informational books, storybooks, multiple creative media forms, singing songs, and telling stories, but mostly through freedom of exploration. I never rushed the children through their work with the worms. It was only through nurturing and time, freedom, patience, and love that Connor, the other toddlers, and I were able to learn and grow with the worms.

Nature provides what manufacturers cannot. No toy company or computer program can duplicate the intricacies, the colors, the shapes, the smells, the textures, the sounds, and the unique qualities of every item produced by nature. How can you provide an experience indoors that equals that of watching a bee dance from flower to flower, hearing its faint buzz? Or that of sitting in the garden while a soft breeze gently blows with the scent of the flowers wafting through the air? Infants and toddlers need nature. They need to go outdoors to experience it. They need it in their classrooms. And they need teachers who value nature and are willing to enjoy it with them.

Chapter 7

Universal Garden Learning Experiences

People often comment that children in their early years have short attention spans. We take exception to this theory. Children have short attention spans when adults direct their learning and determine for them how they should spend their time. However, when children are allowed to participate in decision making about what they will do, often they will spend immense amounts of time in study. Any teacher who has worked with children in a classroom that allows for child choice can attest to this.

As you make your way through a garden study, you will be amazed at the interest some children have in the earth and the plants and animals that inhabit it. You will find that many activities are child initiated or rise naturally from your experiences in the garden. With a little ingenuity, your garden project will be uniquely yours and full of surprises.

When we began our garden, we were frustrated with books on gardening with children. Many of the books consisted of ideas for growing many plants and maybe one activity that could be done with each plant. Since we didn't want to grow a new plant every day, and since plants take time to grow, these books didn't fit our needs. Therefore, our goal in this chapter is to describe experiences that are not dependent on what plants are being grown but can be done in any garden. We hope the following experiences meet that criterion as you seek new adventures in your garden.

Deconstructing Flowers

Concepts
- Flowers have many different parts.
- Flower parts vary by size, shape, texture, color, and smell.
- The parts of a flower have names, such as stem, leaf, petal, stamen, and stigma.

Materials

cut flowers

scissors (optional)

paper

markers or colored pencils

Description

1 Set the flowers out on the table or on the floor. Allow the children to explore the flowers freely. As the children explore the flowers, allow them to take the flowers apart and examine the different parts.

2 Share language to help the children identify the different parts of the flower. If you have more than one type of flower, you can help the children compare the petals and the leaves of the different flowers so that they notice the differences.

3 Encourage children who are interested to draw the flowers or the parts of the flowers. Be sure that you have available markers or colored pencils that are similar to the colors of the flowers.

Extensions
- Share the book *Eyewitness: Plant*, listed in appendix 1, with the children. This book shows and names parts of a flower on several pages.
- Set out square wooden boards for the children to use to arrange the parts of the plants on. This will encourage the children to use the plants to make designs or patterns.
- Provide a balance scale. The children will use the scale to test the weight of the different plant parts.

Safety Considerations

Avoid using commercially-grown roses as these flowers are heavily sprayed with pesticides and fungicides. Also, only share home-grown flowers with children if you are sure that they are free of chemicals.

Drink It Up

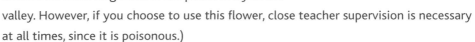

Concepts
- Plants need water to live.
- Flowers take up water through their stems.
- Flowers have veins throughout their stems, leaves, and petals.

Materials

flowers (For best effect, experiment with a variety of flowers. The best for deep color are those with many tiny petals, such as Queen Anne's lace or bridal wreath spirea, but the experiment will work with most white flowers. One of the most dramatic flowers for observing veins in the petals is lily of the valley. However, if you choose to use this flower, close teacher supervision is necessary at all times, since it is poisonous.)

clear vases or other containers (liter soda bottles with the tops cut off work well and won't break)

water

food coloring

knife or scissors for cutting stems

Description

1. Fill the vase or other container with water. Add a few drops of food coloring to the water.
2. Make a fresh cut on the stems of the flowers. If the stems are soft, you can cut them with scissors, but if they are woody, make a diagonal cut with a knife for best results.
3. Place the flowers in the colored water and observe. Within a few hours, you should start to see the color from the water in the petals of the flowers.
4. With the children, study the petals carefully. A magnifying glass will help in seeing the individual veins of the petals.

Extensions
- Before placing the flowers in the water, leave some of them out of water for a while. Don't cut the stems of these immediately before placing the flowers in the colored water. Use two separate vases so you can compare the absorption rates of flowers with freshly cut stems to the rates of those that have been left out of the water.
- Split the stem lengthwise. Put half in one color of water and the other half in another color. (You will have to place two vases side by side to do this. It will be easiest if you use thin vases, such as water bottles. To avoid having to cut the stems too high, you can cut the water bottles to a few inches high. You may need to tape the flowers to hold them in place.) Observe what happens.
- Use several varieties of flowers, and compare the results.

Safety Considerations

Only the teacher should use a sharp knife. Children may be able to cut with table knives if the stems are not too hard.

Little Sprouts

Concepts
- Plants grow from seeds.
- Seeds need moisture to grow.
- Seeds grow roots as well as leaves and stems.

Materials

sensory table or large tub

potting soil

bean seeds

water

trowels and cultivators

Description

1   Guide the children in filling the sensory table or tub at least half full with potting soil.

2   Have the children add water until the soil is moist throughout. This may take a lot of water if the mix is very dry, but be careful not to saturate it to the point where water is standing on the bottom.

3   Add the bean seeds to the tub. The larger the seeds you use, the easier it will be for the children to observe the changes that occur.

4   Let the children use the trowels and cultivators to manipulate the soil and to bury and dig up the beans. Leave the soil and seeds in the tub. Do not cover the table, because doing so may cause mold to grow. Check the beans every day, and allow the children to continue to dig in the soil.

5   Notice changes in the seeds as the days pass. They will swell and start to sprout. Roots will form. Let the children handle the seeds, and guide them in observing changes.

6   Avoid removing the seeds before the children have had plenty of opportunities to observe the plant growth, but after the seeds are fully sprouted, you may want to transplant the seeds to a planter or to the garden. Have the children carefully tuck the seedlings, roots down, into the soil.

Extensions
- Have the children draw pictures of the seeds at various stages of development.
- Photograph or let the children photograph the seeds every couple of days, and display the photos of the seeds at various stages.
- Take dictation as children describe the changes they see in the seeds, or have older children write about the changes they see.
- Try this activity with different seeds, some small and some large. Compare the different varieties of seeds.

Safety Considerations

Avoid using potting soil with fertilizer or other additives. Use trowels and cultivators with curved, rather than sharp, edges. Be sure children are adequately supervised when using hand tools.

What's Inside?

Concepts	• Fruits and vegetables are made up of different parts.
	• Many fruits and vegetables have seeds on the inside.
	• Seeds come in many different sizes, shapes, and textures.

Materials
two or three kinds of fruits or vegetables with seeds
knife
trays on which to explore produce and seeds

Description

1 Set out the fruits or vegetables on the table. Engage the children in a discussion about what they know about the produce so far.

2 Discuss what the children know about seeds. Did they plant seeds in their garden? Where do they think those seeds came from? What do they think they will find if they cut the fruits/vegetables open?

3 Cut the fruits/vegetables. If the produce is soft enough, the children can cut it themselves with table knives. If the produce is large or hard, the adult should use a sharp knife to cut it. Encourage the children to observe the seeds. How are the seeds alike? How are they different? What words could you use to describe the seeds?

Extensions

• Cut open a large fruit, such as a birdhouse gourd or swan neck gourd. For this task, the children can use woodworking tools, such as a hammer. Be sure they wear goggles while attempting to open the gourd. They will first make a small hole in the gourd, and further work with the hammer should make the hole bigger. Soon they should be able to get seeds and pulp out of the gourd.

• If you have seed packets, compare the seeds the children find in the fruits and vegetables with the seeds in the packets for those plants. Are they similar?

Texture Walk

Concepts
- Plants can be identified through the sense of touch.
- Plants can feel smooth, fuzzy, prickly, soft, hard, slick, or bumpy.
- Plants have parts, such as stems, leaves, stalks, vines, petals, fruits, and vegetables.

Materials

note cards

marker

chart paper or clipboard with paper

a garden in full bloom

Description

1 Prepare for this activity by writing one texture word on each note card: *fuzzy*, *smooth*, *prickly*, *soft*, *hard*, *slick*, and *bumpy*.

2 Invite six or seven children to come to the garden with you for a texture walk. Once in the garden, ask children to tell you how plants feel. Accept and acknowledge all answers. Explain that they will be going on a texture walk to find plants that feel a certain way. Show the children the cards one at a time and have them try to read the word. Ask the children if they can think of any things that feel smooth. Repeat this process with each card.

3 Tell the children that each will be given a card with a texture word on it. Then each will go into the garden and try to find a plant that feels the same as the word on the card. Emphasize to children that they must be gentle when touching plants so as not to hurt or kill the plants. Explain that it is not a race, so they will be walking slowly and carefully looking for a plant that matches their card.

4 Remind the children that plants have many parts. Ask the children to name some parts of a plant. Print the parts they list on the chart paper or clipboard. Call attention to any plant parts they may have forgotten. Tell them to check the different plant parts to find out how they feel (for example, the vine may be prickly, but the vegetable may be smooth). Give one card to each child. Make sure each child understands the meaning of the word on his or her card. Release the children into the garden one at a time to minimize their urge to race.

5 Follow the children into the garden to provide support as they locate each texture. See if they can name the part of the plant they are feeling.

6 Encourage the children to trade cards and locate new textures until each child has completed all the cards.

Extensions

- After going on several texture walks, children will be ready for this extension. Gather children together near the edge of the garden. Blindfold one child at a time with a handkerchief. Lead the child to a prickly plant (such as cucumber), and place her hands on it. Ask the child to guess the name of the prickly plant. Repeat with another child and another plant (such as fuzzy lamb's ears or a bumpy pumpkin). Continue until all children have had a turn.

- Peel several large crayons. Take clipboards; thin, white paper like onion skin or tracing paper; and peeled crayons to the garden. Invite the children to make a texture rubbing. Place the plant part (such as a hosta or fern leaf) between the paper and clipboard, or place the paper directly on top of the plant (such as a pumpkin). Unless the plant is ready for harvest or grows abundantly in your garden, supervise to be sure that the plant remains intact throughout this process.

What's That Smell?

Concepts
- Plants have leaves and roots.
- Many herbs have a distinct smell.
- Herbs are used in many foods we eat.

Materials

sensory table

an herb with a strong scent (such as chives, mint, basil, or bee balm)

Description

Preparation: Before the children arrive, go to the garden and pick several stalks of a plentiful herb, such as mint. (If you have a lot, pull it up by the roots so children will be able to examine the whole plant.) If you want, pick a couple of different herbs. Place the freshly picked herbs in the sensory table. If you don't have a sensory table, you can put them on a regular table.

1. Invite children to come to the sensory table to examine the herbs. Allow them time to play in this area and explore the herbs.

2. Encourage the children to examine the different parts of the herb. Ask them what they notice. Have them smell the plants. Show them how rubbing the leaves between a finger and the thumb makes the smell stronger. Ask them if the smell reminds them of anything.

3. Discuss the kinds of foods the herbs are used in (for example, for mint you could discuss candy, tea, ice cream, gum, and so on).

Extensions
- Add water and utensils to the sensory table so the children can pretend they are cooking.
- Use fresh herbs to cook real food with the children.
- After cooking with the herbs, read and discuss the recipes with the children, and then post them near the sensory table for children to refer to in their dramatic play.
- Prepare a "Smell the Same" game using fragrant flowers and herbs. Collect small opaque containers with lids, and poke a few small holes in the lid of each. Go to the garden, and collect two samples of each fragrant flower or herb (such as rose petals or sage leaves). Place these inside the containers. Write the name of the flower or herb on the underside of each cap with a permanent marker, and replace it. Ask the children to smell each container until they find two that smell the same. To check their conclusions, show them how to open the container and check to see if the plant names match.

Garden Leaf Memory Game

Concepts
- Plants have leaves.
- Each plant has leaves of a specific shape, size, and color.
- Plants can be identified by studying their leaves.

Materials

blank note cards

marker

clear, self-adhesive paper or laminating film

pairs of leaves from garden plants

Description

1 Find at least ten pairs of matching leaves from the garden. The older your children are, the more pairs you will need to make this game challenging. The younger the children, the more distinct the leaves will need to be (parsley versus pumpkin leaf versus basil). You may want to take leaves from your most abundant plants, but you can use clippers to take small cuttings from other plants with unique leaves.

2 Use clear, self-adhesive paper to adhere one leaf to each note card, or affix the leaves and then laminate the cards.

3 Gather the children together in a small group on the floor or at a table to play a memory game. Mix the cards thoroughly, and place them upside down in even rows.

4 Decide which child will start. Have each child turn over two cards. Help the children read the names on the cards and notice the details of the leaves. If the cards match, the child keeps the pair and takes another turn. If they do not match, encourage the children to try to remember what they are and then place them face down. Moving clockwise around the table, the next child takes a turn.

5 When all matches are made, the cards are shuffled, and the game begins again. (We prefer to avoid using the term *win* to refer to the child with the most cards. Instead, we focus on finishing and starting again.)

Extensions
- When this game becomes too easy, ask the children to go into the garden with you to find new pairs of leaves to add to the game. Allow them to assist you in attaching the leaves and printing the plant names on the new cards.
- Repeat this process with pictures of flowers from seed catalogs, seed packets, or with actual flower petals.
- Older children can find and press leaves from the garden or from the trees surrounding your school for a memory game.

You Fill Up My Senses

Concepts

- Plants are made up of many parts.
- Each plant has its own unique look.
- Plants have varied textures.
- Some plants have distinct smells.
- Some plants make noise.
- Some plants are edible.

Materials

five large trays (such as copy paper box lids,
  cookie sheets, cafeteria trays)
colored markers
poster board strips
plants that make noise
plants with a strong fragrance
plants that can be eaten
plants that are brightly colored
plants that have an interesting texture

Description

1 Label each tray with a word and picture representing one of the five senses (look, touch, listen, smell, and taste).

2 Ask children to brainstorm garden items that could be displayed on each tray. Work with children in small groups to collect items from the garden for each tray, such as the following:

  1 Listen: wind chime, Chinese lanterns, dried gourds, dried money plants, northern sea oats

  2 Look: Canterbury bells, zinnias, snapdragons, alyssums, geraniums

  3 Touch: lamb's ears, dusty millers, Autumn Joy sedums, strawflowers, cockscombs, hens and chicks

  4 Smell: thyme, sage, basil, chives, cucumber slices

  5 Taste: parsley, strawberries, cherry tomatoes, carrots, pansies, nasturtiums

3 Place trays in an area where they can be visited and manipulated by children or guests.

4 Guide children as they explore, and encourage them to use their senses as they manipulate the objects.

Extensions

Assign children to four groups (touch, smell, look, listen). Give each group a clipboard, and take a sensory walk through the playground, neighborhood, or nearby park. (If cameras are available, children can also take photos.) Encourage the children to find interesting items to write on their list (such as touch the cool gravel or hot asphalt, look for insects, smell food from a nearby restaurant, listen for birds singing). Return to the room, and ask each group to report what they found. Post their records for parents to see at the end of the day.

Seed-to-Plant Matchup

Concepts	• Many plants begin as seeds.
	• Each seed becomes a specific type of plant.
	• Seeds can be identified by size, shape, and color.

Materials

twenty note cards

ten pairs of different seeds

seed catalogs, empty seed packets, or old garden magazines

glue

marker

Description

1 You will need two seeds each of ten types (for example, pumpkin, corn, pea, tomato, lima bean, sunflower, gourd, watermelon, carrot, and love in a puff) and a picture of the plant produced by each seed. Glue a seed to each of twenty blank note cards so you have two sets of ten. Set aside one set. Turn the other set over, and affix a picture of the plant the seed produces to the opposite side of the card. You will now have one set of cards with a seed on each card and one set of cards with a seed on one side and the corresponding plant on the other. Write the name of the plant below each picture with a marker. For younger children, offer only five sets of cards at one time.

2 Place the matchup game on the table in the science area during center time with ten cards showing plants and ten cards showing seeds.

3 When children show interest, ask them if they can match the plants to the seeds that they come from without picking up the cards.

4 Once ten pairs have been made, show the child how to turn the cards over to see whether the seeds are identical.

Extensions

• Take children on a fieldwork trip to the garden section at a local discount or hardware store. While you are there, visit the seed packet rack, and select seeds to plant in your garden.

• Harvest seeds from your garden at the end of the season for children to plant at school or home next year.

• Prepare pumpkin seeds or sunflower seeds to eat as a snack.

• Collect seeds for sorting in mini muffin tins or condiment cups.

Safety Considerations

Read seed packets carefully to be sure that the seeds have not been treated with any potentially harmful chemicals, and make sure that the seeds are not toxic. (For instance, angel's trumpet and castor bean seeds are highly toxic.)

Forever Flowers

Concepts
- Some plants have flowers with petals of different shapes, sizes, and textures.
- Flowers can be preserved through drying.
- Substances such as sand and cornmeal help the flower hold its shape as it dries.

Materials

shoe box

fine sand or cornmeal

small funnels

flowers for drying

Flowers that dry well in cornmeal or sand

astilbe	Queen Anne's lace
black-eyed Susan	rose
butterfly weed	Shasta daisy
delphinium	snapdragon
hollyhock	stock
marigold	yarrow
peony	zinnia

Flower Preservation

Some flowers, called everlastings, dry easily if you simply gather them together in small bunches, tie the stems with a string or rubber band, and hang them upside down until they are dry. Here are some everlastings you can dry this way:

artemisia	statice
baby's breath	strawflowers
Chinese lanterns	sweet marjoram
chive blossoms	tansy
globe amaranth	yarrow
lavender	

Description	1	If you use sand, start with fine, clean, dry sand, and sift it through a strainer until you have only the finest particles.
	2	Guide the children as they fill the shoe box about one inch deep with the drying medium (cornmeal or sand).
	3	Remove most of the stem from a flower. Have the children place the flower on top of the drying medium. (Do one flower at a time.)
	4	Have a child hold a finger over the tip of the funnel as you fill it with drying medium. Once it is full, show the child how to release her finger and let the sand flow around the flower. (If you don't have a funnel, use a small spoon to gently add the sand.) Try to avoid dumping the sand directly on the flower, but build it up around the sides until it naturally flows over the petals. Your goal is to preserve the shape of the flower by surrounding it with the medium, but don't be too fussy. It is hard for young children to control the medium with precision.
	5	Continue adding flowers and surrounding them with the medium until the box is full.
	6	Let the box sit for about two weeks. To remove the flowers, slowly pour the medium from one corner of the box. As the flowers become visible, remove them with a slotted spoon. Brush off the excess drying medium with a clean paintbrush.

Extensions

- Use sand for one box and cornmeal for the other. Compare the results with the same kind of flower.
- Compare the results with different kinds of flowers. Which look the most natural when dried? Make notes in your garden journal to refer to next time you dry flowers.

Pressed for Time

Concepts
- Each plant has its own identifiable characteristics.
- Plants can be preserved for future study through pressing.
- Plants can be pressed using various methods.

Materials

waxed paper
old newspapers
two wooden boards (about sixteen by twelve inches)
cardboard
sturdy string
or a commercial plant press

Description

1   Gather flowers and leaves for pressing from the garden. Select these early in the morning when they are fresh but the dew has dried. Ask the children if they would like to learn about a way to preserve or save these samples for later use. Gather children around a table where materials are prepared. Explain to the children that they will be learning to preserve plants using a plant press.

2   You can make a plant press by using two wooden boards, newspaper, and cardboard. Start by placing a wooden board on the table. Then place a sheet of newspaper, folded in half, on the board. Open the newspaper, and place a plant inside the fold. Fold the newspaper over again, and place a sheet of cardboard on top. Repeat with another piece of newspaper and another plant.

3   Continue layering newspaper and cardboard until several flowers and leaves have been inserted. Place the second board on the top. Wrap string around the entire stack, pull until it is tight, and tie a knot.

4   Place the press in a warm, dry place. Wait several days before checking the plants. When the plants are dry, take them out and examine them closely. Engage children in a discussion of how the flower or leaf has changed in the pressing process. Pressed plants can be stored at room temperature between two sheets of newspaper or waxed paper.

Extensions
- Make your own concentration matching game by pressing two each of ten to fifteen different flowers, herbs, or leaves.
- Use pressed flowers to decorate greeting cards or garden party invitations.
- Make a book of garden favorites. Have children each select their favorite garden plant and press one leaf or flower from it. Use clear contact paper to adhere these to separate sheets of same-size paper. Encourage each child to label the dried sample with invented spelling or copy the name from the garden label, a seed catalog, or a seed packet. Compile these pages, and bind as a book. Involve children in selecting a title, creating a cover, and making a title page.

Dig a Little Deeper

Concepts
- A plant's roots absorb water and minerals from the soil.
- Roots hold the plant in the ground.
- Lateral roots extend from the main root.
- Root growth occurs at the tip of each root where fine root hairs absorb food from the soil.

Materials

hand trowel

magnifying glasses

pencil and paper or garden journal

various plants from the garden

Eyewitness: Plant (see appendix 1)

Description

1 Take children to the garden, and help them dig up a few plants to study. Herbs work well for this activity since they grow abundantly in most gardens. Try digging up a basil plant, a sage plant, and some parsley or mint. For comparison purposes, you could also choose to dig up a radish, a carrot, a potato, some lettuce, and any nearby weeds.

2 Gather a small group of children to study the various plants using magnifying glasses. Engage the children in a discussion of similarities and differences. Call attention to the roots of each plant.

3 Open *Eyewitness: Plant* to page 8. Have the children examine the plants again to see if they can distinguish between the three types of roots discussed in the book. Continue looking at the roots in the book through page 10 to see if you find other similarities.

4 Take pictures of these plants and their roots for your documentation. Have children choose one plant to draw, and encourage them to draw the plant as it looks both above and below the ground.

Extensions
- Give children rulers, and let them measure the roots of various plants.
- Prepare and cook a vegetable that grows as a root, such as carrots, radishes, or beets.
- Use toothpicks to suspend a clove of garlic, a piece of sweet potato or potato, or an avocado pit in a glass of water with the top sticking out. Watch and take notes as the plant develops roots. Then plant it in a pot of soil until it can later be transplanted into your garden.

Crushed Kaleidoscope

Concepts
- Each plant has leaves with distinct shapes.
- Leaves contain chlorophyll.
- Leaves have veins.
- Flower petals contain pigment, which gives them their color.

Materials

green leaves and brightly colored flowers

hammers or medium-size rocks with at least one smooth side

unbleached muslin, cut in small squares no more than twelve by twelve inches, or one large piece of fabric, such as a sheet or tablecloth

one or more pieces of soft wood, such as pine (at least twelve by twelve inches in size)

pushpins (four for each piece of wood)

safety goggles

permanent marker (optional)

Description

This experience can take place either indoors or outside near the garden. If you want to make one large piece, select a tablecloth or sheet to work with. Use precut muslin if you wish for each child to have his individual piece to work with. Working with individual pieces is a bit less cumbersome. You can have children working with more than one board at a time, but we have found that two boards is the most one adult can supervise with preschool-age children. If you have more than one board, you will need extra pushpins and pounding implements. Rocks seem to work better with preschoolers, while older children, who have more control, can handle hammers. Warning: This activity makes a lot of noise, but it is worth it.

1 Gather a variety of flowers from the garden.

2 Place the piece of wood on a stable surface. Have the child place a leaf or flower on the wooden surface and cover it with the fabric. Fasten the fabric to the board by gently hammering a pushpin in each corner of the board, one at each of the corners. Tap gently and just enough to make the pin stick. Don't try to push it all the way in as you may damage the pushpin and make it hard to remove. The goal is to keep the sheet from slipping about in order to make a clear print.

3   Ask the first child to put on the safety goggles. Hand the child the hammer or stone, and let her pound on the leaf or flower. Encourage the child to pound all around the plant in an even manner. You will see the color from the plant transfer to the fabric. Once the child has finished, if you want, you can have her write the name of the plant under the print with a permanent marker.

4   Carefully remove the tacks when finished. Have the child hold up the sheet for the others to see. Ask the children to describe the details they see in the print and what made the colors you see on the sheet. Explain that a pigment called chlorophyll gives plants their green color. Tell them that chlorophyll helps plants make energy from sunlight. After printing a flower, explain that pigment gives flower petals their color. Add other vocabulary words to the discussion as necessary.

5   If you are using a large cloth instead of smaller sheets of fabric, shift the position of the sheet after each child works to make a new print on a clean area. Repeat this process with each child adding a new plant. Continue until all children have had a turn or until the sheet is evenly covered with prints.

Extensions   Cut up another sheet, or use scraps of fabric to let children make individual prints. Sort leaf prints by the number of points on each leaf. Arrange leaf prints by size, from the smallest to the largest. Select some prints to include in your garden journal. Have children tell why they selected each plant for inclusion in the journal, research these plants, and write details about the plants in the journal.

Safety Considerations   You will need to closely supervise the pounding of the plants to make sure that no one is injured. Have children and teachers wear safety goggles during this portion of the activity.

Exploring What Plants Need to Grow

 Sunflower Heights

We noticed that our sunflowers were growing very tall. One day we decided to measure the tallest sunflower to see how tall it was. Sara got on the ladder and measured the sunflower. Maggie held the tape at the bottom. The sunflower was ten feet tall.

Next, we measured a long piece of paper and cut it so that it was ten feet long—as tall as the sunflower. We brought in another sunflower that had broken off in the wind so that we could examine the details for our drawing.

We drew the sunflower head first, carefully studying the head of the real sunflower, so it would look just right. We noticed that the center, where the seeds grow, is brown, and the surrounding petals are yellow. Next we drew the stem and the leaves. Maggie noticed that the leaves are toothed, and she carefully made a zigzag edge to her sunflower leaf.

Finally, we wondered how tall the sunflower was compared to us. We guessed how many children it would take to be as tall as the sunflower. Then we measured the children against the sunflower. The sunflower was as tall as three preschoolers.

 Learning and Development

The children worked on observing and describing the sunflower and the relationships of its parts. They represented the sunflower through drawing, exploring the relationship between pictures and real objects. They worked on math concepts by measuring the sunflower, both with conventional means of measurement and with less conventional means (their own bodies), which was more meaningful to them. They studied spatial relationships, observing the live erect sunflower and comparing it to the sunflower that had broken off and was lying on the floor.

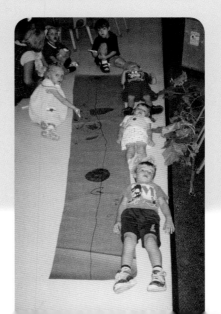

How Big?

Measuring plants can become a regular part of your garden project as you study the growth of plants.

Concepts
- Plants continue to grow throughout their lives.
- We can find out how much a plant has grown by measuring it.

Materials

one tall plant to measure (sunflower, corn, hollyhocks)

ladder (if plant is too tall for teacher to reach the top)

tape measure

roll of paper

markers

flowers and/or leaves from another plant of the same variety (such as another sunflower or hollyhock plant)

Description

1 Gather together by the plant you have selected. Using the tape measure, determine the height of the plant, using a ladder if necessary. (Only the teacher should climb the ladder.)

2 Roll out the paper and measure a distance equal to the height of the plant on the paper. Cut the paper at that length.

3 Show the children the leaves and flowers from the other plant. Encourage them to examine the two closely. Talk about things you observe, such as any visible seeds, the shape and color of the petals, the shape of the leaves, and so on.

4 Have the children draw the plant life-size on the long paper.

5 After the work is complete, measure the plant with people or objects from the classroom. How many children does it take to equal the height of the plant? How many blocks? How many baby dolls? Try a number of different objects, and write your results on the paper or an accompanying chart.

6 Display your representation of the plant and your conclusions. (Our sunflower ended up being taller than the wall, and we had to bend it over onto the ceiling. We added to our list of conclusions, "The sunflower is taller than the wall.")

Extensions

- Since children don't have any special understanding of inches and feet or of metrics, you can use anything to measure. For small plants, Unifix cubes work well. Children can chart the growth of a plant from week to week by measuring with the cubes, then draw around the cubes on a graph to come up with a visual representation of the plant's growth. For bigger plants, you can use other familiar objects from the classroom, such as unit blocks, to measure.

- Compare the sizes of different varieties of flowers. For instance, compare the size of a Russian Mammoth sunflower to a smaller variety.

- Represent a number of small and large flowers this way. Label each flower. Make a wall collage by pasting the representations side by side.

Soiled Again!

Concepts
- Plants need soil to grow.
- People can make soil for plants by mixing various materials.
- Some materials are good for plants because they provide moisture and/or nutrients.

Materials

large container for mixing soil (for example, sensory table, washtub, or wheelbarrow)

smaller container for measuring soil (for example, bucket or cup measure)

topsoil

peat moss

perlite

water

Description

1 Have children explore the three ingredients for the soil. Compare textures, color, and other attributes.

2 Mix in the large container one part each of the topsoil, peat moss, and perlite. (So that you can adapt the activity to the size of your container, we have listed the ingredients in parts instead of in quantities. You can use measuring cups if you are just making enough soil for a few pots, or you can use buckets or flowerpots if you are making a large quantity of soil.)

3 Add water until the mixture is moistened. At this point, you may want to leave the potting soil out for a few days for the children to explore in the sensory table.

4 Use the soil mixture in pots or in the garden.

Extensions
- Add water to each ingredient separately before mixing. Compare the absorption rates of the different media.

Safety Considerations

Be sure children do not put materials in their mouths. Do not use any materials to which chemical fertilizer have been added.

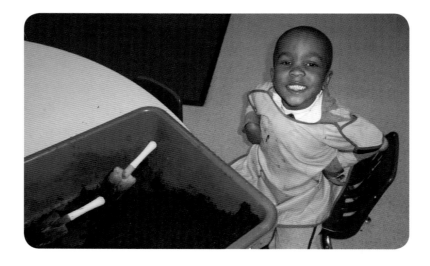

Making the Most of Compost

Concepts
- Plants need food to grow.
- Plants decompose over time and turn into rich compost, which can be used to help other plants grow.
- Food scraps can also be used to make compost for the garden.
- Decomposing plants generate heat.

Materials

large rectangular laundry basket

utility knife (to be used by adult only)

hand trowels

soil

compost materials, such as dry leaves, grass clippings, garden clippings, vegetable and fruit scraps, coffee grounds, and eggshells

Description

1 Use a utility knife to cut out the bottom of the laundry basket.

2 Select an area in or near your garden. Guide the children in digging a hole that is the right size for the laundry basket to sit in. Dig down four to six inches.

3 Place the laundry basket in the hole. Have the children add a layer of compost materials about four inches deep. Sprinkle with a layer of soil. Repeat the layering until you have used up all your compost materials or the basket is full. (If your basket is not full, you can continue adding to it during the next few weeks.)

4 Wet the pile with water. To maintain the compost pile, stir it up periodically. Because of its small size, children should be able to do this with hand cultivators. Also keep the pile moist but not flooded. When the organic matter has turned brown and crumbly, you have compost.

Extensions

- Build two compost piles. Put different ingredients in each one, and compare the results. Does one kind of organic matter break down more quickly than the other? Do they look the same?
- Build two compost piles, one in the sun and one in the shade. Add the same ingredients to each. Do they take the same amount of time to decompose?
- Take the temperature of the compost pile, and graph it. Compost produces heat. How does the temperature in the compost pile compare to the air temperature? Let the children put their hands in the pile and feel the heat.

Safety Considerations

Some people worry that compost will attract rats. This shouldn't be a problem so long as you avoid adding meat or dairy products to your compost. Snakes are sometimes attracted to the warmth of a compost pile but are usually harmless. If you live in an area where snakes are in residence, keep an eye out for them.

Stinky Tea

Concepts	
	• Plants need nutrients to grow.
	• Nutrients can come from other plants.
	• Heat from the sun makes plants break down into nutrients faster.
	• Decomposing matter often has a strong odor.

Materials

alfalfa pellets (available from feed stores)

water

large container with lid

Description

1. Guide the children in selecting a sunny spot for your alfalfa tea to brew. Place your container in this spot.
2. Examine the alfalfa pellets. Discuss their shape. Smell them. Break them apart and examine the texture.
3. Have the children put some alfalfa pellets in the container. Use about one cup of alfalfa pellets for every three gallons of water the container holds. (You don't have to have exact amounts, so don't worry.)
4. Fill the container with water.
5. Cover the container with the lid and set it in the sun. Check the tea each day. Observe the appearance and the smell. It will take about two weeks for the tea to brew. You will know it is finished when it smells really bad. If it doesn't stink, it isn't ready yet. Once it is done, dip it out and put it on the plants. They love stinky alfalfa tea.

Extensions

- There are many organic fertilizers you can buy that children can put on the garden. Check your garden center to find a selection of cottonseed meal, fish meal, bonemeal, Epsom salts, and others. These can be applied dry by broadcasting around the plants. Other fertilizers need to be mixed with water. Fish emulsion fertilizer is a good choice because it won't burn the plants even if children spill it on the leaves, and it smells terrible, which never fails to delight young children.
- Record observations of the tea as it brews.
- Compare the growth of a plant that is fertilized with alfalfa tea to a plant that is not. Start with two plants that are the same size and growing under the same conditions. Feed alfalfa tea to one, and give no fertilizer to the other. What happens?
- If you have access to manure, you can make manure tea instead of alfalfa tea. Follow the same procedure, except substitute manure for the alfalfa. Since manure often has weed seeds in it, you may want to wrap the manure in burlap or cheesecloth and tie the cloth with string before adding it to the water. This will keep the seeds out of your garden. Note: Never put fresh manure directly in your garden. It will burn your plants.

Safety Considerations

Five-gallon buckets work well for making alfalfa or manure tea. However, these buckets have been implicated in drowning deaths of toddlers. We recommend that you use smaller containers.

Feeling Fine

Concepts	• Soil is made up of a variety of substances that help plants grow. • Some substances in soil hold water for the plants. • Some substances in soil help water drain.

Materials

sensory table or large tub

growing medium, such as peat moss, perlite, sand, clay, topsoil

water

hand tools, such as trowels and cultivators

buckets or other containers

Description

1. Use only one type of growing medium at a time so children can explore the specific characteristics of that material. Fill the sensory table or tub with the medium.

2. Add water as needed. For materials such as perlite and peat moss, which contain dust, be sure to add water so the children don't inhale the dust. Other substances, such as topsoil, sand, and clay, can be explored both wet and dry.

3. Allow the children to explore the materials with their hands and with tools. Ask questions that encourage thinking and observation, helping them determine whether the substance holds or repels water and how water affects the material.

4. After children have explored one type of medium, remove it and try another.

Extensions

Use several tubs containing different materials so that children can compare the textures and properties.

Safety Considerations

Be sure that children do not put materials in their mouths.

Mulch Madness

Concepts
- Adding a layer of mulch after planting helps soil to retain moisture.
- Adding a layer of mulch after planting helps to control weed growth.
- Many materials may be used as mulch.
- The effectiveness of mulch varies by the material used.

Materials

seedlings

soil

shovels or hand trowels

newspaper

straw

wood chips

grass clippings

coffee grounds

cloth scraps

black plastic

water

measuring cups or watering can

sprinkler

handheld rulers

Description

1   Send a note home with the children asking parents to save and donate grass clippings, coffee grounds, cloth scraps, and old newspapers.

2   Select seedlings and plant them in your garden, or choose an area of your existing garden that has been weeded, but not mulched, for this activity. Water the seedlings evenly. For a large space, use a sprinkler to do this. For a container garden with containers that are similar in size, use measuring cups or a small watering can to add the same amount of water to each container.

3   Allow children to explore various materials used for mulching. Try layered newspaper, with holes cut to fit around each seedling. Collect and try traditional wood chips, straw, grass clippings, coffee grounds, black plastic, and cloth scraps. Encourage children to come up with their own creative ideas to try.

4   Demonstrate to children how to apply mulch around, not on top of, a seedling. Divide the garden in even sections. Have children select and apply one type of mulch to each section. Explain that this experiment works best if the thickness of the mulch is about the same in each section. Give kids handheld rulers to measure the depth of their mulch material as they apply it.

5   Work with children to make a sketch of the garden, recording the type of mulch used in each section.

6   Remind the children to monitor the amount of moisture in each section daily to determine which types of mulch are the most effective in holding water.

7   Help the children to watch for weeds and count the number in each section. After two weeks, create a graph showing the types of mulch used and the number of weeds in each corresponding section.

8   Discuss the results with the children, and encourage them to draw some conclusions or repeat the experiment to test the accuracy of their results.

Extensions Use a field guide to identify the weeds you find in the garden. Make a weed journal by pressing weeds and attaching them to the pages with contact paper. Then add factual information and children's dictation about each weed.

Compare areas that are mulched to areas that are not mulched.

Safety Considerations If children use shovels to apply mulch materials, supervise closely to prevent injury to other children and to plants.

Measuring Up

Concepts

- Plants need water to live.
- Rainfall can be measured with a rain gauge.
- Rain gauges come in various sizes and styles.
- Rainfall can be charted on a line graph.

Materials

two to three rain gauges of various sizes and styles

chart paper or garden journal

markers

Description

Preparation: Before you start this activity, you'll need to purchase or borrow two to three styles and sizes of rain gauges (fence mount, ground mount, large easy-to-read numbers, and so on).

1   Place the gauges at various locations around the garden. Have the children help. Teach the children not to disturb or empty the gauges during playtime, so that an accurate measure can be taken.

2   Encourage the children to check these gauges daily. Assist the children by demonstrating how to read the water level. Compare the water level in each gauge to see if they each measured the same amount of rainfall. Then show the children how to empty each gauge so that it is ready to measure the next rainfall.

3   Chart rainfall in a garden journal or floorbook or on chart paper for two to four weeks. If it does not rain, encourage children to observe the effect of dryness on the plants. Describe this in the garden journal or floorbook before asking children to assist in watering the garden.

4   Use a sprinkler to water the garden if you continue to have no rain. Check the rain gauges to see if the sprinkler is watering evenly.

Extensions

Plan a walk for a rainy day. Send a note to parents asking them to send boots, jackets, and umbrellas with the children. Begin collecting rain gear so that you will always have extra boots and raincoats on hand for walks such as this. On the first rainy day, adjust your plans and take a walk. Encourage the children to notice the sound, smell, and feel of the rain. Sing songs about rainy weather, such as "If All of the Raindrops Were Lemondrops and Gumdrops" or "It's Raining, It's Pouring," as you walk. Upon return to the classroom, take dictation from the children about the experience, including their estimates as to how much rain will be in the gauges. When the rain stops, take them outside to check their predictions.

Exploring Garden Creatures

Rulers of the Deep

Concepts

- Worms eat paper as well as food that we might otherwise throw away.
- Worms need moisture to live.
- As the food passes through their bodies, the worms turn it into castings, which are rich in nutrients that plants like.
- Composting with worms is called vermiculture.
- We must care for the worms, adding food and moisture periodically, so that they remain healthy.

Materials

large, shallow container (eight to twelve inches deep), such as a storage box or galvanized washtub

shredded paper or newspaper

a cup of soil

water

one pound red worms (Purchase red worms for your worm compost bin. You can find many sources online and listed in appendix 3. Do not substitute another type of worm, since they may have very specific requirements that you will not be able to meet.)

Description

1 Have the children fill the container with shredded paper.
2 Guide the children as they add water, a cup at a time, until the paper is evenly moistened. It should be thoroughly damp, but water should not sit in the bottom of the container. This mixture is called worm bedding.
3 Add the cup of soil. This will help the worms digest the paper.

4   Investigate the worms with the children. They will probably want to hold and examine them. Take lots of time for this step. Show the children how to gently handle the worms by holding their hands flat and letting the worms crawl on the palm. Look closely at the worms. Notice the small band (clitellum) around one end. Discuss how the worms feel.

5   Place the worms in the box. Cover it lightly with a sheet of heavy plastic or the lid to the container. (If you use an unventilated lid, drill a few holes in it so the worms will get oxygen.)

6   Your worms will be fine for a while because they will eat the paper, but the children will soon want to add food scraps for the worms to eat. You can feed the worms vegetable and fruit scraps or leftovers, eggshells, and leftover bread or cereal products. Avoid milk or meat products, as these will draw pests. When the children add food to the compost bin, have them bury it under some of the paper. Rotate the area where you bury the food so you are putting it in a different spot each time.

7   Keep the compost moist. The vegetation you feed will add some moisture, so don't overdo it. A good way to add moisture is to let the children spray water with a spray bottle.

8   Remove the worms, if you want to continue using them, when you notice that much of your bedding has turned into castings, which are dark and fine. (Alternatively, you can put the whole mixture, worms included, in the garden.) To sort the worms from the compost, put small piles of compost on a large sheet of plastic. Shine a bright light on each pile. The worms will crawl away from the light toward the middle of the pile. (This takes a while, but children love it.) Gradually scrape the compost off the pile, giving the worms plenty of time to flee. You should eventually be left with a ball of worms. Use the compost for your garden, and start a new box for the worms.
Note: Chant the following worm-sorting song to hurry the process along.

> Worms, worms, run from the light.
> Worms, worms, get out of sight.

Safety Considerations   Always have the children wash their hands before and after handling the worms or compost materials.

Slippery When Wet

Concepts
- Worms need moisture to live.
- Worms will move toward moisture.

Materials
earthworms
paper towels
large pan with a shallow rim
water

Description

1. Have the children wet some paper towels so they are damp but not dripping. Spread them so they cover half the pan. Next, place a dry paper towel so the edges of the wet and dry towels touch.
2. Place several worms in the pan so they are partly on the dry and partly on the wet towel. Observe the worms. Talk about where they go and what they do. Do they stay where they are or move to one of the towels?
3. Take the worms off and repeat the experiment. This time try putting some worms on each paper towel, some on the wet and some on the dry. Discuss what happens.

Extensions

Try using one worm at a time. Use a timer to see how long it takes each worm to choose a side. Count how many are on each towel after five minutes.

Record your results on a graph, with one side labeled "wet" and the other "dry." Mark which side each worm prefers. Compare the results.

Safety Considerations

The main safety concern in worm experiments is for the worm. When we expose children to living creatures, we must model respect. Young children need to be closely supervised while handling fragile living beings such as worms. Be careful not to leave the worms out so long that the paper dries out, because the worms will too.

Who's Afraid of the Dark?

Concepts	Worms prefer dark to light. Worms move away from the light.

Materials

earthworms
pan or box with shallow sides (a cake pan is a good choice)
cardboard or dark paper
paper towels
water

Description

1 Have the children dampen the paper towels and line the entire bottom of the box or pan with them.
2 Cover half of the box or pan by resting dark paper or cardboard on the sides of the pan or box to keep out the light. Leave the other half uncovered.
3 Put several worms in the middle of the box. Observe and discuss what you see. Where do the worms go?
4 When you are satisfied the worms have decided where they want to be, put them back in their home and try the experiment with some other worms. Do the new worms do the same thing?

Extensions

Record your results on a graph, with one side labeled "light" and the other side labeled "dark." Mark the side each worm prefers. Compare the results.

Safety Considerations

As in the previous activity, the main safety concern in worm experiments is for the worm. When we expose children to living creatures, we must model respect. Young children need to be closely supervised while handling fragile living beings such as worms. Be careful not to leave the worms out so long that the paper dries out, because the worms will too.

A Touching Experience

Concepts
- Worms respond to touch.
- Some parts of a worm's body are more sensitive to touch than others.
- The banded area of the worm is called the clitellum (klih-TEL-um).

Materials

earthworms

moist paper towel

Description

1 Place the worm on the moist paper towel. Observe it for a minute and discuss what it does.

2 Very gently, touch the worm on its head, in the middle, and then on its tail. (The worm's tail is the pointed end. The head is closest to the banded area, which is called the clitellum.)

3 Talk about which parts of the worm move most actively when touched. Which move the least?

4 Repeat several times with different worms to see if you get the same results.

Extensions

Record your results on a graph. One way to do this is to divide the graph into three sections labeled "head," "middle," and "tail." For each worm, mark which part responds most actively to touch. Compare your results for several worms.

Safety Considerations

As in previous worm activities, the main safety issue in worm experiments is for the worm. If we are to expose children to living creatures, we must model respect. Young children need to be closely supervised while handling fragile living beings such as worms. Be careful not to leave the worms out so long that the paper dries out, because the worms will too.

Bird-Watching Backpack

Concepts

- Birds can be identified by their size, shape, color, and behavior.
- Birds can be attracted with food, shelter, and water.
- Certain birds live in certain regions of the country.
- Male and female birds of the same species are often different colors.

Materials

backpack or other small bag with handles

small field guide with color photos or sketches (see the list in appendix 1)

magnifying glasses

ruler or small tape measure

colored pencils

sketch pad or small unlined notebook

binoculars (child- or adult-size)

Description

1   Gather the materials and place them in the backpack or other portable container.

2   Meet with children in small groups to introduce the backpack, discuss the idea of observing birds on the playground, and demonstrate the use of the materials in the kit. Allow children time to practice focusing the binoculars, observing with the magnifying glass, and measuring the length of common classroom items using the ruler or tape measure.

3   Show the field guide to the children, and explain that this book will help them to learn about the birds they see outdoors. Show and explain key features of the book, such as regional maps and drawings or photographs. Ask the children to name a bird they have seen on the playground. Use the index to locate the number of the page that describes this bird. Read the text to the children. Then call attention to the key information given about this bird, such as the size, physical characteristics, behavior, diet, song, and the differences between males and females.

4   Explain that the colored pencils and sketchbook can be used to record as many details about the bird as possible, such as colors, specific markings, and other key features. The children can also draw pictures of feathers, fallen nests, or empty eggshells found on walks or on the playground.

5   Explain that the bird-watching backpack will be available at all outdoor times and that children may use it freely as long as they return all of the materials to the backpack before returning indoors. (You may want to enclose a laminated, illustrated list of all items that should be in the bag.) Talk to the children about how to sit quietly near the garden, birdbath, or feeders and wait for birds to visit.

6   At the next scheduled outdoor playtime, remind the children about the backpack (depending on the size of your group and the children's level of interest, you may want to have a sign-up sheet to assist in turn taking and use of the backpack). Remember that birds are more active and therefore more likely to be seen early in the day. Keeping your feeders full and your birdbath fresh will likely attract more birds. You may want to discuss this with

the children and encourage them to take responsibility for monitoring and maintenance of the feeders and birdbath.

7 Assist children as necessary with use of the field guide, recording important data, labeling sketches, and drawing conclusions. As you observe birds with the children, call attention to bird behavior. Is the bird hopping, walking, or running? Does it climb up a tree trunk or work down the tree headfirst? Does it eat from the feeder or probe the ground for worms? Teach children to use the field guide to incorporate this information into the identification process.

8 Discuss their observations at small- or large-group times over the next few weeks.

Extensions
- Include a camera so children can take photos of what they discover.
- Plan a visit to the bird section of a local pet store or a local bird refuge to study, sketch, and observe various types of birds.
- After becoming familiar with the birds common to your region, create a chart showing the birds you have observed in your garden or near your playground. Hang the chart outdoors, or take it outside each time you go to the playground. Encourage children to make a tally mark next to each species of bird when they see one visit the school yard. After one week, total the tally marks and discuss the results.
- Build bird feeders out of wood, pop bottles, and other recycled materials to hang in the garden.
- Experiment with various types of bird food to see if you can attract new species of birds to your garden.
- Place small scraps of yarn, string, tissue paper, or cloth in a small box near the feeder. Watch to see if birds take some of these materials to use in building their nests.

Safety Considerations
Avoid disturbing birds while watching them. Be extra careful when observing parent birds with their young. Always require children to wash their hands thoroughly after handling feathers, nests, eggshells, or dead birds.

Critter Hunting

Concepts
- Earthworms burrow into the ground by swallowing soil as they move.
- Earthworms, pill bugs, sow bugs, and ants need moisture to live.
- Pill bugs and sow bugs are arthropods but not insects.
- Pill bugs will roll up to protect themselves, while sow bugs will run away.

Materials

shovel or hand trowel

containers for collecting critters

shallow trays or pans for observation

magnifying glasses

paper and pencils

reference books, such as the following:

> *Insects* (Golden Guide) by Clarence Cottam and Herbert Zim (St. Martin's Press, 2002)
>
> *National Wildlife Federation Field Guide to Insects and Spiders & Related Species of North America* by Arthur V. Evans (Sterling, 2007)
>
> *Wiggling Worms at Work* by Wendy Pfeffer (HarperCollins, 2004)
>
> *National Audubon Society First Field Guide: Insects* by Christina Wilsdon (Scholastic, 1998)
>
> *Those Amazing Ants* by Patricia Brennan Demuth (Simon & Schuster, 2012)
>
> *Yucky Worms* by Vivian French (Candlewick Press, 2010)
>
> *Garden Wigglers: Earthworms in Your Backyard* by Nancy Loewen (Picture Window Books, 2006)

Description

1. Ask the children if they would like to go outside and look for critters on the playground or in the garden. Have them chart their predictions of the critters they think they may find and where they could look.

2. Go outside and look in some of the places suggested. If no critters are found, try looking in damp places, underneath rocks or boards, in rotting logs or cement cracks, and in piles of damp rubbish. You will likely find sow bugs and pill bugs, as well as earthworms. Earthworms may also be found on wet sidewalks just after a rain or by digging directly into your garden soil. Smaller worms should be near the soil's surface, and larger worms, much deeper. Try digging down about six to twelve inches with a shovel or hand trowel if you can do so without disturbing your plants.

3. You may also want to search for ant trails and follow them to see if you can find the colony. Anthills can often be found on loose, dry soil. If you find anthills, be sure to teach children to avoid stepping on the ants or disturbing them. Explain that the hill is the ants' home and no one wants their home to be ruined.

4. Once you have located some critters, carefully collect a few of each type to study for the day. Place a homemade critter container, such as a baby food jar with small holes in the lid, on the ground near the critters and scoop them up.

5. Take these critters to the classroom, a nearby picnic table, or a blanket on the ground for observation. Often it is helpful to take some of the critter's natural habitat with you, such

as a piece of rotting bark, some wet leaves, or a chunk of wet soil. Overwhelmed critters may want to hide, and observing this behavior will add to the learning experience. Worms, sow bugs, and pill bugs can be held safely when placed in the flat, open hand of a child.

6   At the observation area, you may want to remove the critters from their containers and place them in several shallow trays for observation. Old cafeteria trays or cookie sheets work well for this, as do shoe box lids. Encourage the children to observe with magnifying glasses.

7   Give the children paper and pencils to record what they observe. If you are working outside on a blanket, give children clipboards or large, flat books to place under their paper so that writing and drawing are easier. This type of documentation can also be entered directly into a garden journal or floorbook.

8   Ask children to note key aspects, such as body parts, color, appearance, and behavior. This will encourage children to observe carefully. Older children can choose two different critters to compare, such as sow bugs and pill bugs. Take dictation for children who do not yet write using invented spelling.

9   Provide children with reference books, and encourage them to find and read books about the critters they are observing. Some of this information can be shared with peers and added to their drawings.

10 Release all critters back into their original surroundings by the end of the same day to preserve their life and the natural environment around your school. Be sure that all their needs are met while they are in your care. For instance, if you do not provide moisture in the form of damp paper towels or soil, worms may dry out. Paying attention to the needs of creatures like these and returning them to their natural habitat teach children to respect living things.

Extensions

- At group time, have children use their bodies to dramatically represent for the rest of the group the critters they observed.
- Start an earthworm compost box in your classroom.
- Help children make critter containers to take home by assisting them as they use a hammer and nail to poke small holes in the lids of recycled margarine or whipped cream containers.

Safety Considerations

Supervise children closely to make sure they do not disturb insects that could cause them harm, such as bees, wasps, or biting ants. Supervise children using shovels very closely, and remind them to keep the shovel down near the ground. Avoid removing ants from their critter containers if observing them indoors, since they could escape into your classroom. Glass baby food jars can break if dropped and should be closely supervised. Avoid sending glass jars home with children.

Up Close and Personal with Insects

Concepts
- Insects are arthropods.
- The life cycle of an insect is called metamorphosis.
- Egg, larva, pupa, and adult are the stages of metamorphosis.
- Insects have six legs.
- Each insect has a hard exoskeleton covering all parts of its body.
- Each order, or group, of insects has its own unique characteristics.
- Butterflies and ladybugs are beneficial to plants.
- The body of an insect has three divisions: head, thorax, and abdomen.

Materials

insect eggs or larvae (Ladybugs, butterflies, and ants are good subjects to study because they will likely be visible in your garden at one time or another. Ladybug or butterfly eggs or larvae can be ordered from educational supply catalogs, such as *Insect Lore*. Ant farms are readily available from a variety of sources.)

transparent insect container with holes in the lid or a mesh cage

magnifying glasses

paper and colored pencils or crayons

preferred food of the selected insect (such as fresh leaves, live plants, fresh fruit, cotton balls soaked with sugar water, or honey)

reference books (see appendix 1)

Description

1   Read through all instructions carefully, and research the needs of the insect before beginning the project. Make plans in advance for how and when the insects will be released into the environment. This will affect the timing of your project. For example, releasing live insects into the outdoors would be inappropriate in cold winter weather. Remember that one of your goals should be to teach children respect for all living things.

2   Once the insects arrive, introduce the project to the children. Follow all directions with great care to be sure your insects live to adulthood.

3   Be sure to surround the children with many informational resources throughout the life of the project, as they will be motivated to learn everything they can about these live visitors. Consider making available several fiction and nonfiction library books, website addresses, posters, and three-dimensional insect models. Research how the insect interacts with plant life. Is it harmful or helpful? What types of plants does it prefer?

4   Place the insect container in a safe place at children's eye level. A sturdy shelf or table works well. Some butterfly-net cages need to be hung from the ceiling. Choose an area of the classroom that is relatively calm, such as the reading or science area.

5   Place magnifying glasses near the container, and provide time each day for children to observe the development of the insects in small groups. One way to do this is to place just enough chairs in the area for the number of children it can safely hold. Allowing too many children to crowd around the cage may lead to accidents. You don't want the ant farm to fall to the floor, resulting in ants being crushed or quickly escaping.

6   Place several journals or clipboards with paper and writing utensils near the insect container. This will foster documentation of metamorphosis. Hang posters showing the four stages of the insect life cycle and the parts of the insect nearby. Provide vocabulary to children as appropriate, taking advantage of each teachable moment. Record children's comments, or encourage them to use invented spelling to write down key information and label artwork. Children's drawings will become more detailed as they gain more and more factual knowledge about the selected insect.

7   Ask children to share their observations at large-group time each day. Ask the group, "What's going on with the ladybugs today?" or "Has anyone noticed anything different about the caterpillars?" Take down children's dictation, date it, and post it near the insect container.

8   Learn alongside the children. Don't be afraid to admit that you don't know all the details. Emphasize your own curiosity, and model for children how to find answers to hard questions.

Safety Considerations   For the safety of your insects, teach children never to shake, move, or bang on the container—especially if it is made of glass. In addition, teach children to leave the lid on the container at all times so insects do not escape into your classroom. Explain to the children that it is better for the insects to stay in the container until it is time for them to be released into the outdoors where they belong.

Calling All Ants!

Concepts
- Ants collect food and transport it to their nest.
- Ants prefer some foods to others.
- Ants are insects, and insects are arthropods.

Materials

shoe box lid or large, flat piece of cardboard

baby food jar or lid

marker

various foods, such as jelly, syrup, small bits of meat, granulated sugar, a slice of lime,
    crumbled crackers, shredded cheese, and so on

books about ants (see book list in appendix 1)

Description

1   Using the baby food jar and marker, have the children trace six circles onto the box lid or cardboard.

2   Have the children fill each circle with a different type of food. Ask the children to predict which food they think will be the ants' favorite and why. Take dictation on a chart or in a garden journal.

3   Take the cardboard or lid into the garden, and with the children, place it where it will not be disturbed by children or noticed by birds. You may want to interview children to find out where they have previously spotted ants or anthills in the garden and place it in that location.

4   Encourage the children to leave the area and allow ants to notice the food. Meanwhile, read several books about ants and arthropods.

5   Return at regular intervals to check the progress of the ants and notice their activity. Encourage the children to observe which foods are preferred and which, if any, are undisturbed.

6   Use a field guide on insects to identify the type of ants you attract.

7   Revisit the site many times throughout the day to track progress, check children's predictions, and draw conclusions about preferred foods.

Extensions
- Encourage the children to draw pictures of the harvesting ants. Take dictation about the process.
- Ask the children for other food suggestions, and repeat the process several days in a row. You could even try putting out larger items (such as a whole graham cracker, half an apple, or a slice of cheese) to see how it affects the harvest. Chart and compare the results as you go.

Safety Considerations

As the children observe, discourage them from disturbing the ants. Some ants do bite.

One Step at a Time

Concepts
- Stepping-stones show us where to walk in the garden.
- People often add decorations to their gardens.

Materials

dishpan or other container for mixing concrete

concrete mix

water

trowel

gloves

mold (You can purchase a concrete mold or use a plastic storage container. Size and shape can vary, but the finished stone should be about three inches deep.)

vegetable oil

decorations such as ceramic pieces, shells, marbles, glass globules, buttons, stones

Description

1 Have the children grease the mold by coating it lightly with vegetable oil. This will make it easier to get the stone out later.

2 Put concrete mix in the dishpan. The amount you need will depend on the size of your stone. Don't worry about getting it exact; you can make more if you need it. (Have the children stand back while you pour the concrete so they won't breathe in the dust.)

3 Have the children add water a little bit at a time, mixing it in gently with the trowel. Add just enough water to dampen the concrete thoroughly. It should be dry enough that you can form a ball with it.

4 Fill the mold with the concrete mixture. Bang the mold a few times on a solid surface to help release air bubbles. Have the children level the top with the trowel.

5 Let the children decorate the top of the stone with the objects you have selected.

6 Let the stone dry for three days before removing it from the mold.

7 Note: Large stones should be reinforced with a layer of hardware cloth or chicken wire. Cut it about one inch smaller than the mold. Put about one inch of concrete in the mold, lay down the wire, and then fill the mold the rest of the way.

Extensions

Have children make individual stepping-stones with their names, handprints, and other small objects. Then use them to make a pathway to or through the garden.

Safety Considerations
- Be careful not to breathe in the concrete dust. You may want to wear a mask.
- Adults and children should wear gloves when handling the concrete, as it can be irritating to the skin.
- Children who are still consistently putting sensory materials in their mouths should not participate in this activity.

For the Birds

Concepts
- Birds need water to drink and bathe.
- People can attract birds by providing them with fresh water.
- A birdbath is an effective way to provide fresh water for birds.

Materials

washtub or other large container for mixing concrete

thirty-two-gallon plastic garbage can with lid (with straight sides so the birdbath will be easy to remove)

concrete mix

water hose (attached to water source)

trowels

gloves

old tire

vegetable oil

chicken wire or hardware cloth cut about one inch smaller than the garbage can lid

decorations, such as ceramic pieces, shells, marbles, glass globules, buttons, stones

Description

1 Have the children coat the inside of the garbage can lid with vegetable oil. This will make the birdbath easier to remove. An alternative is to line the lid with plastic.

2 Have the children place the garbage can lid inside the tire so it sits level. If you don't have a tire, you can dig a hole in the ground or in the sandbox to hold the lid level.

3 Pour concrete into the washtub. Have the children stand back while you do this so they won't breathe in the dust. You'll need enough concrete mix to fill the lid to about two inches from the top. Don't worry about being too exact. You can make more if needed, or use the extra for stepping-stones.

4 Have the children add water a little bit at a time, mixing it in gently with the trowels. Add just enough water to dampen the concrete thoroughly. It should be dry enough that you can form a ball with it.

5 Guide the children in filling the lid mold with the concrete mixture to about one inch deep. Place the chicken wire or hardware cloth on the concrete, pressing firmly so it stays in place. Put another inch of concrete on top of the wire. (The wire will add strength to the birdbath.)

6 Set the garbage can upright inside the lid and in the middle of the concrete. Push down hard so that the concrete starts to come up around the garbage can.

7 Using the hose, fill the garbage can one-quarter full with water. As you fill the garbage can, the weight should push the concrete down even further, making a well in the middle of the birdbath and forming the rim.

8 Fill in any empty areas of the lid with concrete and smooth the edges.

9 Let the children decorate the outside rim of the birdbath with the objects you have selected, pushing them firmly in to the concrete.

10 Remove the garbage can after the concrete has set for about an hour and is able to hold its shape. Let the children decorate the inside of the birdbath.

11 Cover the concrete loosely with plastic wrap so that it will dry slowly. Let the birdbath dry for three days before removing from the mold. Place the finished birdbath in the garden on a tree stump or other sturdy pedestal, ensuring it cannot fall or be tipped over if a child leans on it.

Extensions　Have children clean and fill the birdbath regularly. Encourage them to record observations of birds that visit the birdbath in the form of charts, sketches, photographs, and narratives.

Safety
- Be careful not to breathe in the concrete dust. You may want to wear a mask as you mix the concrete.
- Adults and children should wear gloves and dust masks when handling the concrete, as it can be irritating to the skin.
- Children who are still consistently putting sensory materials in their mouths should not participate in this activity.

A-B-C You in the Garden

Concepts
- Garden plants have a variety of names.
- All books have a common format (such as cover, title page, binding)
- Gardens require a variety of tools, materials, and equipment—these all have names.

Materials

three-ring binder or fastening brads

twenty-six pieces of paper with one alphabet letter on each page

three-hole punch

garden magazines or seed catalogs

photographs of plants in your garden

crayons or colored pencils

scissors

glue or tape

camera or extra garden photos

garden alphabet books (see appendix 1)

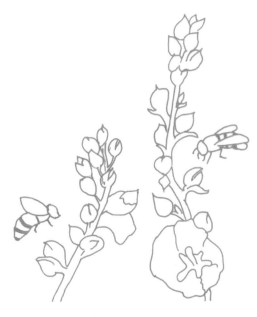

Description

1 Prepare by placing materials on a table. Read a garden-related alphabet book to a group of children before inviting them to make their own garden alphabet book. Explain that this book can be about anything needed to take care of a garden or any plants you have in your current garden.

2 Assist the children in creating a cover for the book and a title page with the title, authors' names, and "publisher" (such as the name of your school or class).

3 Allow each child to choose a letter of the alphabet (such as the first letter of their first name).

4 Encourage the children to think of a plant, garden tool, creature, or activity that they have seen in the garden. For example, they might think of ants for the letter *A*, bulbs for the letter *B*, and coneflower for the letter *C*.

5. Have each child write the word they choose on their letter page. If some children cannot write, write the words for them. You could also show them how to type and print the word at the computer to cut and paste to their page.

6. Allow the children to a cut a picture of the object that their plant- or garden-related word represents from the garden catalogs and magazines. If pictures are not available, the children can draw their own or use an instant or digital camera to take a photo for their page. Duplicate prints of the photos you may have taken for your garden journal also work well for this project.

7. Once each child has drawn or glued his picture, he can either look for another item that begins with that letter or start a new alphabet page.

8. Once the glue has dried and all pages are complete, bind them together in a three-ring binder or fasten them using brass brads. If you do not have a three-hole punch, magnetic photo albums make nice books and help you avoid the wait for glue to dry.

9. Place the finished book in the reading area, and encourage the "authors" to read it to other children, parents, and guests throughout the week.

Extensions

With a small group of children, take a set of alphabet cards out to the garden (one letter on each card with a picture to illustrate the letter, such as *A* is for alligator) for an alphabet scavenger hunt. Give each child a card, and challenge him to find a plant or garden item that begins with that letter. For example, *D* is for dirt, *S* is for sprinkler, *Z* is for zinnias. If children want, you can add these discoveries as new pages to the alphabet book.

Children's Books about Gardens and Garden Creatures

Note: An asterisk denotes a book with very simple text. These would be appropriate for infants and toddlers but also have excellent photographs that make them useful with older children.

FICTION

Bugs: Insects, Spiders, Centipedes, Millipedes, and Other Closely Related Anthropods by Frank Lowenstein and Sheryl Lechner (Black Dog and Leventhal Publishers, 1999)

Bugs! Bugs! Bugs! by Bob Barner (Chronicle Books, 1999)

Bugs for Lunch by Margery Facklam (Charlesbridge, 1999)

The Carrot Seed by Ruth Krauss (HarperCollins, 1945)

City Green by DyAnne DiSalvo-Ryan (Marrow Junior Books, 1994)

Compost Stew: An A to Z Recipe for the Earth by Mary McKenna Siddals (Tricycle Press, 2010)

Counting Is for the Birds by Frank Mazzola Jr. (Charlesbridge, 1997)

The Curious Garden by Peter Brown (Little, Brown and Company, 2009)

Flower Garden by Eve Bunting (Harcourt, 1994)

From Caterpillar to Butterfly by Deborah Heiligman (HarperCollins, 1996)

The Gardener by Sarah Stewart (Square Fish, 1997)

Growing Vegetable Soup by Lois Ehlert (Harcourt, 1987)*

How Groundhog's Garden Grew by Lynne Cherry (Blue Sky Press, 2003)

In the Garden with Van Gogh by Julie Merberg and Suzanne Bober (Chronicle, 2002)*

Inch by Inch: The Garden Song by David Mallett (HarperCollins, 1995)

Jack's Garden by Henry Cole (Greenwillow Books, 1995)

The Little Red Hen and the Ear of Wheat by Mary Finch (Barefoot Books, 1999)

The Magic School Bus Gets Ants in Its Pants: A Book about Ants by Joanna Cole (Scholastic, 1996)

One Bean by Anne Rockwell (Walker Publishing Company, 1998)

One Hundred Hungry Ants by Elinor J. Pinczes (Houghton Mifflin, 1993)

Our Community Garden by Barbara Pollak (Beyond Words Publishing, 2004)

Our School Garden by Rick Swann (Readers to Eaters, 2012)

Princess Chamomile's Garden by Hiawyn Oram (Dutton Children's Books, 2000)

Rah, Rah, Radishes!: A Vegetable Chant by April Pulley Sayre (Beach Lane Books, 2011)*

Sunflower House by Eve Bunting (Harcourt Brace and Company, 1996)

This Year's Garden by Cynthia Rylant (Aladdin Paperbacks, 1984)

Tiny Green Thumbs by C. Z. Guest (Hyperion Books for Children, 2000)

Tops and Bottoms by Janet Stevens (Harcourt, 1995)

Two Bad Ants by Chris Van Allsburg (Houghton Mifflin, 1988)

The Ugly Vegetables by Grace Lin (Charlesbridge, 1999)

Water, Weed, and Wait by Edith Hope Fine and Angela Demos Halpin (Tricycle
    Press, 2010)

Weslandia by Paul Fleischman (Candlewick Press, 1999)

NONFICTION

Ants by Cheryl Coughlan (Pebble Books, 1999)*

Ant Cities by Arthur Dorros (HarperCollins, 1987)

Bees by Kevin J. Holmes (Bridgestone Books, 1998)*

Birds: A Guide to Familiar Birds of North America (Golden Guide) by Herbert S. Zim
    and Ira N. Gabrielson (St. Martin's Press, 2001)

Bugs! by Christopher Nicholas (McClanahan Book Company, 1998)

Bugs, Bugs, Bugs! by Mary Reid and Betsey Chessen (Scholastic, 1998)*

Bumble Bees by Cheryl Coughlan (Pebble Books, 1999)*

Butterflies by Kevin J. Holmes (Bridgestone Books, 1998)*

Butterflies and Moths (Golden Guide) by Robert T. Mitchell and Herbert S. Zim
    (St. Martin's Press, 2002)

A Butterfly Is Patient by Dianna Hutts Aston (Chronicle Books, 2011)

Composting: Nature's Recyclers by Robin Michal Koontz (Picture Window Books, 2007)

Down to Earth: Garden Secrets! Garden Stories! Garden Projects You Can Do!
    by Michael J. Rosen (Harcourt Brace, 1998)

Earthworms by Kevin J. Holmes (Bridgestone Books, 1998)*

Eyewitness: Bird by David Burnie (DK Publishing, 2008)

Eyewitness: Butterfly and Moth by Paul Whalley (DK Publishing, 2012)

Eyewitness: Insect by Laurence Mound (DK Publishing, 2007)

Eyewitness: Plant by David Burnie (DK Publishing, 2011)

Flowers by Gail Saunders-Smith (Pebble Books, 1998)*

Flowers: A Guide to Familiar American Wildflowers by Herbert S. Zim and
    Alexander C. Martin (Golden Press, 1987)

From Flower to Honey by Robin Nelson (Lerner Publications Company, 2003)

From the Garden: A Counting Book about Growing Food by Michael Dahl (Picture
    Window Books, 2004)

From Seed to Plants by Gail Gibbons (Holiday House, 1991)

Garbage Helps Our Garden Grow: A Compost Story by Linda Glaser (Millbrook
    Press, 2010)

Garden Wigglers: Earthworms in Your Backyard by Nancy Loewen (Picture Window Books, 2006)

A Handful of Dirt by Raymond Bial (Walker and Company, 2000)

Insects (Golden Guide) by Clarence Cottam and Herbert S. Zim (St. Martin's Press, 2002)

It Could Still Be a Flower by Allan Fowler (Children's Press, 2001)

It's Our Garden: From Seeds to Harvest in a School Garden by George Ancona (Candlewick Press, 2013)

Ladybugs by Cheryl Coughlan (Pebble Books, 1999)*

National Audubon Society First Field Guide: Insects by Christina Wilsdon (Scholastic, 1998)

Oh Say Can You Seed?: All about Flowering Plants by Bonnie Worth (Random House, 2001)

Plant Secrets by Emily Goodman (Charlesbridge, 2009)

Ready Set Grow!: Quick and Easy Gardening Projects by DK Publishing (DK Publishing, 2010)

A Seed Is Sleepy by Dianna Hutts Aston (Chronicle Books, 2007)

Seeds by Gail Saunders-Smith (Pebble Books, 1998)*

Spiders by Gail Gibbons (Holiday House, 1993)

Sunflower Houses: Inspiration from the Garden—A Book for Children and Their Grown-Ups by Sharon Lovejoy (Workman Publishing, 2001)

Those Amazing Ants by Patricia Brennan Demuth (Simon and Schuster, 1994)

The Vegetables We Eat by Gail Gibbons (Holiday House, 2007)

Very First Things to Know about Ants by Patricia Grossman (Workman Publishing, 1997)

Weeds (Golden Guide) by Alexander C. Martin (Golden Press, 1972)

What Do Insects Do? by Susan Canizares and Pamela Chanko (Scholastic, 1998)*

What Do Roots Do? by Kathleen V. Kudlinski (NorthWord Books, 2005)

Where Butterflies Grow by Joanne Ryder (Lodestar Books, 1989)

Where Do Insects Live? by Susan Canizares and Mary Reid (Scholastic, 1998)*

Wiggling Worms at Work by Wendy Pfeffer (HarperCollins, 2004)

Yucky Worms by Vivan French (Candlewick Press, 2010)

ALPHABET BOOKS

The ABC's of Fruits and Vegetables and Beyond by Steve Charney and David Goldbeck (Ceres Press, 2007)

The Butterfly Alphabet Book by Brian Cassie and Jerry Pallotta (Charlesbridge, 1995)

Eating the Alphabet: Fruits and Vegetables from A to Z by Lois Ehlert (Harcourt, 1989)

An Edible Alphabet: 26 Reasons to Love the Farm by Carol Watterson (Tricycle Press, 2011)

The Flower Alphabet Book by Jerry Pallotta and Leslie Evans (Charlesbridge, 1988)

A Garden Alphabet by Isabel Wilner (Dutton Children's Books, 1991)

A Gardener's Alphabet by Mary Azarian (Houghton Mifflin, 2000)

The Vegetable Alphabet Book by Jerry Pallotta and Bob Thompson (Charlesbridge, 1992)

The Yummy Alphabet Book: Herbs, Spices, and Other Natural Flavors by Jerry Pallotta (Charlesbridge, 1994)

BOARD BOOKS FOR TODDLERS

My Garden/Mi Jardin by Rebecca Emberley (Little, Brown and Company 2005)

A Green, Green Garden by Mercer Mayer (Harper, 2011)

In the Garden by Leslie Bockol (Innovative Kids, 2009)

In the Garden by Elizabeth Spurr (Peachtree, 2012)

The Little Composter by Jan Gerardi (Random House Children's Books, 2010)

The Little Gardener by Jan Gerardi (Random House Children's Books, 2012)

My First Garden by Wendy Lewison (Little Simon, 2009)

What's in My Garden?: A Book of Colors by Cheryl Christian (Star Bright Books, 2013)

Reference Books about Garden Creatures

The Complete Idiot's Guide to Composting: Turn Your Organic Wastematerial into Black Gold by Chris McLaughlin (Alpha Books, 2010)

Composting for Dummies by Cathy Cromell and The National Gardening Association (Wiley Publishing, 2010)

Garden Insects of North America: The Ultimate Guide to Backyard Bugs by Whitney Cranshaw (Princeton University Press, 2004)

Good Bug Bad Bug: Who's Who, What They Do, and How to Manage Them Organically (All You Need to Know about the Insects in Your Garden) by Jessica Walliser (St. Lynn's Press, 2008)

Organic Gardening for Dummies, second edition, by Ann Whitman, Suzanne DeJohn, and the National Gardening Association (Wiley Publishing, 2009)

Snail Trails and Tadpole Tales by Richard Cohen and Betty Phillips Tunick (Redleaf Press, 1993)

What's Wrong with my Vegetable Garden?: 100% Organic Solutions for All Your Vegetables, from Artichokes to Zucchini by David Deardorff and Kathryn Wadsworth (Timber Press, 2011)

Worms Eat My Garbage: How to Set Up and Maintain a Worm Composting System, second edition, by Mary Appelhof (Flower Press, 1997)

APPENDIX 3 Garden and Environmental Education Books and Supplies

Including Sources for Insects, Worms, and Other Beneficial Creatures

Acorn Naturalists
180 South Prospect Avenue, Suite 230
Tustin, CA 92780
800-422-8886
www.acornnaturalists.com

Gardens Alive!
5100 Schenley Place
Lawrenceburg, IN 47025
513-354-1482
www.gardensalive.com

Happy D Ranch
PO Box 301
Visalia, CA 93278
559-738-9301
www.happydranch.com

Insect Lore
PO Box 1535
Shafter, CA 93263
800-548-3284
www.insectlore.com

Kids Gardening
National Gardening Association
237 Commerce Street, Suite 101
Williston, VT 05495
800-538-7476
www.kidsgardening.org

Montessori Services
11 West 9th Street
Santa Rosa, CA 95401
888-274-4003
www.forsmallhands.com

Nasco
901 Janesville Avenue
PO Box 901
Fort Atkinson, WI 53538
800-558-9595
www.enasco.com

Nature Explore
1010 Lincoln Mall, Suite 103
Lincoln, NE 68508
402-467-6112
www.natureexplore.org

Nature's Control
PO Box 35
Medford, OR 97501
541-245-6033
www.naturescontrol.com

Seeds and Garden Supplies

A. M. Leonard
241 Fox Drive
PO Box 816
Piqua, OH 45356
800-543-8955
www.amleo.com

Burpee
W. Atlee Burpee & Co.
300 Park Avenue
Warminster, PA 18974
800-888-1447
www.burpee.com

The Cook's Garden
PO Box C5030
Warminster, PA 18974
800-457-9703
www.cooksgarden.com

Gardener's Supply Company
128 Intervale Road
Burlington, VT 05401
800-876-5520
www.gardeners.com

Harris Seeds
355 Paul Road
Rochester, NY 14624
800-544-7938
www.harrisseeds.com

Johnny's Selected Seeds
PO Box 299
Waterville, ME 04903
877-564-6697
www.johnnyseeds.com

Park Seed
One Parkton Avenue
Greenwood, SC 29647
800-845-3369
www.parkseed.com

Peaceful Valley Farm Supply
125 Clydesdale Court
Grass Valley, CA 95945
888-784-1722
www.groworganic.com

Renee's Garden
6060 Graham Hill Road
Felton, CA 95018
888-880-7228
www.reneesgarden.com

Sage Vertical Garden Systems LLC
730 West Randolph Street. Suite 300
Chicago, IL
312-234-9655
www.sageverticalgardens.com

Seeds of Change
PO Box 4908
Rancho Dominguez, CA 90220
888-762-7333
www.seedsofchange.com

Select Seeds—Antique Flowers
180 Stickney Hill Road
Union, CT 06076
800-684-0395
www.selectseeds.com

Smart Pots
High Caliper Growing-Root Control, Inc.
7000 North Robinson
Oklahoma City, OK 73116
405-842-7700
www.smartpots.com

Territorial Seed Company
PO Box 158
Cottage Grove, OR 97424
800-626-0866
www.territorialseed.com

Thompson & Morgan Seedsmen, Inc.
PO Box 397
Aurora, IN 47001
800-274-7333
www.tmseeds.com

Totally Tomatoes
334 West Stroud Street
Randolph, WI 53956
800-345-5977
www.totallytomato.com

Vermont Bean Seed Company
334 West Stroud Street
Randolph, WI 53956
800-349-1071
www.vermontbean.com

Wildseed Farms
100 Legacy Drive
Fredericksburg, TX 78624
800-848-0078
www.wildseedfarms.com

Common and Botanical Names of Plants Mentioned

Common Name	Botanical Name	Common Name	Botanical Name
agave	*Agave* species	chamomile	*Chamaemelum nobile*
aloe	*Aloe* species	chaparral sage	*Salvia clevelandii*
amaryllis	*Hippeastrum* hybrids	Chinese lantern	*Physalis alkekengii*
angel's trumpet	*Brugmansia arborea*	chocolate mint	*Mentha* species
astilbe	*Astilbe arendsii*	chocolate plant	*Berlandiera lyrata*
azalea	*Rhododendron* species	cockscomb	*Celosia argentea*
banana pepper	*Capsicum Anaheim "banana"*	columbine	*Aquilegia* hybrids
barberry	*Berberis* species	coreopsis	*Coreopsis tinctoria*
basil	*Ocimum basilicum*	corn	*Zea mays*
bean	*Phaseolus vulgaris*	cosmos	*Cosmos bipinnatus*
bee balm	*Monarda didyma*	crocus	*Crocus sativus*
belladonna	*Atropa belladonna*	cucumber	*Cucumis sativus*
Bermuda grass	*Cynodon dactylon*	daffodil	*Narcissus* species
blackberry	*Rubus* species	dahlia	*Dahlia* species
blanketflower	*Gaillardia × grandiflora*	desert marigold	*Baileya* species
bleeding heart	*Dicentra spectabilis*	dusty miller	*Senecio cineraria*
blueberry	*Vaccinium* species	eggplant	*Solanum melongena "Dusky"*
blue salvia	*Salvia farinacea*	English ivy	*Hedera helix*
bok choy	*Brassica rapa chinensis*	ferns	*Matteuccia* variety
bridal wreath	*Spiraea prunifolia*	foxglove	*Digitalis* species
broccoli	*Brassica oleracea* (*Italica* group)	garlic	*Allium sativum*
buttercup	*Primula floribunda*	geranium	*Pelargonium* species
butterfly bush	*Buddleia davidii*	ginkgo	*Ginkgo biloba*
butterfly weed	*Asclepia tuberosa*	gourd	*Cucurbita pepo*
cabbage	*Brassica oleracea* (*capitata* group)	gourd, birdhouse	*Lagenaria* species
cauliflower	*Brassica oleracea* (*botrytis* group)	grasses that rustle	*Chasmanthium latifolium*
canna	*Canna* hybrids	green beans	*Phaseolus vulgaris*
carrot	*Daucus carota*	green pepper	*Capsicum annuum*
castor bean	*Ricinus communis*		*Gaura* species

Common Name	Botanical Name
hens and chicks	*Sempervivum* species
hollyhock	*Alcea rosea*
hosta	*Hosta* species
hyacinth	*Hyacinthus* species
impatiens	*Impatiens* species
indigo	*Indigofera* species
iris	*Iris* species
jalapeño pepper	*Capsicum annuum*
jonquil	*Narcissus* species
lamb's ears	*Stachys byzantina*
lemon balm	*Melissa officinalis*
lemon mint	*Mentha citrata*
lettuce	*Lactuca sativa*
lilac	*Syringa patula*
lime mint	*Mentha citrata*
marigold	*Tagetes* species
melon	*Cucumis melo*
Mexican hat	*Ratibida columnifera*
money plant	*Lunaria annua*
mum	*Chrysanthemum* species
nasturtium	*Tropaeolum majus*
nutsedge	*Cyperus esculentus*
onion	*Allium* species
oregano	*Origanum vulgare*
pansy	*Viola* species
paperwhite narcissus	*Narcissus* species

Common Name	Botanical Name
parsley	*Petroselinum crispum*
pinks	*Dianthus* species
popcorn	*Zea mays* var. *everta*
potato	*Solanum tuberosum*
pumpkin	*Cucurbita pepo*
purple coneflower	*Echinacea* species
Queen Anne's lace	*Daucus carota*
radish	*Raphanus sativus*
red salvia	*Salvia* species
rose	*Rosa* species
sage	*Salvia officinalis*
sedum	*Sedum* species
shrub rose	*Rosa gallica*
snapdragon	*Antirrhinum majus*
spinach	*Spinacia oleracea*
squash	*Cucurbita pepo*
statice	*Limonium sinuatum*
strawberry	*Fragaria* species
strawflower	*Xerochrysum bracteatum*
sweet alyssum	*Lobularia maritime*
tansy	*Tanacetum vulgare*
thyme	*Thymus vulgaris*
tomato	*Lycopersicon* species
tulip	*Tulipa* species
violets	*Viola* species
zinnia	*Zinnia* species

Poisonous Plants

Common Name	Botanical Name	Toxic Parts	Symptoms
autumn crocus	*Colchicum autumnale*	all parts, particularly the bulb	burning sensation in the mouth, vomiting, nausea, severe diarrhea
azaleas	*Rhododendron* species	all parts, particularly leaves and flowers	nausea, vomiting, depression, difficulty breathing, low blood pressure, convulsions; can be fatal
bittersweet	*Solanum dulcamara*	leaves, roots, and berries	vomiting, nausea, abdominal pain, diarrhea, drowsiness, tremors, weakness; may cause difficulty in breathing
black locust	*Robinia pseudoacacia*	bark, leaves, and seeds	burning pain in the mouth, abdominal pain, nausea, vomiting, severe diarrhea
bleeding heart	*Dicentra spectabilis*	foliage and roots	may be poisonous in large amounts
caladium	*Caladium* species	all parts	intense burning and irritation of the mouth, tongue, throat, and lips; swollen lips and tongue; can cause suffocation

Common Name	Botanical Name	Toxic Parts	Symptoms
calla lily	*Zantedeschia* species	all parts, especially the leaves and root	intense burning of the lips and mouth
castor bean	*Ricinus communis*	seed, if chewed (toxic substance: ricin)	burning sensation in the mouth, abdominal pain, nausea, vomiting, severe diarrhea, kidney failure; can be fatal
Christmas rose	*Helleborus niger*	all parts	stomach, intestinal, and skin irritation
crown-of-thorns	*Euphorbia milii*	all parts	intense burning and irritation of the mouth, tongue, throat, and lips; swollen lips and tongue; skin and eye irritation
daffodil	*Narcissus* species	bulbs	stomach pain, vomiting, abdominal pain, diarrhea
daphne	*Daphne* species	all parts, especially berries, bark, and leaves (toxic substance: daphnin)	burning of the mouth and throat, abdominal pain, vomiting, diarrhea, kidney damage; can be fatal
dieffenbachia, dumbcane	*Dieffenbachia* species	all parts	intense burning and irritation of the mouth, tongue, throat, and lips; swollen lips and tongue; can cause suffocation
elderberry	*Sambucus* species	stems, roots, and unripe or raw berries (ripe berries are edible)	nausea, vomiting, diarrhea
elephant ears	*Colocasia* species	leaves	intense burning and irritation of the mouth, tongue, throat, and lips; swollen lips and tongue; can cause suffocation
English ivy	*Hedera helix*	all parts, especially berries and leaves	excess salivation, nausea, vomiting, thirst, severe diarrhea, abdominal pain; may cause difficulty in breathing
foxglove	*Digitalis* species	all parts, especially leaves, seeds, and flowers	stomach pain, nausea, vomiting, abdominal pain, diarrhea, irritation of mouth; may produce an irregular heartbeat; can be fatal
golden chain	*Laburnum* species	all parts, especially bark, leaves, and seeds	abdominal pains, nausea, vomiting, headache, dizziness, skin and mouth irritation, convulsions; can be fatal
hyacinth	*Hyacinthus* species	all parts, especially bulbs	vomiting, abdominal pain, diarrhea; can be fatal

Common Name	Botanical Name	Toxic Parts	Symptoms
holly	Ilex aquifolium	berries	nausea, vomiting, abdominal pain, diarrhea
iris	Iris species	leaves and roots	stomach pain, nausea, vomiting, abdominal pain, diarrhea, burning of the mouth
jack-in-the-pulpit	Arisaema triphyllum	all parts, especially leaves	intense burning of the mouth, tongue, throat, and lips; swollen lips and tongue; may interfere with speaking, swallowing, or breathing
Japanese yew	Taxus cuspidata	leaves and seeds	abdominal pain, vomiting; in severe cases, muscular weakness, and cardiac and respiratory disturbances
jasmine	Jasminum officinale	berries	digestive and nervous symptoms; can be fatal
Jerusalem cherry	Solanum pseudocapscium	all parts, especially leaves and fruit (unripe fruit)	nausea, vomiting, abdominal pain, diarrhea, dilation of pupils, drowsiness
lantana	Lantana species	all parts, especially the green berries	stomach upset, vomiting, diarrhea, weakness, visual disturbances
larkspur	Delphinium species	plant seeds	stomach upset, nervousness, irritability, depression
lily of the valley	Convallaria majalis	all parts, especially roots, leaves, flowers, and fruit	stomach pain, nausea, vomiting, abdominal pain, diarrhea; may produce an irregular heartbeat
mayapple	Podophyllum peltatum	rootstalk, leaves, stems, and green fruit	abdominal pain, vomiting, diarrhea, pulse irregularities
mistletoe	Phoradendron serotinum	leaves, stems, and berries	vomiting, diarrhea, dilated pupils, confusion, respiratory distress
monkshood	Aconitum napellus	all parts, especially the root and leaves	throat congestion, increased salivation, weakness, nausea, vomiting, tingling sensation, cold and moist skin; poisoning of the system
moonseed	Menispermum canadense	mature fruit	convulsions, poisoning of the system; can be fatal
morning glory	Ipomoea purpurea	all parts, especially seeds	hallucinations; poisoning of the system

Common Name	Botanical Name	Toxic Parts	Symptoms
star-of-Bethlehem	*Ornithogalum* species	flowers and bulbs	stomach pain, vomiting, abdominal pain, diarrhea
sweet pea	*Lathyrus odoratus*	seeds	poisoning of the system if ingested in large amounts
tomato	*Lycopersicon, Lycopersicum* species	leaves, vines, and sprouts	headache, abdominal pain, vomiting, diarrhea; can cause circulatory and respiratory depression
Virginia creeper, American ivy	*Parthenocissus quinquefolia*	berries and leaves (toxic substance: oxalic acid)	nausea, vomiting, abdominal pain, diarrhea, headache
wisteria	*Wisteria* species	pods and seeds	abdominal pain, nausea, vomiting, diarrhea
yellow jessamine, Carolina jessamine	*Gelsemium sempervirens*	all parts	heart arrest, visual disturbances, dizziness, headache, dryness of mouth; can be fatal
yellow sage, red sage	*Lantana camara*	leaves and immature fruit (green berries)	stomach pain, vomiting, abdominal pain, diarrhea, lethargy, pupil dilation, unconsciousness, difficulty in breathing, weakness; can be fatal